Legal Guide for Police

Legal Guide for Police, 10th Edition, is a valuable tool for criminal justice students and law enforcement professionals, bringing them up-to-date with developments in the law of arrest, search and seizure, police authority to detain, questioning suspects and pretrial identification procedures, police power and its limitations, and civil liability of police officers and agencies. Including specific case examples, this revised edition provides the most current information for students and law enforcement professionals needing to develop a modern understanding of the law.

Authors Walker and Hemmens have added introductory and summary chapters to this edition, which aid readers in understanding the context, importance, and applicability of the case law. All chapters have been updated to reflect U.S. Supreme Court decisions up to and including the 2013 term of court. Among the important new cases covered are: *Bailey v. United States* (2013), *Berghuis v. Thompkins* (2010), *Kentucky v. King* (2010), *Maryland v. King* (2013), and *Michigan v. Bryant* (2011). A helpful Appendix contains the Bill of Rights and the Fourteenth Amendment, and a Table of Cases lists every case referenced in the text.

Jeffery T. Walker is a professor of Criminal Justice and Criminology and Chair of the Department of Criminal Justice at the University of Arkansas, Little Rock, where he has worked since 1990. Dr. Walker has written 10 books and over 70 journal articles and book chapters. He has obtained over $9 million in grants from the Department of Justice, National Institute of Drug Abuse, and others. He is a past President of the Academy of Criminal Justice Sciences. His editorial experience includes service as Editor of the *Journal of Criminal Justice Education*, and *Journal of Critical Criminology*. Previous publications include articles in *Justice Quarterly, Journal of Quantitative Criminology*, and *Journal of Criminal Justice Education*, and the books *Leading Cases in Law Enforcement* (9th Edition) and *Statistics in Criminal Justice and Criminology: Analysis and Interpretation* (4th Edition). Dr. Walker also served as a Special Agent with the Air Force Office of Special Investigations (AFOSI), conducting major felony crime investigations. In September 2001, Dr. Walker was mobilized to provide counterintelligence, protective services, and force protection support to military personnel in U.S. and overseas locations. His final assignment was Superintendent of Counterintelligence Investigations at Headquarters/AFOSI in Washington, D.C.

Craig Hemmens is Chair and Professor in the Department of Criminal Justice and Criminology at Washington State University. He holds a J.D. from North Carolina Central University School of Law and a Ph.D. in Criminal Justice from Sam Houston State University. He has previously served as Chair of the Department of Criminology and Criminal Justice at Missouri State University, as well as Chair of the Department of Criminal Justice at Boise State University. He is a past President of the Academy of Criminal Justice Sciences. Professor Hemmens has published 19 books and more than 100 articles on a variety of criminal justice-related topics.

Titles of Related Interest from Routledge/Anderson

The Policing of Terrorism: Organizational and Global Perspectives by Mathieu Deflem

Community Policing: A Police-Citizen Partnership by Michael Palmiotto

Corrections: Foundations for the Future, 2nd Edition by Jeanne B. Stinchcomb

Voices from Criminal Justice: Thinking and Reflecting on the System edited by Heith Copes and Mark Pogrebin

Briefs of Leading Cases in Law Enforcement, 9th Edition by Rolando V. del Carmen and Jeffery T. Walker

Criminal Investigation: A Method for Reconstructing the Past, 7th Edition by James W. Osterburg and Richard H. Ward

Policing in America, 8th Edition by Larry K. Gaines and Victor E. Kappeler

Police Administration, 8th Edition by Gary W. Cordner

The Police Manager, 7th Edition by Egan K. Green, Ronald G. Lynch and Scott R. Lynch

Effective Police Supervision, 7th Edition by Harry W. More and Larry S. Miller

Social Media Investigation for Law Enforcement by Joshua L. Brunty and Katherine Helenek

Community Policing: A Contemporary Perspective, 7th Edition by Victor E. Kappeler and Larry K. Gaines

Legal Guide for Police

Constitutional Issues

10th Edition

By
Jeffery T. Walker
Craig Hemmens

Routledge
Taylor & Francis Group

NEW YORK AND LONDON

First edition published in 1977
by Anderson Publishing

Ninth edition published in 2011
by Elsevier

Tenth edition published 2015
by Routledge
711 Third Avenue, New York, NY 10017

and by Routledge
2 Park Square, Milton Park, Abingdon, Oxon, OX14 4RN

Routledge is an imprint of the Taylor & Francis Group, an informa business

© 2015 Taylor & Francis

The right of Jeffery T. Walker and Craig Hemmens to be identified as author of this work has been asserted by them in accordance with sections 77 and 78 of the Copyright, Designs and Patents Act 1988.

Library of Congress Cataloging-in-Publication Data
Walker, Jeffery T., author.
  Legal guide for police : constitutional issues / By Jeffery T. Walker, Craig Hemmens.—
10th edition.
    p. cm.
  Includes bibliographical references and index.
  1. Criminal investigation—United States.   2. Preliminary examinations (Criminal procedure)—
United States.   3. Civil rights—United States.   4. Police—United States—Handbooks, manuals, etc.
I. Hemmens, Craig, author.   II. Title.
  KF9619.85.W35 2015
  345.73′052–dc23
  2014034931

ISBN: 978-1-138-84984-6 (hbk)
ISBN: 978-0-323-32297-3 (pbk)
ISBN: 978-1-315-72515-4 (ebk)

Typeset in Times New Roman
by Apex CoVantage, LLC

Contents

Chapter 1
Introduction

§ 1.1   Criminal Procedure

A question that concerns all democratic societies is how much authority to grant to the government vis-à-vis the individual citizen. Social contract theory as enunciated by Thomas Hobbes and John Locke states that by choosing to live among others, individuals give up some of their liberties and permit the state to intervene in their lives. The state provides certain protections that individuals could not achieve on their own. But how much intervention and in what manner the state may do so are vital questions with which the courts have struggled over the centuries.

In this book we examine the law of criminal procedure. Criminal procedure law sets forth the appropriate behavior for the police, as agents of the state, as they investigate possible criminal activity. Whereas criminal law sets forth the appropriate code of conduct for all citizens, criminal procedure comprises the rules that govern the manner in which the state may go about depriving an individual of his or her liberty. Balancing the rights of the individual and the authority of the state and its agents is a difficult but crucial process.

§ 1.2   Sources of Criminal Procedure Law

The legal foundation for most criminal procedural decisions is the United States Constitution, including the Bill of Rights and the Fourteenth Amendment. The Bill of Rights sets forth 23 individual rights, and the Fourteenth Amendment's guarantee of "due process" has been interpreted by the U.S. Supreme Court to incorporate much of the Bill of Rights. The Bill of Rights originally was conceived as applying only to the federal government; but during the twentieth century, the Supreme Court interpreted the due process clause of the Fourteenth Amendment as including, or incorporating, many of the individual rights contained in the Bill of Rights, thus making these rights applicable to the states. These include most of the procedural criminal provisions of the Fourth, Fifth, Sixth, and Eighth Amendments.

Incorporation means that the individual right (such as the Fourth Amendment right to be free from unreasonable searches and seizures) is included in the Fourteenth Amendment's guarantee of due process or equal protection. Rights incorporated in the Fourteenth Amendment are those the Court has deemed "fundamental." These rights are applied against the states and include most of the criminal procedure-related provision of the Fourth, Fifth, Sixth, and Eighth Amendments.

Other sources for criminal procedure law are state constitutions and federal and state statutes. States are free to provide more individual rights than the federal constitution, but states cannot deny or diminish any federal constitutional rights. In the past, states were seen as perhaps less protective of the rights of criminal suspects than the federal government, yet in the last two decades, a number of state courts have interpreted their state constitutions as providing greater protections of individual liberties than the federal government. To say that a piece of legislation passes constitutional muster is to say only that it passes minimal standards of fairness.

Other sources of criminal procedural law come from the provisions of the Bill of Rights, in particular the Fourth, Fifth, and Sixth Amendments. Courts frequently are asked to interpret the meaning of these amendments and to apply them to current fact situations. The Fifth Amendment prohibits compelling people to testify against themselves. But does requiring a person to take a Breathalyzer test or give a blood sample constitute testimony when the results may be used against that person at trial? The Fourth Amendment prohibits the unreasonable seizure and search of persons, places, and effects, but what is an "effect"? And what is "unreasonable"? Courts must answer these questions to determine when the police have exceeded the scope of their authority, either intentionally or unintentionally.

The U.S. Supreme Court has the final word on the constitutionality of any state action that is challenged as violating a constitutional right. Consequently, much of criminal procedure law comes from Supreme Court decisions. As courts decide only the case before them, and do not issue policy directives, criminal procedure law has developed fitfully, on a case-by-case basis. Much of criminal procedural law has been written in the past 50 years, since the Supreme Court began to apply the provisions of the Bill of Rights to the states, which conduct the bulk of criminal investigation and prosecution. In this book we focus on Supreme Court decisions involving criminal procedure, and use lower court cases to illustrate the principles enunciated by the Supreme Court. Before we do this, however, we need to discuss the role of the judiciary in criminal justice.

§ 1.3   Judicial Functions

Courts provide several functions. First, courts settle disputes by providing a forum for obtaining justice and resolving disputes through the application of legal rules and principles. It is in court that injured parties may seek compensation and the state may seek to punish wrongdoers. While the courtroom is obviously not the only place that people may go to settle disputes, Americans traditionally have turned to the courts for redress.

Second, courts make public policy decisions. Policymaking involves the allocation of limited resources (such as money and property) to competing interests. America has a long tradition of settling difficult policy questions in the courtroom rather than in the legislature. This is because politicians often avoid settling complex and/ or difficult problems for fear of alienating their constituents or because the competing interests are unable to compromise. In addition, the rights of minorities are often unprotected by the legislature, which by its very nature represents primarily the interests of the majority, so courts are forced to step into the breach.

Third, courts serve to clarify the law through interpretation of statutes and the application of general principles to specific fact patterns. Courts are different from the other branches of government in many ways, but perhaps the most significant difference is that courts are reactive—courts do not initiate cases but rather serve to settle controversies brought to them by others—plaintiffs and defendants, in legal parlance. This frequently involves the interpretation of statutes written by the legislature.

Statutes are enacted by the legislature under the authority granted to it by the Constitution. A constitution creates a government—it literally *constitutes* the government. Legislatures are given authority to act in certain areas, and within these areas, they may pass legislative enactments or bills, often referred to as statutes, which are collected into codes, such as the criminal code.

Acts of the legislature are not, however, lawful *per se*. In other words, just because a legislature passes a bill does not mean the bill is a lawful exercise of the legislature's authority. Acts of the legislature may not limit the constitution under which the legislation was created. For instance, the U.S. Congress may not lawfully pass legislation that abridges the Fourth Amendment.

Who decides when the legislature has acted beyond the scope of its authority? In the United States, the Supreme Court has the final say as to the constitutionality of statutes passed by either state or federal legislatures. This is known as the power of judicial review.

Statutes often are written broadly, leaving much room for interpretation. This is also true of the U.S. Constitution. For example, the Fourth Amendment prohibits "unreasonable searches and seizures." But what is unreasonable? What constitutes a search or a seizure? There are no easy answers to these questions.

Why are statutes ambiguous? Why does the legislature not write more clearly and explain exactly what it means? There are several reasons. First, it is difficult to define, in a few sentences, something involving human conduct—there is an almost infinite range of possible actions by individuals.

Second, legislators are politicians, and politics involves compromise. Thus, a statute may be written so that it appeals to the greatest possible number of legislators, but in doing this, the language of the statute may be watered down and made less precise rather than more precise.

§ 1.4   The Supreme Court and the Police

Historically, the Supreme Court paid little attention to the activities of state and local police agencies. There were three primary reasons for this lack of attention: police forces remained relatively small and unorganized until the twentieth century, defendants in criminal cases rarely challenged the means by which police obtained evidence, and the Fourth Amendment, which today is the primary tool for controlling police conduct, did not apply to the activities of state and local police.

The Supreme Court in *Barron v. Baltimore* (1833) held that the Bill of Rights, of which the Fourth Amendment is a part, did not apply to the actions of state and local governmental agencies, but instead was intended to apply only to the activities of federal agencies. As the bulk of police work was conducted by state and local agencies, the decision in *Barron* meant that there were relatively few instances in which the Supreme Court was called upon to interpret the meaning of the Fourth Amendment.

In *Weeks v. United States* (1914) the Court held that evidence illegally obtained by federal law enforcement officers must be excluded in all federal criminal prosecutions. As the Court had not at that time applied the provisions of the Fourth Amendment to the states, this decision led to a practice commonly known as the "silver platter doctrine," in which federal courts admitted evidence illegally obtained by state law enforcement officers, who then turned over the evidence to federal agents. Under this doctrine, such evidence was deemed admissible because the illegal search and seizure was committed by state agents.

correct way, the defendant is not legally guilty and cannot be held accountable for the crime with which he is charged.

The due process model, then, resembles an obstacle course in which cases must navigate hurdles set up to ensure that determinations of guilt are reliable. The key to this is formal, adjudicative, and adversarial fact-finding procedures with constant scrutiny of outcomes to ensure that mistakes have not been made. Defendants are presumed to be innocent until proven guilty, legally as well as factually.

In an ideal world, judges and other criminal justice officials would balance due process and crime control ideals. They would strive for efficiency while insisting on reliability. In the real world, this is probably not possible; many decisions tip in one direction or another. High caseloads, limited resources, and concerns about protecting the community may lead to shortcuts that threaten reliability or to decisions that chip away at the procedural regulations that protect the rights of criminal defendants. Similarly, concerns about restraining the power of criminal justice officials may lead to decisions that make it more difficult for the criminal process to apprehend and convict those who commit crimes.

A good example of an issue where use of the crime control and due process models would lead to different conclusions is plea bargaining. According to the crime control model, the criminal process is operating most efficiently when defendants who are not screened out by police and prosecutors plead guilty at the earliest possible moment. The criminal process would break down if too many defendants insisted on taking their cases to trial. The crime control model thus sees nothing wrong with allowing prosecutors to reduce charges or drop counts in exchange for guilty pleas or permitting judges to make it clear to defendants that those who plead guilty will be treated more leniently than those who insist on a trial. Although plea bargaining may result in guilty pleas by those who are innocent, this type of mistake is likely to be rare, as those who have survived the screening process are in all probability guilty. Disposing of a large proportion of cases as quickly as possible via guilty pleas is, according to this model, the only feasible means of achieving the goal of crime control.

It is no surprise that use of the due process model leads to a different conclusion. According to this model, guilty pleas, which effectively preclude any oversight of the early, informal stages of the process, should be discouraged. The due process model values reliability and contends that mistakes are likely early in the process; because of this, guilty pleas that occur soon after the prosecutor makes a decision to charge have a high probability of producing unreliable factual determinations of guilt. In addition, the model would not allow prosecutors or judges to promise defendants leniency in return for a guilty plea. Defendants, no matter how overwhelming the evidence, have the right to have the charges against them tried using the procedures required by law; they should not be coerced to enter a guilty plea or punished for exercising their constitutionally protected rights. Moreover, before accepting a guilty plea, the judge adjudicating the case should be required to both establish the defendant's factual guilt and ensure that the process that brought the defendant into court has been free of mistakes. According to the due process model, it is only by following these rules that reliability of outcomes can be guaranteed and mistakes minimized.

§ 1.6   Summary

Criminal procedure law is constantly evolving as police resort to new tactics and technologies in their war on crime. The courts, as interpreters of the Constitution, are continually struggling to maintain the proper balance between the competing interests of law enforcement and individual privacy. The Bill of Rights provides a number of broad individual protections, and the Supreme Court has endeavored to develop more precise, understandable parameters of these protections.

The Fourth Amendment prohibits unreasonable searches and seizures, but the Court has not applied this standard blindly, developing the concepts of reasonable suspicion and permitting techniques such as stop-and-frisks. In some instances the Court has created clear rules for police conduct, such as the exclusionary rule and the *Miranda* warnings. In other instances the Court has resorted to a case-by-case mode of analysis, sometimes leaving law enforcement unsure of what is permitted in a particular case. This confusion is to some degree unavoidable as the abstract legal doctrines comprising criminal procedure law are constantly challenged by new technologies, new fact patterns, and a changing political climate.

The Supreme Court is both a legal and political institution, and its decisions invariably are affected to some degree by public opinion about crime. What is unreasonable today may not have been unreasonable 50 years ago. In this book we will attempt to explain the complex world of criminal procedure law. Criminal procedure law is not static—it changes as the times change. But there are certain principles that the courts consistently rely upon; we will focus on these and provide the reader with examples to illustrate these principles.

Chapter 2
Results of Failure to Comply with Constitutional Mandates

The question in this case is whether a reasonably well-trained officer in petitioner's position would have known that his affidavit failed to establish probable cause and that he should not have applied for the warrant.

Malley v. Briggs, 475 U.S. 335 (1986)

The failure of law enforcement officers to comply with the mandates of the U.S. Constitution, as interpreted by the courts, results not only in the dismissal and loss of cases, but also in possible liability on the part of the officer, as well as the administrator and the agency. Failure on the part of the agency to properly train or supervise officers, or to enact and enforce guidelines that are consistent with constitutional provisions, often results in civil actions in state courts and actions in federal courts under the civil rights statutes. In this chapter, the admissibility of evidence for failure to abide by constitutional mandates and areas of potential liability are discussed. In

11

the chapters that follow, the constitutional requirements of searches, seizures, and interrogations are discussed in greater detail.

§ 2.1   The Exclusionary Rule

The adoption of the exclusionary rule by the Supreme Court in 1914 made it essential that all law enforcement officials be aware of the rules surrounding search and seizure. The exclusionary rule provides that evidence obtained by an unreasonable search and seizure will not be admissible in court. This rule of exclusion is not a provision of the Fourth Amendment; it is a rule that was created by the courts as a remedy for a violation of the Fourth Amendment. Because it is a court-made requirement, the courts, if they so decide, may reverse it in some cases and allow evidence to be admitted in a criminal trial that may not have been admitted previously.

There are arguments for and against the exclusionary rule. In England and Canada, evidence is admitted even though obtained in violation of search and seizure rules. The reasoning is that the evidence is relevant and reliable "even if the constable blundered in obtaining it." By weighing the protection of individual rights against the protection of society, the English courts would agree with one New York judge, who questions why "the criminal is to go free because the constable has blundered?"[1] On the other hand, those who advocate strict application of the exclusionary rule argue it is the only means by which the protection provided by the Fourth Amendment can be guaranteed.

Prior to 1961, the U.S. Supreme Court refused to apply the exclusionary rule to the states even though it had been applied to the federal government since 1914. In 1949, a majority of the Court recognized that state officers, in making an illegal search, violated the Fourth Amendment, but the Court refused to force upon the states an evidence rule that would limit the powers of state courts.[2] This changed in 1961 with the ruling in *Mapp v. Ohio*.

§ 2.2   Extension of the Exclusionary Rule to All Courts: *Mapp v. Ohio*

In 1961, the U.S. Supreme Court reversed all previous cases and stated that henceforth, with some exceptions, evidence obtained by procedures that violated Fourth Amendment standards would no longer be admissible in federal or state courts.[3] To

---

[1]   *People v. Defore*, 150 N.E. 585 (1926).
[2]   *Wolf v. Colorado*, 338 U.S. 25 (1949).
[3]   *Mapp v. Ohio*, 367 U.S. 643 (1961).

bring the implications of this decision into focus, the facts of *Mapp* are briefly summarized here. Three Cleveland police officers arrived at Dollree Mapp's residence pursuant to information that a person who was wanted for questioning in connection with a recent bombing was hiding in Mapp's home. Mapp refused to admit the officers when they attempted to enter without a search warrant. Three hours later, the officers returned with reinforcements and again sought entrance. When she did not respond, one of the doors was forcibly opened by the officers so they could gain entry. At this point, Mapp demanded to see the search warrant. A paper claimed by officers to be the warrant was held up by one of the officers. Mapp grabbed for the paper and placed it in her bosom. A struggle ensued in which the officers recovered the piece of paper and handcuffed Mapp. A search of the home was conducted. Obscene paraphernalia was discovered as a result of the search, and Mapp was convicted of possession of obscene paraphernalia.

At court, the police admitted they did not have a warrant. The prosecutor argued that even if the search was illegal, the evidence obtained was nevertheless admissible under the rule established by the Supreme Court in *Wolf v. Colorado*.[4] They also argued that the state of Ohio did not follow the exclusionary rule and that the Supreme Court should not override a decision of the Ohio Supreme Court. In denying the state's argument, the U.S. Supreme Court specifically overruled previous decisions and held that *all* evidence obtained by searches and seizures in violation of the U.S. Constitution is inadmissible in state court.

§ 2.3 Application and Modification of the Exclusionary Rule

Some legal scholars claim that the foundation on which the exclusionary rule was built has become outdated. Numerous cases are cited in which pertinent evidence is excluded and criminals are released, even when the officer has a reasonable degree of training and education concerning proper search and seizure procedure.[5] There have been several arguments for limiting or eliminating the exclusionary rule, including: (1) there is no provision in the Constitution that requires evidence to be excluded; (2) society and victims of crime are denied the protection of the law; (3) the laws relating to search and seizure are so complex that officers cannot comprehend them; and (4) police officers are now more informed and court-imposed methods for "policing the police officer" are no longer justified.

---

4   *Wolf v. Colorado*, 338 U.S. 25 (1949).
5   See, for example, *Bivens v. Six Unknown Fed. Narcotics Agents*, 403 U.S. 388 (1971) and *Malley v. Briggs*, 475 U.S. 335 (1986).

The Supreme Court has considered the arguments in favor of limiting or eliminating the rule, and has made some modifications that make it possible to introduce evidence even though technical rules were violated. These are discussed in the paragraphs that follow.

A. Good Faith Exception

Probably the most far-reaching exception to the exclusionary rule is the good faith exceptions put forth in *United States v. Leon*.[6] In *Leon*, a confidential informant of unproven reliability informed an officer that certain individuals were selling controlled substances from a specific residence. On the basis of this information, police initiated an investigation, focusing on the residence identified by the informant and later two other residences. With two affidavits summarizing the police officer's observations, an application for a warrant to search the three residences and the suspects' automobiles was prepared, reviewed by the deputy district attorney, and submitted to a judge. The judge, after evaluating the evidence, issued a facially valid warrant, which, when executed by police officers, resulted in the seizure of a large quantity of drugs.

The defendants moved to suppress the evidence, claiming that the affidavit to support the warrant was insufficient to establish probable cause. The Supreme Court found that the officer's reliance on the search warrant was reasonable and the evidence should not have been suppressed. The Court based their holding on the fact that:

> The Fourth Amendment Exclusionary Rule does not bar the use of evidence obtained
> in good faith by officers acting in reasonable reliance on a search warrant issued by
> a detached magistrate but ultimately found to be invalid.

Contrary to some commentators, who argued that the exclusionary rule had been abandoned, this case found only that if a search warrant was issued by a magistrate but ultimately found invalid for one reason or another, the evidence will be admissible because the officer executed the warrant in good faith.

An issue that arose following *Leon* was how much officers can rely on a search warrant issued by a judge. In *Massachusetts v. Sheppard*,[7] an officer wrote an application for a search warrant, but could not find the proper form for this kind of search and instead used an old form for controlled substances. The district attorney reviewed the

---

6   *United States v. Leon*, 468 U.S. 897 (1984).
7   *Massachusetts v. Sheppard*, 468 U.S. 981 (1984).

paperwork and it was then presented to a judge. The judge was told of the improper form and informed that some changes might be needed. The judge made some changes and returned the warrant with the assurance of its veracity. At trial, the search warrant was declared to be invalid and Sheppard sought to have the evidence suppressed, arguing that the officer should have known the warrant was invalid. The Supreme Court ruled that a law enforcement officer does not have to second-guess a magistrate in issues of law and search warrants. If the judge states that the warrant is valid, officers may act on it in good faith, even if the warrant is later declared invalid.

The good faith exception typically is limited to errors made by a magistrate, as in *Leon*, or perhaps the law (see below). This rule was extended to court employees in *Arizona v. Evans*.[8] This same logic was more recently used in *Herring v. United States*[9] to extend the good faith rule to others upon whom police officers rely for information. In *Herring*, officers asked a county clerk about an outstanding warrant for Herring. The clerk reported that there was an outstanding warrant based on the electronic database of the county. Based on that information, officers arrested Herring and discovered illegal contraband during a search incident to the arrest. When the clerk went to retrieve the paper copy of the warrant, she discovered it had been withdrawn but the electronic database had not been updated. Officers learned of this error after booking Herring. At trial, the Supreme Court ruled the arrest was illegal, but that the search was valid because the officers were relying on information only later determined to be in error. Thus, the evidence of the search incident to the arrest was admitted in court.

Extending the logic of *Leon*, the Supreme Court in 1987 applied the "good faith exception" to a case in which officers seized evidence from a wrecking yard without a warrant.[10] In this case, the officers acted under a statute that authorized inspection of a business that engaged in buying and selling motor vehicles, parts, and scrap metal. The day after the search, a federal court ruled that such a statute was unconstitutional. The Supreme Court, in reversing the lower court's decision prohibiting admission of the evidence, determined that the evidence should have been admitted even though the statute was later found to be unconstitutional. The Court reiterated that application of the exclusionary rule is never a "right" of the criminal defendant and the courts are to apply the rule only when the purpose of the rule is served. Allowing the evidence to be introduced, the Supreme Court concluded:

> Application of the Exclusionary Rule "is neither intended nor able to cure the invasion of the defendant's rights which he has already suffered" . . . Rather the rule "operates as a judicially created remedy designed to safeguard Fourth Amendment

---

8   *Arizona v. Evans*, 514 U.S. 1 (1995).
9   *Herring v. United States*, 555 U.S. 135 (2009).
10 *Illinois v. Krull*, 480 U.S. 340 (1987).

rights generally through its effect, rather than as a personal constitutional right of the party aggrieved." (Internal citations omitted.)

Although the good faith exception has opened some doors to the use of relevant evidence, significant caveats must be clarified. First, the good faith exception does not apply if the officer cannot establish that he or she was relying in good faith on information from a court official or other person authorized to give official information to police. Second, if the affidavit supporting the warrant is deliberately or recklessly false, it cannot be executed in good faith. Third, if the warrant is so facially deficient as to prohibit objectivity in its execution, there can be no reasonable reliance on its validity.

B. Use of Illegally Seized Evidence for
Impeachment Purposes

In the case of *United States v. Havens*,[11] the Supreme Court authorized the use of illegally seized evidence for impeachment purposes if the defendant takes the stand and makes statements that are contrary to evidence acquired by the illegal search. In *Havens*, police officers found cocaine sewn in a makeshift pocket in a T-shirt worn by a companion of Havens. Havens' companion implicated him and Havens' bag was searched. In the search, customs officers discovered a T-shirt from which pieces had been cut and found that these matched the pieces that were sewn to the shirt in which the narcotics were found. This evidence was not introduced when the prosecution presented its case, but was used on rebuttal after Havens stated on the stand that, to his knowledge, the T-shirt was not in his luggage. As the illegally seized evidence was introduced only for impeachment purposes to discredit the testimony given by the defendant on cross-examination, the Supreme Court determined that introduction of the evidence was proper. The rationale was that arriving at the truth in a criminal case is a fundamental goal of the legal system, and that when a defendant takes the stand, the government should be permitted to conduct an effective cross-examination in an attempt to elicit the truth.

C. Use of Illegally Seized Evidence in Grand
Jury Proceedings

In another exception to the exclusion of illegally seized evidence, the Supreme Court refused to allow a grand jury witness to invoke the exclusionary rule, pointing out that this would unduly interfere with the effective and expeditious discharge of

---

[11]   *United States v. Havens*, 446 U.S. 620 (1980).

the grand jury's duties.[12] The Court reasoned that the judicially created remedy to safeguard Fourth Amendment rights should not be interpreted to proscribe the use of illegally seized evidence at grand jury proceedings.

D. Use of Evidence in Proceedings Other Than Those Related to Criminal Matters

Expanding the rule that the exclusionary rule does not apply in grand jury proceedings, the Supreme Court ruled that it applies only to proceedings that involve criminal prosecutions.[13] The Supreme Court reasoned that the Fourth Amendment exclusion policy cannot be justified when weighed against the importance of having all relevant evidence admitted in noncriminal cases; therefore, courts have approved the use of illegally seized search and seizure evidence at parole hearings and in civil trials.[14] It should be noted, however, that even though the evidence might be admissible in noncriminal cases, there is a possibility that the officer or officers could be civilly or criminally liable.

E. Inevitable Discovery Exception

The final exception to the exclusionary rule discussed here provides that evidence discovered without a warrant is admissible if it would have been discovered anyway. According to this doctrine, if the government can show that discovery of the evidence by lawful means was inevitable, the evidence will be admitted even though it was initially obtained unlawfully.[15] This exception stems from *Nix v. Williams*. In this case, a young girl disappeared from a YMCA building. Williams was seen leaving the building with a large bundle wrapped in a blanket and "two legs in it and they were skinny and white." When Williams' car was found with clothing belonging to the missing child, a search was begun between that spot and the YMCA. Williams was arrested and convicted of murder. After having his case overturned because he was illegally interrogated during his arrest, Williams was tried again. At the second trial, the prosecutor did not offer Williams' statements into evidence, but did admit the body. Williams again appealed admission of the body. This time, the Supreme Court ruled that because the body was found about two miles from one of the search

---

[12] *United States v. Calandra*, 414 U.S. 338 (1974).

[13] *Nix v. Williams*, 467 U.S. 431 (1984).

[14] *United State v. Lamas*, 930 F.2d 199 (5th Cir. 1991).

[15] *Nix v. Williams*, 467 U.S. 431 (1984).

teams and the team was heading toward the body, that it would have been found even if Williams had not confessed and led police to the body.

Although the inevitable discovery rule is a valid exception to the exclusionary rule, it is not particularly easy for the government to invoke. For the inevitable discovery exception to apply, the government must establish by a preponderance of evidence the reasonable probability that the contested evidence would have been discovered by lawful means, in the absence of any police misconduct, and that the government was actually pursuing a substantial alternative line of investigation at the time of the constitutional violation.[16]

§ 2.4   Civil Liabilities

In addition to evidence being excluded from trial if it is obtained in violation of the constitution, law enforcement officers may face civil liability for their unconstitutional actions. When a civil action is initiated against a police officer or a police administrator, it is generally brought under the tort law of the jurisdiction. The plaintiff in a tort action must prove that: (1) the defendant had a duty; (2) the defendant breached that duty; (3) there was a causal connection between the breach of the duty and the plaintiff's injury; and (4) the injury to the plaintiff resulted from that breach.

When determining whether a duty does in fact exist, the courts look to the Constitution of the United States, the constitutions of the various states, state statutes, municipal ordinances, departmental regulations, and cases decided by the courts. For example, if an arrest violates the Fourth Amendment as interpreted by the Supreme Court, that arrest may serve as the basis for a state tort action for false arrest, as well as a federal action under the civil rights statutes for violation of the constitutional right to be free from unreasonable searches and seizures.

More actions are initiated in civil court against police officers and administrators than in criminal court because it is less difficult to prove that a duty has been breached and the plaintiff is more likely to obtain a civil judgment. The reason for this is that in a civil action, the plaintiff is required to show a breach of duty only by a *preponderance* of the evidence, rather than *beyond a reasonable doubt*. The preponderance of the evidence standard requires less proof than the beyond a reasonable doubt standard. Also, in a tort action, judgment may be rendered by a nonunanimous jury, whereas criminal cases generally require a unanimous jury.

---

[16] *United States v. Janis*, 428 U.S. 433 (1976).

§ 2.5   Civil Rights Actions

A. Civil Actions

Although the civil rights statutes under which most actions are initiated against police for failure to comply with constitutional mandates were passed just after the Civil War, it is only recently that they have been used extensively. The civil rights statute that provides civil remedies for official misconduct was enacted by Congress in 1871, and now is codified as Title 42 United States Code § 1983. Lawsuits under this statute are commonly referred to as § 1983 actions.

This statute provides:

> Every person who, under color of any statute, ordinance, regulation, custom, or usage, of any State or Territory or the District of Columbia, subjects, causes, or causes to be subjected, any citizen of the United States or other person within the jurisdiction thereof to the deprivation of any rights, privileges, or immunities secured by the Constitution and laws, shall be liable to the party injured in an action at law, suit in equity, or other proper proceeding for redress, except that in any action brought against a judicial officer for an act or omission taken in such officer's judicial capacity, injunctive relief shall not be granted unless a declaratory decree was violated or declaratory relief was unavailable. For the purposes of this section, any Act of Congress applicable exclusively to the District of Columbia shall be considered to be a statute of the District of Columbia.

To successfully pursue an action in federal court under § 1983, the person who claims an injury must establish: (1) that the defendant deprived the injured party of "rights, privileges, or immunities" secured by the Constitution or the laws of the United States; *and* (2) that the defendant against whom the action is brought acted "under color of any statute, ordinance, regulation, custom, or usage."

The first concern of the plaintiff in a civil rights action under § 1983 is to show that the defendant officer deprived the plaintiff of a constitutional right provided by the Constitution, federal statute, or court decision.[17] When such a decision is made and the constitutional right is determined, the police are presumed to know that such a right exists. This requires that police and administrators not only be familiar with constitutional rights as interpreted by the U.S. Supreme Court and other courts, but also keep up to date as new decisions are handed down.

---

[17] *Albright v. Oliver,* 510 U.S. 266 (1994).

The second concern of the plaintiff in a civil rights action under § 1983 is to show that the officer acted under "color of law." A police officer acts under color of law when he or she has authority under state law. For example, an officer acts under color of law when investigating crimes, making arrests, conducting searches, quelling disturbances of the peace, or conducting other law enforcement activities. A police officer does not act under color of law if his or her behavior does not take place in the line of duty, or is not made possible because of his or her legal authority. For example, a police officer acts as a private citizen when engaged in an off-duty fight that arises out of a private matter.

When initiating an action under § 1983, the plaintiff alleges that the defendant acted under color of law and deprived the plaintiff of his or her constitutional rights. The plaintiff will also ask that damages be awarded. These are usually money damages and, occasionally, an order not to engage in similar conduct in the future.

The defendant then considers the defenses available. One defense that has been the basis of many court decisions is the defense of "qualified immunity." Discussion of some federal court decisions will clarify the scope of the "qualified immunity" defense.

The Ninth Circuit Court of Appeals explained that the doctrine of qualified immunity protects government officials performing *discretionary functions* from liability for civil damages insofar as their conduct does not violate clearly established statutory or constitutional rights of which a *reasonable person would have known*.[18] After indicating that "qualified immunity" protects all but the plainly incompetent or those who knowingly violate the law, the court explained that the determination of whether an official is entitled to qualified immunity involves a two-step analysis, asking: (1) whether the law governing the official conduct was *clearly established*; and (2) whether, under the law, a reasonable officer could have believed the conduct was lawful. For a right to be "clearly established" for qualified immunity purposes, its contours must be sufficiently clear that, at the time of the alleged unlawful action, a reasonable official will understand that what he or she is doing violates that right.

Using similar language, the Fifth Circuit Court of Appeals explained that the court conducts a bifurcated analysis to determine whether a defendant is entitled to qualified immunity.[19] The first step is to determine whether the plaintiff has alleged a violation of a clearly established constitutional right. The second step is to determine whether the defendant's conduct was "objectively reasonable." In defining "objectively reasonable," the court said that "objective reasonableness" supporting a claim of qualified immunity is assessed in light of legal rules clearly established at the time of the incident, and an officer's conduct is not "objectively reasonable" when

---

[18]   *Headwaters Forest Defense v. County of Humboldt,* 211 F.3d 1121 (9th Cir. 2000).
[19]   *Wooley v. City of Baton Rouge,* 211 F.3d 913 (5th Cir. 2000).

reasonable officials would have realized that the particular officer's conduct violated a particular constitutional provision.

After many lower court decisions, the "qualified immunity" issue reached the United States Supreme Court in 2001.[20] The plaintiff in this case filed a suit, pursuant to *Bivens v. Six Unknown Federal Narcotics Agents*, against Saucier, a military police officer. Katz (the plaintiff) alleged, among other things, that Saucier had violated his Fourth Amendment rights by using excessive force in arresting him while he protested during then-Vice President Al Gore's speech at a San Francisco army base.[21] The district court declined to grant Saucier summary judgment on qualified immunity grounds, as did the Ninth Circuit Court of Appeals.

The United States Supreme Court disagreed with the lower courts, explaining that when the defendant claims qualified immunity, a ruling on that issue should be made early in the proceedings so the cost and expense of a trial are avoided where the qualified immunity defense is dispositive. The Court noted that, in determining that the defense of qualified immunity is appropriate, two questions must be answered. The first inquiry is whether a constitutional right would have been violated on the facts alleged. The second inquiry, assuming that the violation is established, is the question of whether the right was clearly established must be considered on a more specific level than that recognized by the Court of Appeals. If it is determined that there has been a violation of a constitutional right, the next step is to determine whether the right was clearly established. This inquiry must be undertaken in light of the case's specific context, not as a broad and general proposition. The relevant, dispositive inquiry in determining whether a right is clearly established is whether it would be clear to a reasonable officer that the conduct was unlawful in the situation he or she confronted.

Applying this rationale, the court concluded with this paragraph:

> In the circumstances presented to this officer, which included the duty to protect the safety and security of the Vice President of the United States from persons unknown in number, neither respondent nor the Court of Appeals has identified any case demonstrating a clearly established rule prohibiting the officer from acting as he did, nor are we aware of any such rule. Our conclusion is confirmed by the uncontested fact that the force was not so excessive that the respondent suffered hurt or injury. On these premises, petitioner was entitled to qualified immunity, and the suit should have been dismissed at an early stage in the proceedings.

---

[20] *Saucier v. Katz,* 533 U.S. 194 (2001).

[21] See *Bivens v. Six Unknown Fed. Narcotics Agents,* 403 U.S. 388 (1971), which held that action could be brought against federal officers following legal principles developed where actions are brought against state officers under § 1983.

Attempts by states to immunize conduct otherwise subject to suit under § 1983 have been unsuccessful. Federal courts have held that a state law that immunizes government conduct otherwise subject to suit under § 1983 is preempted by the supremacy clause of the U.S. Constitution.[22]

B. Criminal Actions

Failing to comply with constitutional mandates as interpreted by the courts may also result in criminal action against the officer in federal court. The federal law that defines the criminal violation was enacted in 1886 and is now codified as Title 18 United States Code § 242. It provides:

> Whoever, under color of any law, statute, ordinance, regulation, or custom, willfully subjects any person in any State, Territory, Commonwealth, Possession, or District, to the deprivation of any rights, privileges, or immunities secured or protected by the Constitution or laws of the United States, or to different punishments, pains, or penalties, on account of such person being an alien, or by reason of his color, or race, than are prescribed for the punishment of citizens, shall be fined under this title or imprisoned not more than one year, or both; and if bodily injury results from the acts committed in violation of this section or if such acts include the use, attempted use, or threatened use of a dangerous weapon, explosives, or fire, shall be fined under this title or imprisoned not more than ten years, or both; and if death results from the acts committed in violation of this section or if such acts include kidnapping or an attempt to kidnap, aggravated sexual abuse, or an attempt to commit aggravated sexual abuse, or an attempt to kill, shall be fined under this title, or imprisoned for any term of years or for life, or both, or may be sentenced to death.

Title 18 § 242 requires that the federal prosecutor introduce evidence to show: (1) that the person charged was acting under color of law; (2) that there was a deprivation of rights protected by the Constitution or laws of the United States; and (3) that the defendant acted willfully or intentionally to deprive a person of their rights. The first two requirements are similar to those required when an action is filed in civil court under § 1983. A third requirement is added, however, that requires the prosecution to show that the officer who acted under color of law did so *willfully* or *intentionally*.

In discussing the "willfully" element, a federal court explained that for purposes of a federal civil rights criminal prosecution, the defendant's act is done with the

---

[22]   See, for example, *Silva v. University of New Hampshire*, 888 F. Supp. 293 (D.N.H. 1994).

requisite willfulness if it is done "voluntarily and intentionally," and with the specific intent to do something the law forbids.[23]

Willfulness essentially means that the defendant intended to commit an act without necessarily intending to do the act for the specific purpose of depriving another of their constitutional rights.[24] To act "willfully," for purposes of the statute, the defendant must intend to commit an act that results in the deprivation of an established constitutional right. The defendant acts willfully if he or she *deliberately*, as opposed to accidentally or negligently, brings about a result that is forbidden by the Constitution, even though he or she is not thinking about violating a constitutional right. If an officer knowingly or unknowingly willfully deprives a person of a right that is protected by the Constitution, he or she may be liable under § 242 as well as § 1983.

Ordinarily, private citizens are not prosecuted under § 242. However, if private citizens are jointly engaged with police officers in the prohibited action, they could be convicted of deprivation of rights under color of law.[25] Although it is more difficult to prove a criminal case under § 242 than to successfully pursue a civil action under § 1983, there is no doubt that a police officer who, acting in the scope of his or her employment, deprives a person of a constitutional right, may be prosecuted in federal court.

§ 2.6   Liability of Supervisors, Administrators, and Agencies

Not only is an officer who deprives a person of a constitutional right civilly liable for failure to protect those rights, but the supervisor, administrator, or agency may also be held liable under a theory that is referred to as *vicarious liability*. Although some government agencies, especially state agencies, still cannot be held liable due to the doctrine of *sovereign immunity*, this doctrine has been rejected in many states by statute or court decision.

Some courts have used the *respondeat superior* doctrine to hold agencies liable for the acts of officers who deprive citizens of rights protected by state or federal constitution, laws of the states, ordinances of political subdivisions, departmental regulations, or court decisions.

Under the *respondeat superior* doctrine, a master is liable for the acts of a servant. Thus, when the tortious conduct of the employee is so closely connected in time, place, and causation that it is regarded as a risk of harm fairly attributable to

---

[23]   *United States v. Reese*, 2 F.3d 870 (9th Cir. 1993).

[24]   *United States v. Bradley*, 196 F.3d 762 (7th Cir. 1999).

[25]   *United States v. Causey*, 185 F.3d 407 (5th Cir. 1999).

the employer or business, the employer can be held liable. For example, the Supreme Court of Louisiana decided that the tortious conduct of a police officer toward an individual outside the geographical limits of the town was such as to render the town vicariously liable under the doctrine of *respondeat superior* when the officer was acting within the scope of his employment. In this case, the officer, acting within the scope of his employment, was accused of striking the plaintiff on the head without just cause while investigating a traffic violation and an intoxication offense.[26]

Vicarious liability makes it essential that supervisors and agencies provide appropriate training and oversight. Failure to do so may well result in liability for wrongdoing on the part of individual law enforcement officers.

A. Vicarious Liability Under Title 42 United States Code § 1983

In earlier cases, the U.S. Supreme Court held that police agencies were not "persons" under § 1983 and therefore could not be held liable when officers of the agency deprived citizens of their constitutional rights. However, in 1978, the Court made it clear that local government officials, sued in their official capacity, *are* "persons" under § 1983 and may be held liable for constitutional deprivations made pursuant to government customs, even if those customs have not received formal approval through the government's official decision-making channels.[27]

In *Monell v. Department of Social Services*, the Supreme Court explained that the language of § 1983 compelled the conclusion that Congress did not intend a local government to be held liable solely because it employs a tortfeasor. That is, it cannot be held liable under the *respondeat superior* theory. However, local governing bodies and local officials *may* be sued directly under § 1983 for monetary, declaratory, and injunctive relief in situations in which the officer's action that is alleged to be unconstitutional implements or executes a policy, ordinance, regulation, or decision officially adopted or promulgated by those whose edicts or acts may fairly be said to represent official policy.

Under this interpretation, the acts of the chief of police and his or her subordinates in their official capacity, whether *de jure* or *de facto*, equate with the acts of the city itself. In a North Carolina case the action was brought against the patrol officer, the city, the command sergeant, the director of the internal affairs division, the chief of police, and the city manager, for an injury received by an arrestee. The court

---

[26] *Lamkin v. Brooks,* 498 So. 2d 1068 (La. 1986).
[27] *Monell v. Department of Social Services,* 436 U.S. 658 (1978).

decided that the evidence supported a finding that the patrol officer assaulted a drug felon during and after arrest and that the assault proximately resulted from a de facto policy developed by supervisory officials.[28]

Although it is clear that a written policy established by an explicit directive will make a city liable for the acts of department employees, official policy may also be established by a de facto policy. In a civil rights action, the burden is on the plaintiff to show that a de facto policy did exist. This becomes difficult in some instances, but the Supreme Court shed some light on this requirement in two cases decided in 1985 and 1986.

In 1985, in *Oklahoma City v. Tuttle,* the Supreme Court held that it was reversible error to allow the jury to infer a policy of inadequate training on the city's part based on a single shooting incident.[29] The court indicated that a de facto policy cannot be established by *one* act of an officer who is not acting in an official decision-making capacity. The court explained that there must be an affirmative link between the municipality's policy and the alleged constitutional violation. If a cause of action is based on allegations of inadequate training, a *pattern* must be established or substantial proof provided that the policy was established or acquiesced in by a municipal policymaker.

One year later, in *Pembaur v. City of Cincinnati*, the Supreme Court decided that municipal liability may be imposed for a single decision *if* the decision is made by a municipal policymaker responsible for establishing final policy.[30] The court reasoned that this case differed from *Tuttle* because in this case, the instructions to "go in and get the employees" came from a county prosecutor who, under Ohio law, was authorized to give instructions to the county sheriff. The county prosecutor therefore was acting as the final decision-maker for the county, and the county could have been held liable under § 1983.

Following these decisions, lower federal courts have expounded on the liability of municipalities and supervisors. Although the courts have been uniform in holding that the doctrine of *respondeat superior* is inapplicable to § 1983 claims,[31] they have also been consistent in holding that municipalities are "persons" within the meaning of § 1983 and may be held liable if constitutional harm suffered was a result of

---

[28] *Spell v. McDaniel,* 604 F. Supp. 641 (E.D.N.C. 1985). However, neither a state nor its officials acting in their official capacity are "persons" under 42 U.S.C. § 1983. *Will v. Michigan Dept. of State Police,* 491 U.S. 58 (1989).

[29] *Oklahoma City v. Tuttle,* 471 U.S. 808 (1985).

[30] *Pembaur v. City of Cincinnati,* 475 U.S. 469 (1986).

[31] *Weimer v. City of Johnston,* New York, 931 F. Supp. 985 (N.D.N.Y. 1996); *Garcia v. Senkowski,* 919 F. Supp. 609 (N.D.N.Y. 1996); *Pugliese v. Cuomo,* 911 F. Supp. 58 (N.D.N.Y. 1996). *Hughes v. City of Hartford,* 96 F. Supp. 2d 114 (D. Conn. 2000).

official policy, custom, or pattern.[32] Municipalities are potentially liable in civil rights suits under § 1983 for policies and customs they consciously and purposefully adopt or if the alleged unconstitutional action implements or executes municipal policy, custom, pattern, or practice.[33]

B. Theories for Attaching Liability

Plaintiffs who file suits against police officers for deprivation of constitutional rights often join supervisors, administrators, and agencies in the lawsuit in order to reach those who have "deep pockets"—defendants with large financial reserves. It can also be assumed that the plaintiff will predicate the action on as many theories of liability as possible. For example, actions may be brought for failure to properly investigate personnel before appointment, failure to properly train, failure to supervise and control, failure to discipline, or failure to terminate officers who have proved unfit for carrying out their duties. For the purposes of this book, the emphasis is placed on the necessity of training police officers, especially regarding constitutional mandates.

The courts have recognized that municipalities and police administrators have an affirmative duty to train the police officers they employ. A breach of that duty, which proximately causes injury to the plaintiff, can result in personal liability on the part of the administrator or liability on the part of the agency. Courts have been particularly willing to find liability for failure to train when the use of firearms is involved.

C. Municipal Liability Under § 1983

In 1989, the U.S. Supreme Court left no doubt that a municipality can be held liable under 42 U.S.C. § 1983 for constitutional violations resulting from its failure to train municipal employees. In *City of Canton v. Harris*, the plaintiff alleged that the city was liable for violating the plaintiff's right, under the due process clause of the Fourteenth Amendment, to receive necessary medical attention while in police custody.[34] The trial court found the city liable, but the state court of appeals reversed, reasoning that the instructions to the jury might have led the jury to believe, incorrectly, that it could find against the city based on the *respondeat superior* doctrine.

The U.S. Supreme Court agreed with the trial court that a city can be held liable under § 1983 for inadequate training of its employees, but only where the failure to

---

[32] *Scott v. Moore,* 86 F.3d 230 (3d Cir. 1996).

[33] *Boyer v. Board of County Commissioners,* 922 F. Supp. 476 (D. Kan. 1996); *Keathley v. Vitale,* 866 F. Supp. 272 (E.D. Va. 1994).

[34] *City of Canton v. Harris,* 489 U.S. 378 (1989).

train amounts to *deliberate indifference* to the rights of people with whom the police come into contact. The Court went on to explain that the failure of the city to provide proper training to specific officers or employees is equivalent to a policy for which the city is responsible and for which the city may be held liable if it results in injury. The Court also indicated that, in order for liability to attach, the deficiency in the city's training program must be closely related to the ultimate injury. That is, there must be a causal connection between the failure to train and the ultimate injury.

After stating that a municipality is not automatically liable under § 1983, even if it inadequately trained or supervised its employees and those employees violated the plaintiff's constitutional rights, the court established some guidelines. To establish that a municipality's failure to train evidenced a deliberate indifference to the rights of its citizens, a plaintiff must present evidence that the municipality knew of a need to train or supervise in a particular area and the municipality made a deliberate choice not to take any action. Plaintiffs may demonstrate this by showing that a need for more or better training was obvious when a pattern of constitutional violations existed, such that the municipality knew or should have known that corrective measures were needed or where the municipal employees face clear constitutional duties in recurrent situations, even without prior incidents, to place the municipality on notice.

In 2005, in *Town of Castle Rock v. Gonzales*,[35] the U.S. Supreme Court clarified when a municipality may be held civilly liable under § 1983. In this case, Gonzales had obtained a restraining order against her estranged husband, requiring him to stay away from her and their children. The order required police officers to arrest her husband if he violated the restraining order. When her husband took their children away, Gonzales contacted the police department and asked them to enforce the order. The police department refused to intervene. Gonzales' husband eventually killed their three children and committed suicide. Gonzales subsequently filed suit against the town of Castle Rock, rather than the police officers or police department. She claimed the town had a custom of not responding properly to complaints of restraining order violations. The town acknowledged that there was indeed a custom of not vigorously enforcing restraining orders, but that this did not constitute a violation of Gonzales' constitutional right to due process. The U.S. Supreme Court agreed, holding there was no civil liability because Gonzales did not have a property interest in police enforcement of the restraining order against her husband, and thus there was no due process violation. The Court did note that state tort law might provide a remedy for the town's misfeasance.

In summary, in order to hold the city or agency liable under § 1983 for failure to train, the plaintiff must introduce evidence to show that: (1) the municipality failed to train the officer for the specific duty assigned; (2) the failure to train amounted

---

[35] *Town of Castle Rock v. Gonzales*, 545 U.S. 748 (2005).

Jessica Gonzales poses with a portrait of her three daughters, from left, Katheryn, Rebecca and Leslie. The three girls were killed by their father, Simon J. Gonzales, who died afterward in a shootout with police in Castle Rock, Colorado. Gonzales asked the U.S. Supreme Court to back her $30 million lawsuit claiming police didn't do enough to prevent her estranged husband from killing their three daughters. (*AP Photo/Craig F. Walker, Denver Post, file*)

to deliberate indifference to the rights of persons with whom the police come into contact; and (3) the deficiency in the city's training program was closely related to the ultimate injury (a causal connection between the duty to train and the injury).

It is extremely important that officers and administrators be aware of constitutional guarantees. An act violating constitutional rights can no more be justified by ignorance or disregard of settled, indisputable law than by the presence of actual malice. The responsibility for knowing constitutional mandates must be shared by the police officer and the administrator. Not only must the officer have a reasonable understanding of these rights, but the officer's knowledge must be continually updated.

D. Liability of Supervisors

Supervisors may also be liable under § 1983 if they were personally involved in the violation or they knowingly, willfully, or recklessly caused the deprivation of the constitutional right. To establish a § 1983 claim against a supervisory official, it must be shown that the official knowingly, willfully, or recklessly caused the alleged deprivation by his or her action or failure to act.

Liability under § 1983 cannot be based on the theory of *respondeat superior.* Personal involvement may be based on the supervisory role of the defendant, and personal involvement may include direct participation in the events. Failure of this supervisory official to remedy the wrong upon learning of it, or the creation, by a supervisory official, of a custom or policy under which the constitutional violations occurred may create liability on the part of the supervisor.

In *Samuels v. LeFevre*, a federal court listed the situations in which supervisory officials can be held liable under § 1983. That court stated that a supervisory official can be held to have been personally involved in constitutional violations and, therefore, is subject to § 1983 liability if he or she: (1) failed to remedy the wrong after hearing of a violation through a report or appeal; (2) created a policy or custom under which the constitutional violations occurred or allowed a custom or a policy to continue; or (3) was grossly negligent in managing the subordinates who committed the violations.[36]

E. Failure to Intervene

The courts have extended liability under § 1983 to police officers who are not in a supervisory position, but are present when a fellow officer deprives a citizen of constitutional rights. In *Crawford v. City of Kansas City*, the plaintiffs alleged that the officer should be liable because he failed to intervene to stop a shooting. The defendants argued that because the officer was not directly involved, there should be no liability. The court disagreed, noting that an officer who has the *opportunity* to prevent, but does *not* prevent, a fellow officer's use of allegedly excessive force may be liable under § 1983.[37]

In an Illinois case, the court held that a police officer who is present and fails to intervene to prevent other officers from infringing the constitutional rights of citizens is liable under § 1983 if that officer had reason to know that excessive force was being used, that the citizen had been unjustifiably arrested, or that any constitutional violation had been committed by law enforcement officers, and the officer had a realistic opportunity to intervene to prevent the harm from occurring.[38]

A police officer cannot be held liable, however, under § 1983 for failing to take reasonable steps to protect a victim of another officer's use of excessive force during

---

[36] *Samuels v. LeFevre,* 885 F. Supp. 32 (N.D.N.Y. 1995).
[37] *Crawford v. City of Kansas City,* 952 F. Supp. 1467 (D. Kan. 1997).
[38] *Lanigan v. Village of East Hazel Crest,* 110 F.3d 467 (7th Cir. 1997).

the course of arrest if he or she has no realistic opportunity to prevent the attack.[39] In this case, the fellow officer did not intervene, but called for back up units. The court held that this was a reasonable course of action under the circumstances and that the officer intervened at the first realistic opportunity to do so.

§ 2.7   Admissibility of Evidence

Perhaps the most costly result of failing to comply with constitutional mandates is that evidence will be inadmissible and people who are guilty of serious crimes will go free. The constitutional violations most often claimed when challenging evidence are summarized below.

A. Search and Seizure Exclusionary Rule

With some exceptions, evidence obtained by a search and seizure that violates Fourth Amendment standards as interpreted by the Supreme Court is inadmissible in criminal cases. This is referred to as the *exclusionary rule*. It was first established in 1914 in *Weeks v. United States*.[40] At the time the rule was established by the Supreme Court, it applied only to *federal* officers. However, in *Mapp v. Ohio*, decided in 1961, the Supreme Court held that the exclusionary rule would be applied in both federal *and* state courts.[41] A result of the exclusionary rule is that, in most instances, if evidence is obtained during an illegal search, it will be inadmissible. There are some exceptions to this rule, such as the "good faith" and "plain view" exceptions.

B. Inadmissibility of Confession Evidence

The *free and voluntary* rule, which prohibits the use of confessions obtained by force or duress, has been in effect in the United States since it was founded. Exceptions to this rule are discussed in Chapter 8.

---

[39]   *Fantasia v. Kinsella,* 956 F. Supp. 1409 (N.D. Ill. 1997).
[40]   *Weeks v. United States,* 232 U.S. 383 (1914).
[41]   *Mapp v. Ohio,* 367 U.S. 643 (1961).

C. The Right to Counsel Exclusionary Rule

The Supreme Court in *Nix v. Williams* noted that the rationale for the exclusionary rule is that the fruit of unlawful police conduct should be excluded, because such a course is needed to deter police from violating constitutional and statutory protections. Under this rule, evidence obtained as a result of failure to comply with the Sixth Amendment's right to counsel provision is excluded, notwithstanding "the high social cost of letting obviously guilty persons go unpunished."[42]

D. Exclusion of In-Court Identification

If the lineup, showup, or other confrontation (these procedures are discussed in future chapters) is so unnecessarily suggestive as to be conducive to irreparable mistaken identification, the procedure violates due process and the in-court identification could be contaminated. In addition, the admissibility of evidence is often challenged if, in obtaining the evidence, the officer violated the self-incrimination or due process provisions of the U.S. Constitution.[43]

§ 2.8   Summary

The exclusionary rule is a remedy created by the U.S. Supreme Court to deal with violations of the Fourth Amendment. It is not a constitutional requirement, but it can nonetheless result in the exclusion of evidence from trial. There are several exceptions to the exclusionary rule, most notably the good faith exception, which weaken its impact on law enforcement practices, but it remains crucial that law enforcement understand the possible consequences of acting unconstitutionally.

Before studying the specific provisions of the Constitution that limit police activity, it is important to understand the effects of failing to comply with the constitutional mandates as interpreted by the courts.

A law enforcement officer, on assuming the responsibilities of his or her office, takes an oath to support the Constitution of the United States. In most instances, however, he or she is unaware of the specific provisions of the Constitution and is not acquainted with the fact that civil and criminal liability can result from this lack of knowledge.

---

[42]   *Nix v. Williams,* 467 U.S. 431 (1984).
[43]   *Albright v. Oliver,* 510 U.S. 266 (1994).

A police officer is subject to civil liability under state tort laws if he or she fails to comply with constitutional provisions, state laws, municipal ordinances, or court decisions.

In addition to liability under state tort laws, a civil action may be brought in federal court under Title 42 United States Code § 1983. Under this title, the officer is liable if he or she acts under color of law and deprives a person of a constitutional right. The officer may also be criminally liable under Title 18 United States Code § 242 for failing to comply with constitutional mandates and acting with willful intent.

Supervisors and administrators cannot escape liability even if they do not take an active part in the violation of a constitutional right. Under the *respondeat superior* doctrine established at common law, agencies may be liable for the acts of their employees when the employees act in the scope of their employment. While the doctrine of *respondeat superior* is inapplicable to § 1983 claims, municipalities and supervisors are "persons" within the meaning of § 1983 and may be held liable. If administrators or supervisors fail to properly train or supervise the employee, they, as well as the agency they represent, may be subject to liability.

In addition to possible liability for failing to comply with constitutional mandates, in many instances, evidence obtained in violation of these provisions is excluded. As a result, pertinent evidence is not admitted even though it would help determine the facts of the case, and even though a person who is obviously guilty might go free.

Although a study of the constitutional mandates will not guarantee that a civil action will not be brought against the officer or administrator, or that evidence will always be admissible, there is no doubt that a thorough knowledge of the most important constitutional provisions will reduce the number of civil and criminal actions and will result in fewer admissibility problems.

Chapter 3
Police Power and Limitations

Due process of law is a summarized constitutional guarantee of respect for those personal immunities which are "so rooted in the traditions and conscience of our people as to be ranked as fundamental" or are "implicit in the concept of ordered liberty."

Rochin v. California, 342 U.S. 165 (1952)

§ 3.1   Police Power, Authority, and Responsibility

The "police power" of the state includes all the general laws and regulations necessary to secure the peace, good order, health, and prosperity of the people, and the regulation and protection of property rights. Police power is inherent in the states and, under this power, the states have passed laws defining crimes, regulating traffic, and providing for criminal procedural rules. In explaining the historic concept that the primary police power resides in the states, the United States Supreme Court stated that there is no better example of the police power, which the framers of the

Constitution denied the national government and gave to the states, than the suppression of violent crime and the vindication of its victims.[1] Under this broad authority, state legislatures may enact laws concerning the health, safety, and welfare of the people, so long as the regulations are not arbitrary or unreasonable.[2]

The federal government has no inherent police power as such. However, Congress may exercise a similar power incidental to the powers conferred to it by the commerce clause of the Constitution. Congress exercised this power sparingly for many years, but the powers granted to federal agencies and the federal government were gradually increased by Congress and approved by the U.S. Supreme Court. This resulted in more police power being given to the federal government and agencies, and state agencies having less power and more restrictions.

"Police authority" is the authority granted to law enforcement officers and agents so they may carry out the duties of their position. This authority is granted by statute, ordinance, and in some instances, court decision.

As a condition of employment, law enforcement officers are required to take an oath to enforce state and federal laws, and often city ordinances. In carrying out the responsibilities as designated by legislation, regulations, and the courts, the officer must often detain, arrest, search, or question suspects. Because of the peculiar position in which officers are placed, they have much more legal authority than the average citizen. Just as importantly, however, the officers have the responsibility to use their authority with prudence and discretion.

§ 3.2   Limits on Police Authority

The state's police power is limited by: (1) the rights guaranteed by the Constitution; (2) the necessity of a legitimate public purpose; and (3) a reasonable exercise of that power.[3]

Although sworn law enforcement officials have greater powers than the average citizen, these powers are not without limits. Article VI of the Constitution mandates that all executive and judicial officers, both of the United States and individual states, be bound by oath or affirmation to support the Constitution of the United States.

If, in carrying out the police powers of the state, there is a conflict between the enforcement of the statutes and protection of the constitutional rights as interpreted by the Supreme Court, the statute must give way. For example, the Supreme Court has determined that only certain types of searches are reasonable under the Constitution.

---

[1]   *United States v. Morrison*, 529 U.S. 598 (2000).

[2]   *State v. Leferink*, 992 Pa. 2d 775 (Idaho 1999).

[3]   *President Riverboat Casino, Inc. v. Missouri Gaming Commission*, 13 S.W.3d 635 (Mo. 2000).

Incoming New York City Police Commissioner William J. Bratton stands with his wife as Mayor Bill de Blasio reads the oath during Bratton's swearing in at police headquarters in New York. Criminal justice personnel are required to enforce state, federal, and local laws, but are bound by oath or affirmation to support the Constitution of the United States. (*AP Photo/Kathy Willen*s)

If, in enforcing a state law, an officer conducts an unreasonable search, the protections as guaranteed by the Fourth Amendment to the Constitution will be given priority.

§ 3.3   Bill of Rights

When the Constitution of the United States was ratified and became effective in 1789, it had no Bill of Rights. Those who opposed a Bill of Rights argued that such a guarantee was unnecessary, inasmuch as the powers granted to Congress were expressed powers, and limiting language was unnecessary. However, most of the states that finally ratified the Constitution submitted amendments to the Constitution to be acted on after the new government became operational.

At the first session of Congress, 10 amendments to the Constitution were approved and later ratified by the states. These first 10 amendments are known collectively as the Bill of Rights.[4] The Bill of Rights was not intended to establish any principles of government, but only to enumerate certain guarantees and immunities that the colonies had inherited from their English ancestors. The Bill of Rights, when adopted, was intended to apply only to the national government. The amendments did not apply to or restrict the states in any way.

The provisions of the Bill of Rights establish the foundation for statutes and court decisions concerning search and seizure, arrest, questioning procedures, the right to counsel, and other restrictions that limit action by public officials. Those of primary concern to law enforcement personnel are summarized here and are discussed in detail in future chapters.

- The Fourth Amendment prohibits unreasonable search and seizure of persons or property.
- The Fifth Amendment enumerates safeguards for persons accused of a crime. It provides, among other things, that no person shall be compelled in any criminal case to be a witness against himself, and no person shall be deprived of life, liberty, or property without due process of law.
- The Sixth Amendment assures that, in criminal prosecutions, the accused shall enjoy the right to a speedy and public trial by an impartial jury, the right to be confronted by witnesses against him, and the right to have the assistance of counsel for his defense.

These three amendments are of primary concern to criminal justice personnel, but they would mean little without court interpretation. The facts, reasoning, and decision of each individual case must be examined to determine the restrictions placed upon those who enforce the law.

§ 3.4   Due Process of Law

The Fifth Amendment, when ratified in 1791, included a provision that: "No person shall be deprived of life, liberty, or property, without due process of law . . ." This provision was adopted because the colonists feared a strong central government. It applied only to the federal government. It was not until 1868 that a federal constitutional due process provision became applicable to the states. In that year, the Fourteenth Amendment was ratified. Part of that amendment states:

> . . . nor shall any State deprive any person of life, liberty, or property, without due process of law.

---

4   See Appendix for the specific wording of the Bill of Rights.

Note that this provision specifically applies *to the states* and not to the federal government. Therefore, if a due process violation is claimed in a state case, the applicable provision is the Fourteenth Amendment due process clause, not the Fifth Amendment due process clause.

When the Fourteenth Amendment was written and ratified, it did not enumerate the specific protections that were included in the concept of "due process." For example, it did not indicate that the *state* shall not issue warrants without probable cause. However, soon after the Fourteenth Amendment was ratified, the U.S. Supreme Court faced the difficult task of determining whether the due process clause of the Fourteenth Amendment protected individual rights against the state in the same manner in which the Bill of Rights protected them against federal action.

After 50 years of cases holding that the due process clause of the Fourteenth Amendment did not incorporate the protections included in the Bill of Rights, the Supreme Court (on a piecemeal basis) began to hold that most of the rights enumerated in the first eight amendments *did* apply to the states. At present, the search and seizure provisions of the Fourth Amendment, the self-incrimination provisions of the Fifth Amendment, and the right to counsel provisions of the Sixth Amendment apply to the states by way of the due process clause of the Fourteenth Amendment.

In addition to using the Fourteenth Amendment due process clause as a vehicle for making most of the protections of the first eight amendments apply to the states, that clause, in a more general sense, *limits* the powers of the states. For example, in *Rochin v. California*, the U.S. Supreme Court applied the due process rationale in holding that forcing a defendant to have his stomach pumped in order to secure evidence violated the due process clause.[5]

§ 3.5   Effects of Broadening the Scope of the Fourteenth Amendment Due Process Clause

By broadly interpreting the due process clause of the Fourteenth Amendment, Congress and the courts have extended the powers of the federal government, and in so doing made it possible to establish guidelines for state officials. In making this power clear, the U.S. Supreme Court stated that the enforcement clause of the Fourteenth Amendment is a positive grant of legislative power that includes the authority to prohibit conduct that is not in itself unconstitutional and to intrude into legislative spheres of autonomy previously reserved to the states.[6]

---

5   *Rochin v. California,* 342 U.S. 165 (1952).
6   *United States v. Morrison,* 529 U.S. 598 (2000).

Where state officials once looked primarily to state court cases for standards and guidelines, they must now look as well to decisions of the U.S. Supreme Court. For example, not so long ago the states were free to establish their own policies concerning the scope of a search following a legal arrest. Now they must follow the mandates of U.S. Supreme Court decisions. In establishing that a provision of the Bill of Rights also limits state action, the Court thereby establishes minimum standards to be applied by state agents in enforcing state laws.[7]

When establishing procedures in criminal cases, including investigative procedures, law enforcement officials must study federal decisions in order to determine minimum protections to be given to people accused of crimes. Standards relating to detention, arrest, search, seizure, questioning, and confrontations for identification are discussed in the chapters that follow.

§ 3.6   Protection of Rights via State Constitutions and Laws

The U.S. Supreme Court establishes only minimum standards of conduct. The states may, through legislation or by court decision, require *stricter* standards of conduct. The states may not, however, either by legislation or constitutional amendment, establish standards that do not meet the minimum standards established by federal courts or Congress.

For many years, state courts that required stricter standards than those established by the U.S. Supreme Court did so by way of federal constitutional provisions, as well as state constitutions and statutes. However, in 1975, the Supreme Court mandated that the states, in requiring stricter standards than the U.S. Supreme Court, must do so by way of their own state constitutions and not by way of the federal constitution.[8] In *Oregon v. Hass*, the Supreme Court held that, as a matter of federal constitutional law, a state may not impose greater restrictions than the federal courts when the Supreme Court specifically refrains from imposing them. For example, if the U.S. Supreme Court finds that the self-incrimination provision of the Fifth Amendment does not prohibit the use of statements without the *Miranda* warnings for impeachment purposes, *states* cannot interpret that protection of the federal constitution in such a way as to prohibit the use of such a "confession for impeachment purposes." The state, by way of its own self-incrimination provision, may limit the use of the confession for impeachment purposes, but it may not use the Fifth Amendment self-incrimination provision in requiring greater restrictions than those mandated by the Supreme Court.

---

[7]   *Withrow v. Williams,* 507 U.S. 680 (1993).

[8]   *Oregon v. Hass,* 420 U.S. 714 (1975).

In a federal case that involved a search and seizure question, the search was valid under federal law but not under state law.[9] The discussion included this comment concerning the validity of state restrictions that are more stringent than federal restrictions:

> The Fourth and Fifth Amendments of the United States Constitution set only the minimum that is required. States are free to enact or to create by judicial fiat provisions additional privileges and immunities going beyond requirements found in the United States Constitution. New York State, through its courts, has chosen to expand upon the constitutional protections in several areas, one of which is a person's right to be free from unreasonable searches and seizures.

Because both federal and state courts may, by interpretation of their respective constitutions, limit authority, state officials must not only be familiar with the state statutes and court decisions, but with federal law and especially federal court decisions that determine police procedures.

§ 3.7   Summary

Criminal justice personnel are required to enforce state, federal, and local laws. On the other hand, they are bound by oath or affirmation to support the Constitution of the United States. Although the Supreme Court has attempted to balance the police power of the government and individual rights, if there is a conflict, the constitutional rights as interpreted by the U.S. Supreme Court take precedence.

Many of the individual rights that must be protected are listed in the Bill of Rights. Although these rights, such as those enumerated by the Fourth, Fifth, and Sixth Amendments, originally applied to the federal government, they now apply to the states by way of the Fourteenth Amendment due process clause. Consequently, decisions of the U.S. Supreme Court must be searched to determine the standards to be applied in such areas as search and seizure, self-incrimination, and right to counsel.

In addition to standards established by the Supreme Court, the states, by way of their constitutions, may establish additional requirements. Justice personnel must be familiar with both the minimum standards required by the federal courts, as well as those required by state law or state court decisions based upon state constitutions.

---

[9]   *Woods v. Candela,* 921 F. Supp. 1140 (S.D.N.Y. 1996).

Chapter 4
Police Authority to Detain

The Fourth Amendment does not require a policeman who lacks the precise level of information necessary for probable cause to arrest to simply shrug his shoulders and allow a crime to occur or a criminal to escape.

Adams v. Williams, 407 U.S. 143 (1972)

§ 4.1   General Considerations

Although most state statutes or codes clearly spell out the authority of a police officer to *arrest*, until recently, there were few such provisions concerning the right to *detain* without probable cause to arrest. Although it was common practice for police officers to stop and question a suspect under such circumstances, the courts and legal writers were sharply divided on the issue of whether such a right actually existed and, if it did exist, its precise limitations. This left police officers in a dilemma. Just one example may bring this troubling question into focus.

If a police officer, walking a beat at 2:00 A.M. in a commercial area where there is a high burglary rate, observes a person running from the back of a place of business and entering a car with its motor running and the lights out, does he have the authority to stop the car and question the occupants? Does the situation change if the occupant of the car refuses to answer any questions or claims that he is not required to answer questions? Is the officer subject to criminal or civil action if he detains the suspect in this situation?

Today, constitutional jurisprudence provides for three types of contact between citizens and the police: (1) consensual encounters; (2) brief detentions under the auspices of *Terry v. Ohio*; and (3) full-fledged arrests. After a brief discussion of the "consensual encounter," the remainder of this chapter will be devoted to a discussion of issues relating to the "stop-and-frisk" rule as stated in *Terry v. Ohio*. In Chapter 5, the requirements for a full arrest will be explored.

§ 4.2   Consensual Encounters

The police do not need reasonable suspicion or probable cause to initiate a voluntary encounter. A police officer may question a citizen concerning his or her identification and conduct without the encounter necessarily evolving into a seizure. If the police do not restrain the suspect's freedom of movement or communicate through words or conduct that compliance with their request is mandatory, they may ask questions about the contents of luggage, the reason for the suspect's presence at a particular place, or other reasonable and pertinent questions. Because a consensual encounter is voluntary, such an encounter does not constitute a "seizure" within the meaning of the Fourth Amendment. An individual is "seized," however, when he or she has an objective reason to believe that he or she is not free to terminate the conversation with the officer.[1] In distinguishing between "consensual encounters" and "detentions," a California court commented that a consensual encounter results in no restraint of an individual's liberty whatsoever and the officer is not required to have an objective justification to stop a citizen, while "detentions" are seizures of an individual that are strictly limited in time, duration, scope, and purpose.[2]

In distinguishing between a consensual encounter and a seizure, a Texas court explained that law enforcement officers are permitted to approach citizens, without any justification, to ask questions or even to request consent to search, and if a reasonable person would feel free to disregard the police and go about his or her

---

[1]   *United States v. Gigley,* 207 F.3d 1212 (10th Cir. 2000).
[2]   *In re Randy G.*, 96 Cal. Rptr. 2d 338 (2000).

business, then the encounter is consensual and merits no further analysis. However, under both federal and state constitutions, a seizure has occurred when a reasonable person would believe that he or she was not free to leave and that person has actually yielded to a show of authority or has been physically forced to yield.[3]

In many cases, there is a fine line between a consensual encounter and a stop-and-frisk situation. During a consensual encounter, a citizen is free to leave at any time or ignore the police officer's questions. If the person interviewed refuses to stop or refuses to answer questions and the officer continues to detain that person, it is no longer a consensual encounter. A court must consider the totality of the circumstances to determine whether the police exercised force or used their authority to effect a stop or whether the police merely sought the voluntary cooperation of a citizen through a consensual encounter.[4]

§ 4.3   *Terry v. Ohio* Stop-and-Frisk Rationale

In *Terry v. Ohio,* the U.S. Supreme Court squarely faced the problem relating to detention without an arrest and laid down some general rules.[5] The facts in *Terry* are similar to those of thousands of other cases in which police officers are confronted with situations that require action. In *Terry*, a police officer (McFadden), while patrolling the streets in downtown Cleveland, observed three men "casing a job—a stick up." The activities of the suspects, which included looking into the store window, walking a short distance, turning back, peering in the same store window, and returning to the corner, caused McFadden to determine that a further inquiry was justified. He therefore approached the three men, identified himself as a police officer, and asked their names. When the men mumbled something in response to his inquiry, McFadden grabbed one suspect (Terry), spun him around, and patted down the outside of his clothing. Feeling a pistol in the pocket of the overcoat, officer McFadden reached inside the overcoat but was unable to remove the weapon. However, he ordered Terry to remove the overcoat and retrieved a handgun. He then ordered all three men to face the wall with their hands raised. During a pat-down of the clothing of one of the other men (Chilton), he discovered a handgun in the pocket of Chilton's overcoat.

At the trial, a motion was made to suppress the guns that were taken from the clothing of the two defendants. Officer McFadden testified that he had only patted down the men to see whether they had weapons and that he did not put his hands beneath the outer garments of either Terry or Chilton until he felt the guns.

---

[3]   *Lewis v. State,* 15 S.W.3d 250 (Tex. 2000).
[4]   *People v. Herrera,* 1 P.3d 234 (Colo. 1999).
[5]   *Terry v. Ohio*, 392 U.S. 1 (1968).

The Court acknowledged that the question was a difficult and troublesome one. In discussing the case, arguments were advanced as to why police officers should not have the right to stop and frisk suspects in such situations. The U.S. Supreme Court upheld the detention and frisk by officer McFadden, stating:

> A police officer may in appropriate circumstances and in an appropriate manner approach a person for purposes of investigating possible criminal behavior *even though there is no probable cause to make an arrest.*

Thus, the U.S. Supreme Court, in distinguishing between an investigatory "stop" and an arrest, upheld the authority of police officers to detain a person when they observe unusual conduct that leads them to reasonably conclude, in light of their experience, that criminal activity may be afoot.

The authority to detain does not authorize a police officer to detain anyone on mere suspicion. The officer must be able to articulate the reasons for his or her belief that criminal activity was being planned or under way. The Supreme Court did say, however, that the officer could give weight to his or her experience and to the reasonable inferences that such familiarity entitles him or her to draw from the facts. The Court explained that the purpose of the *Terry* frisk is not to discover evidence, but rather to protect the police officer and bystanders from harm; the objective is to discover weapons readily available to the suspect that may be used against the officer.

The scope of the *Terry* stop-and-frisk doctrine was examined by the U.S. Supreme Court in 1972. The Court, in *Adams v. Williams*, approved the stopping and questioning of a suspect after an informant had advised the officer that the suspect was carrying narcotics and had a gun stuck under his belt.[6] In *Adams*, part of the officer's information was received from an informant, whereas in *Terry* the information to justify the stop was obtained by personal observation. The Supreme Court nonetheless upheld the stop-and-frisk based on the informant's information.

Although *Terry* clearly gives officers the right to detain a suspect if they can articulate facts upon which they based their belief that criminal activity was afoot, the right to detain is not without limits. In 1983, the U.S. Supreme Court elaborated on the standards to be applied in order to justify a detention without probable cause. In *Kolender v. Lawson*, police officers detained a pedestrian on the basis of a statute that justifies the detention of a person who loiters or wanders upon the streets and who refuses to identify him- or herself.[7] Under this statute, if the person detained refuses to identify him- or herself, he or she may be arrested. The Supreme Court found that the statute violated the due process clause of the Fourteenth Amendment because it

---

6   *Adams v. Williams*, 407 U.S. 143 (1972).
7   *Kolender v. Lawson,* 461 U.S. 352 (1983).

gave police unlimited discretion. The Court acknowledged that the stop might be justified if the requirements of *Terry* were met, but indicated that, in this case, the officers were given more authority to detain than that announced in *Terry v. Ohio*.

The right to stop and frisk under *Terry* requires a lesser degree of proof than that required to make an arrest.[8] In *United States v. Seslar*, the Tenth Circuit Court of Appeals succinctly pointed out the differences in the degree required. In general, there are three types of citizen–police encounters: (1) *consensual encounters*, which involve a citizen's voluntary cooperation with the official's noncoercive questioning and which are not seizures within the meaning of the Fourth Amendment; (2) *investigative detentions*, or *Terry* stops, which are seizures that are justified only if articulable facts and reasonable inferences drawn from those facts support a *reasonable suspicion* that the person has committed or is committing a crime; and (3) *arrests*, which are seizures characterized by a highly intrusive or lengthy detention, and which require probable cause to believe that the arrestee has committed or is committing a crime.[9]

An *investigative stop* is a short detention to determine whether criminal activity is about to take place. In evaluating the reasonableness of the investigative stop, the courts will examine whether the officer's action was justified at its inception, and whether it was reasonably related in scope to the circumstances that justified the interference in the first place.[10]

An investigatory stop is a "seizure" that must be justified by an objective manifestation that the person is or is about to be involved in criminal activity. Therefore, the detaining officer must have knowledge of specific, articulable facts that, if taken together with rational inferences from these facts, reasonably warrant the stop.[11] A seizure of a person occurs if a law enforcement officer intentionally and significantly restricts, interferes with, or otherwise deprives the individual of his or her liberty or freedom of movement, or whenever the individual believes that his or her liberty or freedom of movement has been deprived and such belief is objectively reasonable in the circumstances.[12]

In *Terry*, the U.S. Supreme Court established general guidelines to be followed by police officers when making an investigatory stop. However, the Court did not establish or define a "bright-line" rule. In *Rhodes v. State*, a Texas court noted that while a bright-line rule would be desirable for evaluating whether an investigative detention is unreasonable, common sense and ordinary human experience must

---

8   *United States v. Roberts*, 986 F.2d 1026 (1993).
9   *United States v. Seslar*, 996 F.2d 1058 (10th Cir. 1993). See *United States v. Ruiz*, 961 F. Supp. 1524 (D. Utah 1997) for a definition of consensual encounters.
10 *United States v. Muldrow*, 19 F.3d 1332 (10th Cir. 1994).
11 *State v. Dennis*, 753 So. 2d 296 (La. 1999).
12 *State v. Puffenbarger*, 998 P.2d 788 (Or. 2000).

govern these criteria.[13] The reasonableness of the detention must be judged from the perspective of a reasonable officer at the scene rather than with the advantage of hindsight, and allowances must be made for the fact that officers must often make quick decisions under tense, uncertain, and rapidly changing circumstances.

Reasonable suspicion is a less demanding standard than *probable cause*, because it can be established with information that is different in quality and content and could be less reliable than that required to show probable cause. While the courts have been consistent in holding that an investigative stop must be based on a reasonable and articulable suspicion that the person seized is engaged in criminal activity, there is less certainty concerning the factors that may be considered in determining the existence of "reasonable suspicion."[14] The courts have discussed on a case-by-case basis some specifics that can be considered in determining what amounts to reasonable suspicion. Among these are: (1) information from reliable persons; (2) reports from other agencies; (3) the individual is in an area of expected criminal activity; and (4) unprovoked flight from officers.

In discussing the weight to be given to a report from a known citizen, a Massachusetts court held that a report from a known citizen that a gun is being carried in public calls for investigation by the police.[15] However, an anonymous tip, standing on its own, is insufficient to support a reasonable, articulable suspicion that would justify an investigative stop; rather, to provide reasonable suspicion, either the informant or the information given must exhibit sufficient indicia of reliability.[16] A Virginia court, in discussing the value of an anonymous tip, stated that an anonymous tip that has been sufficiently corroborated may furnish reasonable suspicion justifying an investigative stop if the informant's information is independently corroborated so as to give some degree of reliability to the informant's allegation. In a federal case, the court held that police officers had reasonable suspicion to conduct an investigative stop of the defendant, based on a tip by a known and reliable informant giving a detailed description of the defendant and his automobile, the date and time of the crack cocaine transaction and its location, and the defendant's unprovoked flight from the officers when they approached him.[17]

Police officers may make investigatory stops on the basis of reliable information from another officer or agency. For example, in a Massachusetts case, police officers had articulable facts sufficient to make an investigatory stop when they had received a radio dispatch describing the perpetrators of a robbery at a convenience store. The reliability of the dispatch was substantiated by its detail: the officers observed a car

---

[13] *Rhodes v. State*, 945 S.W.2d 115 (Tex. 1997).
[14] *Jackson v. Sauls*, 206 F.3d 1156 (11th Cir. 2000).
[15] *Commonwealth v. Foster*, 724 N.E.2d 357 (Mass. 2000).
[16] *Giles v. Commonwealth*, 529 S.E.2d 327 (2000). *See also Florida v. J.L.*, 529 U.S. 266 (1999).
[17] *United States v. Hodge*, 89 F. Supp. 2d 668 (D.V.I. 2000).

parked behind another convenience store on the most direct route from the munici-pality in which the robbery occurred, and the clothing of the two men in the car matched the description of the robbery suspects.[18]

Although the fact that the contact by the police occurred at a certain time of the day or night will not in itself justify reasonable suspicion that criminal activity may be afoot, many cases have included the time element, along with other factors, in determining that reasonable suspicion justified the stop. For example, in a Louisiana case, the court held that an investigatory stop of the subject was justified when the subject and two other men were in the parking lot of a closed private business at 3:30 A.M., and the business owner had complained to the police of criminal acts in the parking lot after business hours.[19]

Some recent decisions have questioned the legitimacy of citing the area of con-tact, such as a high-crime area, as a basis for reasonable suspicion. For example, in a Ninth Circuit Court of Appeals decision, the judges indicated that the citing of an area as "high-crime," for purposes of determining whether an investigatory stop in the area is based on reasonable suspicion, requires careful examination by the court because such a description, unless properly limited and factually based, can easily serve as a proxy for race or ethnicity.[20] However, most courts give consideration to the fact that crimes are more likely to occur in some areas. For example, a Louisiana court reasoned that an investigatory stop-and-frisk of the defendant for weapons was justified by an officer's knowledge that the defendant was a suspect in an armed rob-bery, the defendant's presence in the high-crime location, and the defendant's ner-vousness when the officers attempted to question him.[21]

The area of the activity is especially important in drug-related cases. In a Penn-sylvania case, the court held that the investigatory stop of the defendant was based on reasonable suspicion because the officer had made many narcotics arrests and was familiar with drug trafficking that regularly took place in the area. The court noted that the officer had staked out the location necessary for surveillance based on its notorious reputation for open drug sales, the officer had observed an exchange of cash for a small object that appeared to him in light of his experience to be a drug sale, and the officer had conducted an investigatory stop.[22]

---

[18] *Commonwealth v. Barbosa*, 729 N.E.2d 650 (Mass. 2000).

[19] *State v. Lagarde*, 758 So. 2d 279 (La. 2000).

[20] *United States v. Montere-Camargo*, 208 F.3d 1122 (9th Cir. 2000).

[21] *State v. Brumfield*, 745 So. 2d 214 (La. 1999).

[22] *Commonwealth v. Valentin*, 748 A.2d 711 (Pa. 2000). See also *People v. Reyes*, 708 N.Y.S.2d 82 (2000), in which the court included a comment that the observation took place in an area known for drug activity, and *Wise v. State* 751 A.2d 24 (Mass. 2000), in which the court used the term "high narcotics traffic."

The conduct of a suspect, when evaluated in light of the police officer's experience, may furnish the background against which to assess facts relevant to whether reasonable suspicion exists to support an investigatory stop. However, experience does not, in itself, serve as an independent factor in the reasonable suspicion analysis and the inferences the officer draws must be objectively reasonable.[23]

In a New York case, the court held that the police officer had reasonable suspicion to stop and detain a suspect for questioning, given the police officer's experience and training, the large number of drug sales in the area, and his view of a hand-to-hand transaction in which the officer observed the suspect exchanging money for a small item.[24]

The "reasonable suspicion" issue reached the U.S. Supreme Court in *Illinois v. Wardlow*.[25] The evidence presented indicated that Wardlow fled upon seeing police officers patrolling an area known for heavy narcotics trafficking. Two of the officers caught up with Wardlow, stopped him, and conducted a protective pat-down search for weapons. Discovering a .38 caliber handgun, the officers arrested Wardlow, who was convicted of unlawful use of a weapon by a felon. The trial court denied Wardlow's motion to suppress the evidence of the gun, finding that the gun was recovered during a lawful stop-and-frisk in accordance with the *Terry* rule. The state appellate court reversed, declaring that the police did not have reasonable suspicion to make this stop. The state supreme court affirmed, determining that sudden flight in a high-crime area does not create a reasonable suspicion justifying a *Terry* stop, as flight may simply be an exercise of the right to "go on one's way."

The U.S. Supreme Court upheld the conviction, stating that the stop was supported by reasonable suspicion as required by *Terry v. Ohio*. In this decision, the high court considered: (1) whether the individual's presence in an area of expected criminal activity created reasonable, particularized suspicion; and (2) whether flight by a suspect upon seeing the police is in itself sufficient to justify a temporary investigative stop of the kind authorized by *Terry*. On the issue of the individual's presence in the high-crime area, the Court noted that an individual's presence in a "high-crime area," standing alone, is *not* enough to support a reasonable, particularized suspicion of criminal activity. But a location's characteristics are relevant in determining whether the circumstances are sufficiently suspicious to warrant further investigation.

On the issue of flight by a suspect upon the mere sight of a police officer as justifying reasonable suspicion, the Court rejected the proposition that flight in itself is an indication of ongoing criminal activity. Flight is, however, a factor that can be considered. The Court stated that "Headlong flight—wherever it occurs—is the

---

[23]   *United States v. Mattarolo,* 209 F.3d 1153 (9th Cir. 2000).

[24]   *People v. Murphy,* 699 N.Y.S.2d 443 (1999).

[25]   *Illinois v. Wardlow,* 528 U.S. 119 (2000).

consummate act of evasion; it is not necessarily indicative of wrongdoing, but is certainly suggestive of such." The Supreme Court concluded that, based on the total-ity of circumstances, the officer was justified in suspecting that the individual was involved in criminal activity and, therefore, in investigating further.

§ 4.4   Application to Off-Street Situations

Although the detention in *Terry* involved a pedestrian on the street, there is no reason the same rationale could not be applied to a situation in which the suspect is in a building, or even in his or her own home.

The *Terry* detention doctrine has a very practical application when the officer who is executing a search warrant discovers that a person not described in the warrant is on the scene. The officer in this instance may, of course, make an arrest if he or she has probable cause, or if the person commits a crime in his or her presence. On the other hand, there are some situations in which there is no probable cause to make an arrest, but there is information that leads the officer to believe that criminal activity is afoot, as exemplified by *Terry*. If there is a sufficient basis to believe that criminal activity is afoot, the officer, in order to protect himself or herself, may detain the person and pat down his or her outer clothing for weapons.[26]

§ 4.5   Application to Detention of Motorists

Although there is no doubt that a police officer may arrest the driver of an auto-mobile if he or she has probable cause to believe that a felony has been committed, or if a misdemeanor is committed in his or her presence, there are many situations in which it is desirable to have the right to stop an automobile for the purpose of asking questions, even where there is no probable cause to make an arrest. Historically, the law relating to the authority to detain motorists when there was no probable cause to arrest was in doubt. However, in *United States v. Cortez* in 1981, the Supreme Court made it clear that the *Terry* reasoning applied to automobile situations.[27]

In *Cortez*, officers stopped a pickup truck that they believed, in view of their experience, was carrying illegal aliens. Even though the officers did not have the necessary probable cause to make an arrest, they had articulable reasons for believing that the truck carried illegal aliens on the particular route that was followed. The Supreme Court, in approving the investigative stop, explained that the reasoning of

---

[26]   *Ybarra v. Illinois,* 444 U.S. 85 (1979).
[27]   *United States v. Cortez,* 449 U.S. 411 (1981).

Terry v. Ohio applies in automobile situations. In order to make a *Terry* stop, the Court explained, the officer must assess the situation based upon the totality of circumstances. From this assessment, the officer may then draw inferences and make deductions. In making these deductions, the evidence may be weighed as understood by those knowledgeable in the field of law enforcement.

A federal court held that, under *Terry*, law enforcement agents may briefly stop moving vehicles to investigate the reasonable suspicion that its occupants are involved in criminal activity.[28] And a state court commented that police officers can require motorists to stop and respond to investigatory questions if the officers have reasonable suspicion that the individual has committed or is about to commit a crime; the purpose of the detention is reasonable; and the detention itself is reasonable in light of the purpose of the investigatory stop.[29]

Having recognized that a *Terry* stop applies in automobile situations, the Supreme Court in 1985 considered the authority of a police officer to stop a vehicle on the authority of a "wanted" flyer, issued by another department in another state.[30] In *United States v. Hensley*, the officer stopped a vehicle on the basis of information he received on a "wanted" flyer from an adjacent state. During the detention, the officer seized evidence that was later introduced at trial. The defendant complained that the initial stop was illegal; therefore, use of the evidence violated the exclusionary rule. In upholding the stop and detention, the Court recognized that the law enforcement interest at stake in these circumstances outweighs the individual's interest to be free of a detention that is no more extensive than necessary. The Court indicated that when police have reasonable suspicion, grounded in specific and articulable facts, that a person they encounter was involved in or was wanted in connection with a completed felony, then a *Terry* stop may be made to investigate that suspicion.

In 1990, the U.S. Supreme Court was again confronted with the question of whether an informant's tip may carry sufficient indicia of reliability to justify a *Terry* stop, even though it may be insufficient to support an arrest or search warrant.[31] In *Alabama v. White,* police received an anonymous telephone tip that the suspect, White, would be leaving a particular apartment at a particular time, in a particular vehicle, that she would be going to a particular motel, and that she would be in possession of cocaine. The police immediately proceeded to the apartment building, saw a vehicle matching the description given by the caller, observed White as she left the building and entered the vehicle, and followed her along the

---

[28] *United States v. Patch,* 114 F.3d 131 (9th Cir. 1997).
[29] *People v. Melanson,* 937 P.2d 826 (Colo. 1996).
[30] *United States v. Hensley,* 469 U.S. 221 (1985).
[31] *Alabama v. White,* 496 U.S. 325 (1990).

most direct route to the motel, stopping her vehicle just short of the motel. The Alabama appeals court reversed her conviction, holding that the trial court should have suppressed the marijuana and cocaine evidence because the officers did not have the reasonable suspicion necessary under *Terry v. Ohio* to justify the investigatory stop of the vehicle.

The U.S. Supreme Court reversed, concluding that the anonymous tip, as corroborated by independent police work, exhibited sufficient indicia of reliability to provide reasonable suspicion to make the investigatory stop. The Court explained that, standing alone, the tip is completely lacking the necessary indicia of reliability because it provides virtually nothing from which one might conclude that the caller is honest or his or her information is reliable, and gives no indication of the bases for his or her predictions regarding White's criminal activities. However, the Court continued, although it is a close question, the totality of the circumstances demonstrates that significant aspects of the informant's story were sufficiently corroborated by the police to furnish reasonable suspicion. The Court explained that reasonable suspicion that justifies an investigatory stop is a less demanding standard than probable cause, not only in the sense that reasonable suspicion can be established with information that is different in quantity or content than that required to establish probable cause, but also in the sense that reasonable suspicion can arise from information that is less reliable than that required to show probable cause. Referring to the "totality of circumstances" approach for determining whether an informer's tip establishes probable cause for a search warrant as explained in *Illinois v. Gates*,[32] the Court reasoned that the informant's veracity, reliability, and basis of knowledge, which are relevant in determining whether an informer's tip establishes probable cause, are also relevant in the reasonable suspicion context, although an allowance must be made in applying them to the lesser showing required to meet the reasonable suspicion standard.

The authority to stop a vehicle when the officer has reasonable suspicion that a person is involved in criminal activity has been challenged in hundreds of cases. In many of these cases, the courts have found that the stop was unlawful because the officer failed to articulate sufficient facts to justify "reasonable suspicion." Some of these cases are summarized below to give the reader some insight into what the courts consider "reasonable suspicion."

In a decision by the Ninth Circuit Court of Appeals, it was reiterated that the Fourth Amendment allows government officials to conduct an investigatory stop of a vehicle only upon a showing of reasonable suspicion: a particularized and objective basis for suspecting the particular person stopped of criminal activity.[33] The court continued by stating that "reasonable suspicion" permitting an investigatory

[32] *Illinois v. Gates*, 462 U.S. 213 (1983).
[33] *United States v. Thomas*, 211 F.3d 1186 (9th Cir. 2000).

stop of a vehicle requires specific, articulable facts that, together with objective and reasonable inferences, form a basis for suspecting that a particular person is engaged in criminal conduct. After stating these general principles, the court then decided that information local law enforcement agents received from FBI agents, suggesting that the local agent "might want to pay particular attention to a certain house," based on "a suspicion that there was a possibility that there might be some narcotics there," was entirely conjectural and thus did not support a finding of reasonable suspicion to conduct an investigatory stop of a motor vehicle that drove away from the house.

A Florida court succinctly stated that rule: "what is required for a valid vehicle stop is a founded suspicion on the part of the officers effectuating the stop that the occupants have committed or are about to commit a crime."[34] Applying this rule, the court reasoned that information contained in a report to "be on the lookout" (BOLO) for an automobile whose occupants were allegedly involved in a robbery and shooting was sufficiently reliable to justify an investigatory stop of the automobile, even though the source of the information was two witnesses who were never identified, where the officer who issued the BOLO testified that the witnesses approached him upon his arrival at the crime scene with the information that the perpetrator fled in a car and provided a detailed description and tag number of the car, and there was no reason to doubt the veracity of that information.

To illustrate the fine line between a justifiable stop and a stop that is not justified, consider the following cases. In a federal case, the court held that the police had reasonable suspicion that the automobile was stolen, sufficient to support an investigatory stop when the vehicle was the same color and make as a car reported stolen, the driver was of the same race and appeared to be of the same age as the alleged perpetrator of the theft, and a sticker affixed to the windshield in lieu of the license plate was held in place by masking tape, suggesting that it was taken from another vehicle.[35]

In a Maryland case, however, the court held that the police officer was not justified, under the reasonable suspicion standard, in conducting an investigative traffic seizure of the defendant, who was operating his vehicle in compliance with the rules of the road at 3:05 A.M., when the officer had been informed an hour and 15 minutes earlier that a robbery was committed at a hotel two miles away, and that the suspects were three black men who fled in a gold or tan car, and the defendant was a black male, was driving a gold car, and was carrying one black male as a passenger.[36]

---

[34]   *State v. Ramos,* 755 So. 2d 836 (Fla. 2000).

[35]   *United States v. Davis,* 200 F.3d 1053 (7th Cir. 2000).

[36]   *Cartnail v. State,* 753 A.2d 519 (Mass. 2000).

§ 4.6   Detention of Luggage

Having determined that police may detain pedestrians under the *Terry* doctrine and may detain motorists using the same rationale, the Court had little difficulty applying these principles to the detention of luggage. In *United States v. Place*, the Supreme Court approved the detention of luggage when an officer's observations led him to reasonably believe that the luggage contained contraband.[37] The Court indicated that *Terry* principles permitted the officer to detain the luggage temporarily to investigate the circumstances that aroused the officer's suspicion as long as the detention was reasonable as to both time and manner.

It is interesting to note that in the *Place* case, the Court also reasoned that subjecting luggage to a "sniff test" by a trained narcotics detection dog does not constitute a "search" within the meaning of the Fourth Amendment. This holding was recently upheld by the Supreme Court in *Illinois v. Caballes*.[38] In *Caballes,* the Supreme Court held that running a drug detection dog around a vehicle during a traffic stop did not violate the Fourth Amendment.

§ 4.7   Duration of the Detention

To be constitutional, an investigative detention must be justified at its inception and must be reasonably related in scope to the circumstances that justified the interference in the first place; and the length of the detention may not be longer than necessary to confirm or dispel the officer's suspicions regarding the criminal activity for which the investigatory stop was initiated.[39] If a detention continues beyond the time reasonably necessary to effect its initial purpose, the seizure may lose its lawful character.

Although the U.S. Supreme Court has not established any standard time limit for a permissible stop, some guidelines can be gleaned from the cases. In *United States v. Place*, discussed previously, the Court warned that while luggage may be detained, it may only be detained for a reasonable period. In *Place*, a detention of 90 minutes was considered too long.

In *United States v. Sharpe*,[40] Drug Enforcement Administration agents, with the assistance of a state officer, detained vehicles for a period of about 20 minutes. They stopped a truck camper and an automobile based on a reasonable suspicion that the

---

[37] *United States v. Place,* 462 U.S. 696 (1983).
[38] *Illinois v. Caballes,* 543 U.S. 405 (2005).
[39] *Meinert v. City of Prairie Village, Kansas,* 87 F. Supp. 2d 1175 (D. Kan. 2000).
[40] *United States v. Sharpe,* 470 U.S. 675 (1985).

camper was loaded with marijuana. The U.S. Supreme Court noted that, in evaluating the reasonableness of an investigative stop, the Court examines "whether the officer's action was justified at its inception and whether it was reasonably related in scope to the circumstances which justified the interference in the first place." As to the length of a stop or detention, the Court must consider the purposes to be served by a stop as well as the time reasonably needed to effectuate those purposes. The Supreme Court agreed with the trial court that the 20-minute detention was not too long under the circumstances. In this case, the DEA agent had diligently pursued his investigation and no delay unnecessary to the investigation was involved.

In determining the period of detention, it should be noted that the courts will consider whether the officer making the stop diligently pursued the investigation and whether it was related in scope to the circumstances that justified the interference in the first place. While 20 minutes was not too long in this case, it could have been too long had the circumstances been different. On the other hand, had the circumstances justified a more time-consuming investigation—for example, to check whether the car was stolen—then 20 minutes would not necessarily have been too long.

Although the courts have not established any definite limits on the duration of a *Terry* stop, many cases have been considered by the courts. A review of both federal and state cases makes it possible to formulate rules that must be followed by enforcement personnel when considering the legality of an investigative stop.

In a comprehensive decision by a Connecticut court, that court not only decided the case based on the facts, but included in the opinion rules to guide officers in future cases.[41] In this case, the police stopped a vehicle based on reports that the occupants had been involved in a shooting. The officers removed the occupants from the vehicle, searched them, and detained them for one hour. The court decided that one hour of detention was not too long, considering the seriousness of the crimes and the need to check the description and identification of those detained. The court noted that:

> A *Terry* stop that is justified at its inception can become constitutionally infirm if it lasts longer or becomes more intrusive than necessary to complete the investigation for which the stop was made. . . . If, on the contrary, the officer's suspicions are confirmed or further aroused during the *Terry* stop, the stop may be prolonged and the scope enlarged as required by the circumstances.

The constitutional considerations for investigative detention are whether the detention was too long in duration, whether the police officers diligently pursued means of investigation that were likely to confirm or dispel their suspicions quickly, and whether the police were unreasonable in not recognizing alternative, less intrusive

---

[41] *State v. Casey,* 692 A.2d 1312 (Conn. 1997).

means by which their objectives might have been accomplished. If the detention was a result of the defendant's own actions, this fact is considered in determining whether the duration of the stop was too long.

In a Georgia case, the court held that airport drug enforcement agents had a reasonable suspicion that the defendant possessed drugs and this warranted detaining the defendant for 20 minutes before the arrival of a narcotics detection dog.[42] A New York court also agreed that 20 minutes was reasonable when the suspects were held until officers could make inquiries absolving them of the suspicion of a robbery.[43] However, a Florida court determined that the officers no longer had a reasonable basis to justify an investigative detention after the officers had learned the defendant's identity and verified that he was a resident in the neighborhood.[44] The court added that the officer's testimony that the situation still "didn't feel right" to him, however genuine, did not amount to a reasonable and articulable suspicion that the defendant was committing or about to commit a crime.

§ 4.8 Detention to Check Driver's License and Registration

Until 1979, it was common practice for police officers to stop vehicles to check a driver's license, even if there was no articulable reason to believe that the person driving did not have a license. In 1979, the Supreme Court, in *Delaware v. Prouse*, addressed the issue of routine police stops for the purpose of checking drivers' licenses or registration certificates, and halted the practice.[45]

In *Prouse*, a patrol officer stopped an automobile and seized marijuana that was in plain view on the car floor. The patrol officer testified that, prior to stopping the vehicle, he had observed neither traffic nor equipment violations and had no suspicion of any criminal activity. He admitted he made the stop only to check the driver's license and the car's registration.

Although the Court acknowledged that states have a vital interest in ensuring that only those qualified to do so are permitted to operate motor vehicles, the Court also noted that these important ends did not justify the intrusion on the Fourth Amendment interest that such stops involve.

The decision in *Prouse* made it clear that while the police practice of stopping vehicles for the sole purpose of checking operators' licenses would not pass

---

[42] *Gordon v. State*, 528 S.E.2d 838 (Ga. 2000).

[43] *Mendoza v. City of Rome*, 70 F. Supp. 2d 137 (N.D.N.Y. 2000).

[44] *Ikner v. State*, 756 So. 2d 1116 (Fla. 2000).

[45] *Delaware v. Prouse*, 440 U.S. 648 (1979).

constitutional muster, a traffic violation does support an investigatory stop. When such a stop is made, the length and scope of the investigation are limited by circumstances justifying the initial intrusion.

A police officer's investigation during a traffic stop may include asking for the driver's license and registration. To justify the traffic stop and the resulting driver's license check, the officer must be able to articulate facts that would create an objectively reasonable suspicion that the individual is involved in criminal activity.

Although the Supreme Court prohibited future indiscriminate stopping of automobiles to check drivers' licenses and registrations, the Court in *Prouse* approved stopping vehicles if there were articulable and reasonable suspicions that the motorist was unlicensed or that the automobile was not registered. The Court also indicated that the decision did not preclude states from developing methods for spot checks that involve less intrusion or do not involve the unrestrained exercise of discretion.

§ 4.9   Detention at Police Roadblocks

In recent years, the U.S. Supreme Court has been called upon to determine whether the establishment of police roadblocks for the purpose of curbing drunk driving violates the Fourth Amendment to the U.S. Constitution. While acknowledging that stopping an automobile as a part of a highway sobriety checkpoint program constitutes a "seizure" within the meaning of the Fourth Amendment, the Court nevertheless noted that such stops are consistent with the Fourth Amendment.[46]

In *Michigan Department of State Police v. Sitz*, the Michigan State Police had established a highway sobriety checkpoint program with guidelines governing checkpoint operations, site selection, and publicity. During one operation, 126 vehicles passed through the checkpoint with an average delay of 25 seconds per vehicle. Only two drivers were arrested for driving under the influence. The trial court found that the program violated the Fourth Amendment and the state court of appeals affirmed, agreeing with the lower court's findings that sobriety checkpoints are generally ineffective and, therefore, do not significantly further that interest; and that while the checkpoint's objective intrusion on individual liberties is slight, their "subjective intrusion" is substantial.

The U.S. Supreme Court, using a "balancing test," reversed the lower court decision and held that the highway sobriety checkpoint program was consistent with the Fourth Amendment. Noting that drunk drivers cause an annual death toll of more than 25,000, and in the same time span cause nearly one million personal injuries and

---

[46] *Michigan Department of State Police v. Sitz*, 496 U.S. 444 (1990).

Ohio State Highway Patrol troopers hand out survey cards and talk with motorists at a sobriety checkpoint. Courts have upheld the practice of sobriety checkpoints when appropriate procedures have been established. (*AP Photo/David Kohl*)

more than $5 billion in property damage, the Court concluded that the state's interest in preventing drunk driving was significant. When this interest was balanced against the minimal intrusion on individual liberties that the checkpoint entailed, the balancing test weighed in favor of the checkpoint program.

In approving this limited use of sobriety checkpoints, the Court emphasized the fact that the checkpoints in this case were selected pursuant to specific guidelines and that the uniformed police officers stopped every approaching vehicle. Referring to previous cases, the Court stressed that the circumstances surrounding a checkpoint stop-and-search are far less intrusive than those attending a roving patrol stop.[47]

Courts have upheld the practice of sobriety checkpoints when appropriate procedures have been established. In a Tennessee case, the reviewing court, after discussing other cases, agreed that sobriety checkpoints met the requirements of the state as well as the federal Constitution. The court cautioned, however, that such checkpoints, although seizures, can be reasonable, provided they are established and operated in

---

[47]   *United States v. Martinez-Fuerte,* 428 U.S. 543 (1976).

accordance with predetermined operational guidelines and supervisory authority that minimizes the risk of arbitrary intrusion on individuals and limits the discretion of law enforcement officers at the scene.[48] The court noted that the decision to hold a sobriety checkpoint, as well as the decision as to the time and place, should be matters reserved for prior administrative approval, thus removing determination of those matters from the discretion of police officers in the field. In this case, the court held that the sobriety checkpoint was not established and operated in a manner that was consistent with the state constitution, and thus the checkpoint constituted an unreasonable seizure. The court explained that the decision to set up the roadblock was made by an officer in the field, the site selected for the roadblock and the procedure to be used in operating the roadblock were matters left to the discretion of the officer in the field, and no supervisory authority was sought or obtained.

In establishing guidelines for the use of roadblock stops, a Georgia court held that the totality of the circumstances surrounding a police roadblock must show that the roadblock is not being used as a pretext to detain citizens in order to search their cars.[49]

A New Jersey court held that a motor vehicle may be stopped without reasonable suspicion at a roadblock, provided that the time, location, and operation of the roadblock are reasonable, and that it does not bear arbitrarily or oppressively on motorists as a class.[50] The court also warned that the state using a roadblock bears the burden of establishing that government interests are of sufficient importance to justify the intrusion upon the traveling public's federal and state constitutional rights to be free of warrantless seizures.

The validity of using checkpoints in an effort to discover unlawful drugs was addressed by the U.S. Supreme Court in *Indianapolis v. Edmond*.[51] At issue were checkpoints set up on six occasions on the streets of Indianapolis. Motorists were stopped, their licenses were inspected, and detectives circled the cars with dogs to sniff for drugs. After 1,161 motorists were stopped, 55 arrests were made for drug-related crimes. Edmond filed a lawsuit claiming that the roadblocks violated the Fourth Amendment. The Supreme Court held that the checkpoint program to discover unlawful drugs violated the Fourth Amendment. The Court distinguished between establishing roadblocks for the purpose of curbing drunk driving and establishing roadblocks for the purpose of searching for evidence of drug trafficking. Absent an emergency or imminent threat to the lives and safety of the public, roadblocks for the purpose of searching for evidence of drug trafficking violate the Fourth Amendment. The Court noted that roadblocks stop citizens without probable cause or reasonable suspicion to look for evidence of criminal activity,

---

[48] *State v. Downey,* 945 S.W.2d 102 (Tenn. 1997).
[49] *Boyce v. State,* 523 S.E.2d 607 (Ga. 1999).
[50] *State v. Flowers,* 745 A.2d 553 (N.J. 2000).
[51] *Indianapolis v. Edmond,* 531 U.S. 32 (2000).

and the risk that narcotics trafficking poses to the public is not immediate (unlike the problem of drunk driving), as is the risk posed by a person operating a vehicle while under the influence of alcohol.

In 2004, in *Illinois v. Lidster*, the U.S. Supreme Court again examined the constitutionality of a checkpoint program.[52] In this case, police in Lombard, Illinois, set up a roadblock in an effort to obtain information from drivers about a recent hit-and-run accident. The police set up the roadblock at the site of the accident and at the same time of day the accident had occurred. The police thought questioning drivers who were driving in the area might help them locate a witness to the accident. Drivers were stopped for about 15 seconds, asked if they had seen the accident, and handed a flyer with information about the accident. Lidster was stopped after the vehicle he was driving swerved and almost struck an officer as it approached the roadblock. Police smelled alcohol on Lidster's breath, investigated further, and eventually arrested him for drunk driving. On appeal, Lidster argued that the checkpoint was unconstitutional. The Supreme Court upheld the checkpoint, noting that the public interest in solving the hit-and-run accident was great, while the checkpoint itself represented only a minimal intrusion on Fourth Amendment liberties. Balancing the governmental interest against the intrusion on individual liberties, the Court determined that the checkpoint was reasonable.

§ 4.10 Summary

Although the laws of arrest have for some time been spelled out by statutes and court decisions, those relating to detention without probable cause are of more recent origin.

In 1968, the U.S. Supreme Court provided some guidelines for detaining without making an arrest. Under these guidelines, a police officer may, in appropriate circumstances and in an appropriate manner, detain a person for investigation, even without probable cause to arrest, when the officer reasonably believes, in light of his or her experience, that criminal activity may be afoot. This does not grant authority to the police officer to stop a person on mere suspicion, but it does allow the officer to detain someone when he or she can articulate facts that reasonably lead him or her to believe, in light of his or her experience, that criminal activity has occurred, is occurring, or is about to occur.

The *Terry* principle, which authorizes detention without arrest, has been applied in detaining pedestrians on the street as well as people in buildings and apartments if the detaining officer can articulate facts that justify his or her belief that criminal activity is afoot. More recently, the courts have applied the *Terry* reasoning to automobile situations if the detention is not more extensive than necessary under the circumstances.

---

[52] *Illinois v. Lidster*, 540 U.S. 419 (2004).

The *Terry* doctrine, which authorizes the detention of pedestrians without probable cause, has also been applied in determining whether luggage can be detained. If an officer's observations lead him or her to reasonably believe that the luggage contains narcotics or contraband, then the *Terry* principles permit the officer to detain the luggage temporarily to investigate the circumstances that aroused his or her suspicions.

Although the courts have not placed any definite time limitations on a particular detention, they will look to the purpose of the detention and whether the police diligently pursue the investigation to confirm or dispel their suspicions.

A police officer does not have the authority to routinely stop automobiles for the purpose of checking a driver's license or registration certificate; however, the automobile may be detained without probable cause to make an arrest if there is an articulable and reasonable suspicion that the motorist is unlicensed or that the automobile is not registered. Additionally, the courts have approved the establishment of roadblocks or traffic checkpoints to determine whether the driver has a driver's license. The rationale for the roadblock stop is that the driver can see visible signs of the officer's authority, and he or she is less likely to be frightened or annoyed by the intrusion.

Sobriety checkpoints are constitutional as long as checkpoint programs follow specific guidelines. Checkpoints for general crime control or for drug trafficking are not permitted, as the state cannot show the same overriding public interest as with sobriety checkpoints.

Chapter 5
Law of Arrest

. . . It is the command of the Fourth Amendment that no warrants for either searches or arrests shall issue except upon probable cause, supported by oath or affirmation, and particularly describing the place to be searched, and the persons or things to be seized.

Henry v. United States, 361 U.S. 98 (1959)

Section

§ 5.1   General Considerations

Before the criminal justice process can begin, a person must come within the custody and control of the law. In some instances, an arrest immediately follows a detention—for example, when a person is detained and the officer discovers additional information that gives him or her probable cause to make an arrest. But when the officer has probable cause to make an arrest without a warrant, is acting under a warrant, or has witnessed an offense personally, he or she may make the arrest immediately.

61

As indicated in the previous paragraph, not all stops amount to arrests. To better understand the levels of interaction between police and private citizens, courts have indicated the amount of information required to justify stops, and have designated three types of encounters:

1. Consensual encounters: no justification required.
2. Investigative detentions: require reasonable suspicion that criminal activity has occurred or is about to occur.
3. Arrest: requires a showing of probable cause.

Although investigative detentions and arrests are "seizures" under the Fourth Amendment, merely asking a person for identification is not a seizure if the person is free to walk away. If an officer restrains an individual's freedom to walk away, however, a seizure occurs.

The laws of the United States relating to arrest have developed over several centuries and are based primarily on the common law of England. Under the common law, a peace officer or private person could make an arrest if he or she had reasonable grounds to believe that a felony had been committed, even though a crime was not committed in his or her presence. At common law, an arrest could be made for an offense less than a felony only if the crime was committed in the officer's presence. Many of the early cases added that, at common law, a peace officer had no power to arrest except when a breach of the peace had been committed in his presence. However, other cases, as well as common law commentaries, shared the view that the "breach of the peace" requirement did not exist.

To resolve the issue, the U.S. Supreme Court agreed to review the decisions in *Atwater v. City of Lago Vista* in 2001.[1] The Court concluded that the Fourth Amendment does not forbid a warrantless arrest for a minor criminal offense, such as a misdemeanor seat belt violation, that is punishable only by a fine.

Although the Fourth Amendment is often referred to as the *search and seizure* amendment, it also protects individuals from illegal seizures *of their persons*, that is, arrest. Both the express terminology of the amendment and the historical context of its adoption led to this conclusion. In *Henry v. United States*, the Supreme Court dispelled any uncertainty that might previously have existed as to the status of an illegal arrest under the Fourth Amendment by stating:

It is the command of the Fourth Amendment that no warrant either for searches or arrest shall issue except on probable cause.[2]

---

[1]   *Atwater v. City of Lago Vista,* 532 U.S. 318 (2001).
[2]   *Henry v. United States,* 361 U.S. 98 (1959).

Los Angeles County Sheriff's Department commander Charles Heal answers defense questioning concerning the non-lethal use of force while testifying in the trial of former Inglewood, California, police officer Jeremy Morse. Morse is the officer shown making an arrest in the center of the video screen. (*AP Photo/Brad Graverson, Pool*)

Prior to 1962, federal arrests were governed by the Fourth Amendment, whereas similar state procedures were judged by a more flexible standard in the due process clause of the Fourteenth Amendment. However, in 1963, the U.S. Supreme Court in *Ker v. California*[3] held that arrests by state and local police officers are to be judged by the same constitutional standards that apply to the federal government. Thus, in order for an arrest to be valid today, police must comply with the provisions of the Fourth Amendment as well as those of state constitutions and statutes.

To understand the various aspects of the laws of arrest, the discussion in this chapter emphasizes: (1) the statutory provisions that give the police officer authority to arrest; (2) definitions and elements of arrest; (3) the authority to arrest with a warrant; (4) the authority to arrest without a warrant; (5) use of force in making an arrest; (6) the use of the citation and summons; and (7) arrests after fresh pursuit.

---

[3]   *Ker v. California*, 374 U.S. 23 (1963).

§ 5.2   Statutory Authority to Arrest

Each state has a statute or code section that authorizes peace officers to make arrests. The statutes differ from state to state. Two state statutes that authorize a police officer to make an arrest with or without a warrant are included here as examples of statutes that differ in granting authority to arrest.

The Kentucky Revised Statutes provide:

431.005 Arrest by peace officers; by private persons
(1) A peace officer may make an arrest:
   (a) In obedience to a warrant; or
   (b) Without a warrant when a felony is committed in his presence; or
   (c) Without a warrant when he has probable cause to believe that the person being arrested has committed a felony; or
   (d) Without a warrant when a misdemeanor, as defined in KRS 431.060, has been committed in his presence; or
   (e) Without a warrant when a violation of KRS 189.290, 189.393, 189.520, 511.080, or 525.070 has been committed in his presence, except that a violation of KRS 189A.010 or KRS 281A.210 need not be committed in his presence in order to make an arrest without a warrant if the officer has probable cause to believe that the person has violated KRS 189A.010 or KRS 281A.210.[4]
(2) (a) Any peace officer may arrest a person without a warrant when the peace officer has probable cause to believe that the person has intentionally or wantonly caused physical injury to a family member or member of an unmarried couple.
   (b) For the purposes of this subsection, the term "family member" means a spouse, including a former spouse, a parent, a grandparent, a child, a stepchild, or any other person related by consanguinity or affinity within the second degree.
   (c) For the purpose of this subsection, the term "member of an unmarried couple" means each member of an unmarried couple which allegedly has a child in common, any children of that couple, or a member of an unmarried couple who are living together or have formerly lived together.

. . .

---

[4] 189.290 Operator of vehicle to drive carefully; 189.393 Complying with traffic officer's signal; 189.520 Operating vehicle while under influence of intoxicants or drugs; 189.580 Duty in case of accident; 189A.010 Operating a motor vehicle under the influence of alcohol; 281A.210 Operating a commercial vehicle while under the influence of alcohol or other controlled substance; 511.080 Criminal trespass in the third degree; 525.070 Harassment.

(3) A private person may make an arrest when a felony has been committed in fact and he has probable cause to believe that the person being arrested has committed it.[5]

The Illinois statutes provide:

107-2   Arrest by peace officer
107-2 (1) Arrest by peace officer. A peace officer may arrest a person when:
      (a) He has a warrant commanding that such person be arrested; or
      (b) He has reasonable grounds to believe that a warrant for the person's arrest has been issued in this State or in another jurisdiction; or
      (c) He has reasonable grounds to believe that the person is committing or has committed an offense.
(2) Whenever a peace officer arrests a person, the officer shall question the arrestee as to whether he or she has any children under the age of 18 living with him or her who may be neglected as a result of the arrest or otherwise. The peace officer shall assist the arrestee in the placement of the children with a relative or other responsible person designated by the arrestee. If the peace officer has reasonable cause to believe that a child may be a neglected child as defined in the Abused and Neglected Child Reporting Act, he shall report it immediately to the Department of Children and Family Services as provided in that Act.
(3) A peace officer who executes a warrant of arrest in good faith beyond the geographical limitation of the warrant shall not be liable for false arrest.[6]

State statutes have one element in common—that a peace officer may arrest under the authority of an arrest warrant. Also, although the wording is different, all states authorize an officer to make an arrest when he or she has reasonable grounds to believe that the person whom he or she is about to arrest has committed a *felony*.

The statutes differ as to the authority to arrest for a *misdemeanor* committed outside the officer's presence. In some states, a peace officer may make a warrantless misdemeanor arrest *only* if the offense is committed in his or her presence. Other states follow this general rule but have exceptions for certain types of misdemeanors, usually those involving physical violence. However, in some states, including Illinois, peace officers have the authority to make a misdemeanor arrest on reasonable grounds to believe that the person is committing or has committed an "offense."[7]

Because state statutes differ in granting authority to make felony and misdemeanor arrests, it is important that those who act under a particular statute be familiar with the precise provisions of that statute as interpreted by court decisions.

---

[5] KY. REV. STAT. § 431.005 (2005).
[6] 725 ILCS 5/107-2 (West 2005).
[7] 725 ILCS 5/107-2 (West 2000).

The U.S. Supreme Court has determined that so long as an arrest is based upon probable cause, it does not violate the Fourth Amendment even if the arrest is barred under state law. *Virginia v. Moore*[8] involved an arrest in Virginia. Moore was stopped for driving with a suspended license. State law specified the proper police procedure was to issue a citation and a summons to appear in court; arrest was not permitted. Nonetheless, police arrested him and conducted a search incident to the arrest, finding cocaine in Moore's clothing. He was convicted of drug possession and sentenced to five years in prison. He appealed, arguing the arrest violated the Fourth Amendment, and sought to have the seized evidence excluded. The Virginia Supreme Court held that the search violated the Fourth Amendment, as it does not permit a search incident to the issuance of a citation, which was the only state-approved response to Moore's traffic violation.

The U.S. Supreme Court, in a unanimous decision authored by Justice Scalia, held that the police did not violate the Fourth Amendment when they made an arrest based on probable cause that a crime had occurred, even though that arrest was barred by state law. Because the arrest was constitutional, the search incident to the arrest was as well. Justice Scalia noted that though a state is free to provide greater protections under its constitution than those provided by the Fourth Amendment, doing so does not affect the validity of the search under the Fourth Amendment.

State and federal statutes that authorize arrest by a peace officer must be strictly followed. A peace officer who makes an arrest outside his or her own state must follow the laws of the other state. One state cannot give a peace officer authority to act in another state.

§ 5.3   Definition and Elements of Arrest

A. Definition

Although state and federal statutes and codes have provisions specifying when a law enforcement officer may make an arrest without a warrant, few of the statutes attempt to define *arrest*. For this reason, it is necessary to look to court decisions, treatises, and encyclopedias for definitions. Some of the more common definitions include the following:

The term "arrest" has a technical meaning, applicable in legal proceedings. It implies that a person is thereby restrained of his liberty by some officer or agency of the

---

[8]   *Virginia v. Moore,* 553 U.S. 164 (2008).

law, armed with lawful process, authorizing and requiring the arrest to be made. It is intended to serve, and does serve, the end of bringing the person arrested personally within the custody and control of the law, for the purpose specified in, or contemplated by the process.[9]

An arrest is the taking, seizing, or detaining of the person of another, (1) by touching or putting hands on him; or (2) by any act that indicates an intention to take him into custody and that subjects him to the actual control and will of the person making the arrest; or (3) by the consent of the person to be arrested.[10]

An arrest of a person carries with it an element of detention, custody, or control of the accused, and the mere fact that an officer makes the statement to an accused that he is under arrest does not complete that arrest; there must be custody or detention and submission to such arrest.[11]

A person is under "arrest" if he is not free to leave and a reasonable person in his position would not think that the detention was temporary.[12]

None of these definitions is entirely satisfactory. *Arrest* is a term that eludes precise definition. It is a legal conclusion used to describe a complex series of events that has taken place.

In a 1989 civil rights case, the U.S. Supreme Court was called on to determine when a Fourth Amendment "seizure" occurs. In *Brower v. County of Inyo*, a civil rights action was brought, alleging that police officers, acting under color of state law, violated the rights of a driver who was killed when the stolen vehicle that he was driving at high speed to elude police crashed into a police roadblock. The complaint alleged that the "seizure" occurred when the driver of the car was stopped by an 18-wheel truck that was placed completely across the highway in the path of the driver. The district court dismissed the case against the police and the county, concluding that the roadblock was reasonable under the circumstances, and the court of appeals affirmed on the ground that no "seizure" had occurred.[13]

---

[9] *Hadley v. Tinnin*, 86 S.E. 1017 (N.C. 1915), quoting *Lawrence v. Buxton*, 8 S.E. 774 (N.C. 1889).

[10] 5 AM. JUR. 2d *Arrest* § 1 (1962).

[11] *Medford v. State,* 13 S.W.3d 769 (Tex. 2000).

[12] *Green v. State,* 240 Ga. App. 774, 525 S.E.2d 154 (1999).

[13] *Brower v. County of Inyo,* 489 U.S. 593 (1989). See also *California v. Hodari D.*, 499 U.S. 621 (1991), in which the Court held that there was no seizure (arrest) when a suspect failed to comply with the officer's show of authority. As the suspect was not seized until he was tackled by the officer, cocaine abandoned while he was running was not the fruit of an illegal seizure.

The U.S. Supreme Court determined that there was a seizure for the purposes of the Fourth Amendment when the police placed the 18-wheel truck completely across the highway. The Court explained:

> It is clear, in other words, that a Fourth Amendment seizure does not occur whenever there is a governmentally caused termination of an individual's freedom of movement (the innocent passerby), nor even whenever there is a governmentally caused and governmentally *desired* termination of the individual's freedom of movement (the fleeing felon), but only when there is a governmental termination of freedom of movement *through means intentionally applied.* (Emphasis by the Court.)

The Court emphasized that no unconstitutional seizure occurs when a suspect unexpectedly loses control of a car and crashes during a police pursuit. Although the conduct in this case amounted to a "seizure," the case was remanded with instructions for the lower court to determine whether the seizure was also *unreasonable*.

As indicated in the previous chapter, the quantum of evidence required to justify a detention (reasonable suspicion) is less than probable cause, which is required to justify an arrest. In 1985, the Supreme Court was asked to determine at what point an investigative detention for fingerprinting purposes becomes an arrest.[14] In *Hayes v. Florida*, the Court pointed out that at some point in the investigative process, police procedures can qualitatively and quantitatively be so intrusive with respect to the suspect's freedom of movement and privacy interests as to trigger the full protection of the Fourth Amendment. When the line between detention and arrest is crossed, probable cause is required. In defining that line, the Court said:

> The line is crossed when the police, without probable cause or a warrant, forcibly remove a person from his home or other place in which he is entitled to be, and transport him to the police station, where he is detained, although briefly, for investigative purposes.

The Court explained that this does not imply that a brief detention in the field for purposes of fingerprinting is unreasonable even without probable cause; but when there is only reasonable suspicion, transporting a person to the police station is impermissible under the Fourth Amendment. This becomes an arrest, and probable cause is required for the arrest to be legal.

Whether a police officer's actions amount to an arrest can become very important. Frequently, the successful prosecution of a case will depend upon the legality of the arrest. For example, if an arrest is illegal, the search incident to that arrest is not authorized and any evidence secured thereby will not be admissible in court.

---

[14]   *Hayes v. Florida,* 470 U.S. 811 (1985).

Although it is difficult, if not impossible, to frame a comprehensive definition of arrest, by considering the following common elements, it is easier to understand the Court's reasoning in determining when the acts of an officer arc considered an arrest.

B. *Elements of an Arrest*

Legal scholars have attempted to delineate the various elements of an arrest. Different scholars have enumerated three, four, and even five separate elements of arrest. Rather than making an unequivocal statement that there are a certain number of elements, it is preferable to consider the elements that may or may not apply in a given case.

1   Intent on the Part of the Officer to Take the Suspect into Custody

The intent of the arresting officer to take a person into custody is one of the basic elements that distinguish an arrest from lesser forms of detention. Although the intent of the officer is an important factor in every arrest, specific or actual intent is unnecessary. For example, under certain circumstances, the court may infer from the officer's conduct an intent to take a person into custody, when in fact no such intent existed. Thus, in a false arrest case, the officer cannot escape liability by stating that he or she did not intend to make the arrest, if the facts show that the officer did in fact take the person into custody.

Commenting on the police officer's intent, a Louisiana court held that the totality of circumstances determines whether an arrest occurs, but several factors distinguish an arrest from lesser infringements on personal liberty; one factor is whether the totality of the circumstances indicates a police intent to impose an extended restraint on the person's liberty.[15]

2   Real or Assumed Legal Authority of the Arresting Officer

To constitute an "arrest," as the term is used in criminal law, the restraint of the liberty of the individual must be under either actual or assumed authority. If the officer acts under *actual* authority as provided by law and the other elements are present, the arrest is legal.

On the other hand, if the officer acts under *assumed* or *pretended* authority, the arrest is illegal and the officer may be civilly or criminally liable. Common examples

---

[15]   *California v. Hodari D.,* 499 U.S. 621 (1991).

of assumed authority are situations in which an officer acts under a void warrant or makes an arrest for a misdemeanor not committed in his or her presence when such an arrest is not authorized by the law of his or her state.

3   The Person Arrested Must Come within the Custody and Control of the Law

To constitute an arrest, the subject must come within the actual custody and control of the officer.[16] If the person submits voluntarily to the control of the officer, this is an arrest just as if the officer had physically subdued and handcuffed the subject. It is not necessary that there be an application of actual force, touching, or physical restraint. It is sufficient if the arrestee understands that he or she is in the power of the person arresting him or her and submits to that control. Anyone, therefore, may come within the custody and control of the law either by: (1) submission or (2) physical restraint.

Mere words on the part of an officer can constitute an arrest if they are coupled with an intent on the part of the officer to restrain a person and if, in fact, they cause a person to be restrained. On the other hand, mere words do not constitute an arrest if the person to be restrained turns his or her back and walks away and indicates that he or she does not intend to submit to custody. As one court cautioned:

> One person can no more arrest another by simply telling him to consider himself under arrest and then turning on his heel and leaving that person free to go his own way, than one can commit a homicide by merely telling him to consider himself dead.[17]

The last element is often confusing. Some writers have indicated that one element of arrest is that there must be an intent on the part of the arrestee to submit to the arrest. Obviously, this cannot be true in all situations. If it were, a person who was unconscious or intoxicated could not be placed under arrest because he or she could not intend to submit. As a matter of law, a person may be arrested when there is an actual seizure and restraint even though the arrestee does not understand or intend to be arrested.

The custody and control question has received considerable attention since the Supreme Court in *Michigan v. Chesternut* in 1988 considered a different test.[18]

---

[16]   *Commonwealth v. Guillespie,* 745 A.2d 654 (Pa. 2000).

[17]   *Berry v. Bass,* 102 So. 76 (La. 1924). See also *Wilson v. State,* 943 S.W.2d 43 (Tex. 1997), holding that the officer has to assume custody and control over the person arrested.

[18]   *Michigan v. Chesternut,* 486 U.S. 567 (1988).

Although the Court agreed that there was no bright-line rule, the majority noted that the test, as applied in previous cases, is:

> The police can be said to have seized an individual "only if, in view of the circumstances surrounding the incident, a reasonable person would have believed that *he was not free to leave.*" (Emphasis added.)

The Court explained that what constitutes a restraint on liberty, prompting a person to believe he or she is not free to leave, will vary not only with the particular police conduct at issue, but also with the setting in which the conduct occurs.

In *Morgan v. Woessner*, the Ninth Circuit Court of Appeals held that "the essential inquiry is whether the person stopped reasonably believed that he or she was not free to leave." There, the Court observed that a person is "seized only when, by means of physical force or a show of authority, his freedom of movement is restrained . . . as long as the person to whom the questions are put remains free to disregard the questions and walk away, there has been no intrusion on the person's liberty or privacy as would under the Constitution require an objective justification."[19]

A Louisiana court stated that, in order to determine whether an arrest was made, one must look at the totality of circumstances and assess whether there was an intent to impose restraint and whether a reasonable person would consider him- or herself free from restraint.[20] Applying the rule, the Court held that when the defendant voluntarily accompanied police officers to the station, he was not arrested; the officers had invited the defendant and others to accompany them to the station to discuss burglaries and the detectives testified that no one was handcuffed and that they were free to leave at any time.

§ 5.4   Arrest under the Authority of an Arrest Warrant

The primary and most basic source of authority to arrest, recognized under the common law and under modern statutes, is that of a warrant. This is the only authority expressly sanctioned by the Constitution of the United States. The Constitution not only provides that unreasonable searches shall not be made, but states that:

> No Warrants shall issue, but upon probable cause, supported by Oath or affirmation, and particularly describing . . . the persons or things to be seized.

---

[19]   *Morgan v. Woessner*, 975 F.2d 629 (9th Cir. 1992).
[20]   *State v. Normandin*, 750 So. 2d 321 (La. 1999).

The function of an arrest warrant is to protect private citizens from the harassment of unjustified arrests, incarcerations, or criminal prosecutions. The major objection to warrantless arrests is that they bypass the safeguards provided by an objective predetermination of probable cause and substitute the less reliable procedure of an after-the-event justification.[21]

A Texas appeals court explained the purpose of the state and federal constitutional provisions concerned with arrest and seizure, and the preference to be given to an arrest with a warrant, with these comments:

> The basic purpose of both federal and state constitutional provisions is to safeguard the privacy and security of individuals against arbitrary invasions by governmental officials; therefore, an arrest effected without a warrant issued upon probable cause is . . . per se unreasonable, except for a few specifically well-delineated exceptions . . .[22]

Therefore, as a general rule, an officer should obtain a warrant before acting when this is at all practicable. The U.S. Supreme Court has indicated that in doubtful or marginal cases, in which probable cause for an arrest is not clearly made out, action under a warrant will be sustained where action without a warrant would fail. The Court noted that:

> The informed and deliberate determination of magistrates empowered to issue warrants is to be preferred over the hurried actions of officers.[23]

Aside from the fact that the Fourth Amendment provides for the issuance of a warrant and the courts have expressed a preference for an arrest with a warrant, there is a practical reason a police officer should, whenever time permits, obtain a warrant before making an arrest. In most instances, if the warrant is proper on its face and the officer does not abuse his or her authority in executing the warrant, he or she will be protected against civil liability for false arrest or false imprisonment.

It should be noted, however, that if the officer's actions indicate gross incompetence or neglect of duty in presenting supporting affidavits to justify the issuance of an arrest warrant, the officer is not entitled to rely on a judicial officer's judgment in issuing the warrant. In *Malley v. Briggs*, the Supreme Court noted that, under the rule of qualified immunity, a police officer cannot avoid liability for causing an

---

[21] *Beck v. Ohio*, 379 U.S. 89 (1964).
[22] *Peddicord v. State*, 942 S.W.2d 100 (Tex. 1997).
[23] *United States v. Ventresca*, 380 U.S. 102 (1965).

unconstitutional arrest by presenting the judicial officer with a complaint and a supporting affidavit that failed to establish probable cause.[24]

A. Requirements of a Valid Arrest Warrant

Recognizing the preference given to an arrest with a warrant over an arrest without a warrant, it is essential that the officer be aware of the requirements that must be fulfilled if the warrant is to be considered valid. As has been indicated, some of the requirements are constitutional, while others are statutory or have been judicially determined. If any of the requirements is lacking, then the warrant is invalid and the arrest made under that warrant, as well as any search incident to that arrest, is unauthorized.[25] The most common requirements for a valid arrest warrant are discussed below.

1   The Warrant Must Be Supported by Probable Cause

The Fourth Amendment states that no warrant shall be issued to seize a person unless it is supported by probable cause. Probable cause must be found to exist by a magistrate or other judicial officer. In order for the warrant to achieve the protective function that it was designed to achieve, the magistrate must make a neutral and impartial evaluation of the evidence on the basis of the evidence presented in the complaint.

A law enforcement officer can be almost certain that the defense attorney will challenge the arrest warrant, especially if there was a search incident to the arrest and pertinent evidence was obtained. The defense attorney may claim that there was no probable cause to support the arrest warrant or that the information on which probable cause was based was obtained illegally. The challenges to probable cause have centered around two main questions: (1) What is probable cause? and (2) What types of evidence can be considered by the magistrate in determining whether probable cause exists? These questions will be discussed separately.

The first question, "What is probable cause?" has been addressed by many courts. The U.S. Supreme Court has defined probable cause as follows:

> Probable cause exists where the facts and circumstances within their [the arresting officers] knowledge and of which they had reasonably trustworthy information are

---

[24] *Malley v. Briggs,* 475 U.S. 335 (1986).
[25] See *State v. Wilson,* 65 S.W.2d 504 (Tenn. 1999), which held that a void warrant invalidates all subsequent proceedings emanating from the warrant.

sufficient in themselves to warrant a man of reasonable caution in the belief that an offense has been or is being committed.[26]

The key words are "reasonably trustworthy information" and a "man of reasonable caution." These are subjective and are open to review in each case.

Although probable cause cannot be supplied by mere conjecture, suspicion, or a hunch of the officer, the officer is not required to furnish evidence sufficient to establish guilt beyond a reasonable doubt. Somewhere between "mere suspicion" at one end of the spectrum and "beyond a reasonable doubt" at the other, is "probable cause."[27]

One of the cases holding that probable cause for the warrant was insufficient to justify an arrest was *Whiteley v. Warden*.[28] In this case, the basis for an arrest warrant issued by a justice of the peace was a complaint that stated:

> I, C.W. Ogburn, do solemnly swear that on or about the 23 day of November, A.D. 1964, in the County of Carbon and State of Wyoming, the said Harold Whiteley and Jack Daley, defendants, did then and there unlawfully break and enter a locked and sealed building . . .

Reversing the conviction, the U.S. Supreme Court pointed out that the complaint consisted of nothing more than the complainant's conclusion that the individuals named perpetrated the offense described in the complaint. Although the officers in this case had additional information at their disposal, it was not furnished to the magistrate who issued the warrant. The Court explained that the magistrate must base his or her decision on the information presented at the time the warrant is issued.

The second question, "What type of evidence can be considered by a magistrate in determining whether probable cause exists?" has also been discussed by a number of courts. Generally, the officer-affiant supplies the evidence to the magistrate, who then issues an arrest warrant. The information included in the affidavit and submitted to the magistrate may be derived from the officer's personal observations, physical evidence found at the scene of the crime, reliable information from officers of other law enforcement agencies, or eyewitness reports. In addition, informants' tips may provide an invaluable source of information for the arrest warrant.

Until 1983, the Supreme Court had placed restrictions on the use of information from undisclosed informants. In earlier cases, including *Aguilar v. Texas* and *Spinelli v. United States*, the Supreme Court held that information from unnamed informants

---

[26] *Draper v. United States,* 358 U.S. 307 (1959).

[27] *State v. Judge,* 645 A.2d 1224 (N.J. 1994). This case held that "probable cause" is a well-grounded suspicion that a criminal offense is being committed; it is more than bare suspicion but less than legal evidence necessary to convict beyond a reasonable doubt.

[28] 401 U.S. 560 (1971).

could be used in determining probable cause only if two requirements were met:[29] (1) the informant was reliable; and (2) the information from the informant was credible.

In 1983, the Court abandoned the requirement that *both* reliability and credibility be established and that the "totality of circumstances" approach was the proper approach.[30] The opinion included this statement:

> For all these reasons, we conclude that it is wiser to abandon the two-pronged test established by our decisions in *Aguilar* and *Spinelli*. In its place we reaffirm the totality of circumstances analysis that traditionally has informed probable cause determinations. The task of the issuing magistrate is simply to make a practical, commonsense decision whether, given all of the circumstances set forth in the affidavit before him, including the "veracity" and "basis of knowledge" of persons supplying hearsay information, there is a fair probability that contraband or evidence of a crime will be found in a particular place, and the duty of the reviewing court is simply to insure that the magistrate had a "substantial basis for concluding" that probable cause existed.

To avoid problems, it is preferable to clearly establish the reliability of the informant and obtain definite statements concerning the basis of the information. In situations in which the informant has not given valid information on a prior occasion, the officer should verify the information and make an independent investigation to obtain additional information.

As a practical matter, the officer should not rely exclusively on the undisclosed informant's information, but should take steps to corroborate and verify the information and seek additional information. The more information the officer can use to develop probable cause, the better will be his or her chances that the warrant will be held valid.

2   The Affidavit for the Warrant Must Be Supported by Oath or Affirmation

A second requirement for a valid warrant is that the warrant be "supported by oath or affirmation." This requirement is a prerequisite for conferring the magistrate's jurisdiction over the person of the defendant. The officer requesting the warrant must take an oath or affirm that the facts and circumstances described in the affidavit are true.

There is a presumption that an affidavit is supported by an oath or affirmation; however, the defense attorney or the defendant may offer proof that the oath was not

---

[29] *Aguilar v. Texas*, 378 U.S. 108 (1964); *Spinelli v. United States*, 393 U.S. 410 (1969).

[30] *Illinois v. Gates*, 462 U.S. 213 (1983). See Chapter 6 for a discussion of the facts in the *Gates* case.

administered. In such a case, the warrant may be held invalid, and any evidence obtained as a result will be inadmissible.

The responsibility for placing the affiant under oath or requiring an affirmation belongs to the magistrate or judicial officer. Nevertheless, it is advisable that the police officer who is submitting the affidavit remind the magistrate of the requirement if necessary.

3   The Person to Be Seized under the Warrant Must Be Particularly Described

A third requirement included in the Fourth Amendment is that the person to be seized must be *particularly* described. The usual method of designating the person to be arrested is by the insertion of his or her name on the warrant. If the name is not known, the warrant must include a description that is sufficient to identify the person to be arrested with reasonable certainty. This may be done by stating his or her occupation, personal appearance, peculiarities, place of residence, or other means of identification.[31]

The question often arises as to whether a "John Doe" warrant is serveable. It is obvious that if you apply the previous formula, a "John Doe" warrant with no further information does not "particularly describe" the person to be seized. On the other hand, if the warrant is drafted to authorize the arrest of "John Doe" and includes an adequate description that will identify the person to be arrested, such a warrant is valid. For example, the Third Circuit Court of Appeals held that a warrant directing officers to arrest "John Doe, a white male with black wavy hair and stocky build, observed using a telephone in apartment 4C, Patricia Lane, East McKeesport, Pennsylvania," provided a sufficient physical description and indication of the precise location to make the "John Doe" warrant valid.[32]

The preferred procedure is to determine the name and/or alias of the person to be arrested. If this is not possible, and a "John Doe" arrest warrant is issued, every effort should be made to include detailed identifying information, especially information that is peculiar to the individual to be arrested.

4   The Warrant Must State the Nature of the Offense

In addition to the constitutional requirements for warrants, courts and legislative bodies have developed additional requirements. One of these is that the warrant must state the nature of the offense committed. The warrant does not have to contain the

---

[31] *People v. Montoya,* 63 Cal. Rptr. 73 (1967).
[32] *United States v. Ferrone,* 438 F.2d 381 (3d Cir. 1971).

same detail as would appear in an indictment or information, but it must contain a sufficiently clear description of the offense in order to advise the person named in the warrant of the charge against him or her.

5   The Warrant Must Designate the Officer or Class of Officers Directed to Comply with the Order of the Court

To be valid and executable, the warrant must be directed to a *specific officer* or to *a class of officers*. It might be addressed, for example, to all the peace officers of the state of Idaho. It is preferable to designate a class of officers rather than a specific officer, so that all officers within that class will have the authority to execute the warrant.

6   The Warrant Must Be Issued in the Name of the United States or of the Particular State

The police power of the government rests with the individual states. Certain powers are delegated to local officials by the state constitution or by statute. Because the authority is primarily in the state, the name of the state must appear on the warrant, even if issued by a county or city official. A warrant issued by a federal officer must have "United States" on the warrant.

7   The Warrant Must Be Issued and Signed by a Neutral and Detached Judicial Officer

To fulfill the purpose of the warrant, it must be issued by someone who does not have an interest in the outcome of the case. The U.S. Supreme Court has determined that an attorney general is not neutral and detached, and a warrant issued by an attorney general, even though authorized by statute, is not a valid warrant.[33]

B. Execution of the Warrant

Even though a warrant has been properly issued on a showing of probable cause, and sufficiently describes the person to be arrested, the arrest will be invalid unless the warrant is properly executed. The most important requirements relating to the execution of the warrant are stated here.

---

[33] *Coolidge v. New Hampshire,* 403 U.S. 443 (1971).

1   The Executing Officer Must Be Specifically Named or Come within the Class Designated on the Warrant

A common practice is to issue an arrest warrant to "all peace officers in the state." This practice has been approved by the courts and avoids many problems, because the warrant can be executed by anyone within that class. If, however, as was the earlier practice (and still is in some areas), a warrant is issued to a sheriff, as the highest-ranking peace officer within the jurisdiction, then he or she may deputize others to execute it, or deputies may execute the warrant on the grounds that they are acting through the sheriff.[34]

2   The Warrant Must Be Executed within Jurisdictional Limits

The validity of an arrest under a warrant depends upon the territorial jurisdiction of the *issuing* official. Most modern statutes contain provisions authorizing the execution of a warrant in any county of the state, even though it was issued by a magistrate in another county. In the absence of a statute conferring statewide authority on the issuing magistrates, a warrant may not be executed outside the county of its origin.

Because state legislatures only have the power to grant authority to officials operating within that state, a warrant issued for the arrest of a person in one state may not be executed in another state unless the second state has by statute conferred validity on out-of-state warrants. A warrant issued in one state may, however, serve *indirectly* as a basis for an arrest in the second state, even in the absence of legislation. In such a case, it is not the warrant, but the reasonable inference that a police officer in the second state may draw from the fact of its issuance, that forms a basis for the arrest. In addition, an out-of-state warrant may serve as the basis for issuing a fugitive warrant in another state.

3   The Arresting Officer Should Make His or Her Purpose Known

Some states have statutes that require the officer to inform the person who is to be arrested of the reason for the arrest and the fact that a warrant has been issued. When it is possible and when it is not dangerous to the officer, he or she should make it clear that he or she is making the arrest under the authority of a warrant and advise the person of the charge. This is particularly important when the officer is not in uniform, because failure to do so could prove dangerous to the officer, not only physically, but in future legal actions.

---

[34]   *Ex parte Rhodes*, 20 So. 894 (La 1896).

There are logical exceptions to this rule. If the person to be arrested flees or forcibly resists before the officer has an opportunity to advise him or her, or if the giving of such information would imperil the arrest, then notice is not required. If the arrestee flees to another part of the house to hide, he or she cannot complain that the officer did not inform him or her of the intended arrest.[35]

Some states have statutes that require the police, before entering an individual's home without his or her consent, to identify themselves, announce their purpose, and demand admittance. This is referred to as the *knock-and-announce rule* (see Chapter 6).

4   The Officer Generally Must Show the Warrant or Advise the Arrestee That the Warrant Has Been Issued

At common law, the arresting officer was required to show the warrant to the person arrested unless it was dangerous for him or her to do so. Because of the need for quick action in our highly mobile society, however, there has been a trend to relax the requirements of the common law regarding the display of the warrant.

The federal rules and most state codes contain provisions to the effect that the officer need not have the warrant in his or her possession at the time of the arrest, but after the arrest, if the person so requests, the warrant shall be shown to him or her as soon as is practicable.[36]

5   Police Must Have Reason to Believe That the Suspect Is Present in the Home

In *Smith v. Tolley*, a federal court commented that an arrest warrant founded on probable cause implicitly carries with it the limited authority to enter the dwelling in which the suspect lives when there is reason to believe that the suspect is within.[37] The court warned, however, that the officer must have a reasonable belief that the suspect is inside the residence before entering the residence to execute an arrest warrant. This reasonable belief must be based on common sense factors guided by the experience of officers.

Another federal court, in explaining the authority of a police officer to enter a suspect's residence, held that the forced entry into a suspect's home to execute a misdemeanor arrest warrant was proper when the officers reasonably believed the suspect was hiding inside and did not want to acknowledge the uniformed officers who had driven up in marked police cars.

---

[35] *Kirvelaitis v. Warden,* 513 F.2d 213 (6th Cir. 1975).

[36] For example, see KY. R. CRIM. P. 2.10(1) (2004) and FED. R. CRIM. P. 4(d)(3) (2004).

[37] *Smith v. Tolley,* 960 F. Supp. 977 (E.D. Va. 1997).

6   Absent Exigent Circumstances or Consent, the Arrest Warrant May Not Be Executed in the Home of a Third Party

Although it is clear that an arrest warrant may be executed in the home of the person whose name appears on the warrant and may be executed in a public place, it may not be executed in the home of a third party unless there are exigent circumstances, the third party consents, or there is a search warrant for the house of the third party. This rule was clearly established in *Steagald v. United States*.[38]

In *Steagald*, the officers had an arrest warrant for a person named Ricky Lyons. After receiving information that Lyons could be reached at the home of Gary Steagald, the officers entered Steagald's home without a search warrant. Lyons was not found during the search of the house, but the agents discovered cocaine and charged Steagald with possession. Prior to trial, Steagald moved to suppress the evidence on the grounds that it was illegally obtained. The Supreme Court determined that entry into Steagald's house, even with an arrest warrant for Lyons, was illegal.

The rule resulting from this case is that, absent exigent circumstances or consent by the owner, a warrant issued for the arrest of one person does not justify the entry into or search of the house of a third party, without first obtaining a search warrant for the third party's home.

§ 5.5   Arrest without a Warrant

It was recognized at common law that, under certain circumstances, it was impracticable, if not impossible, to obtain an arrest warrant. Common law attempted to strike a balance between the interests of the community in protecting itself and the rights of the citizens to be free of unjustified arrests. The exceptions to the rule requiring a warrant were based on the strictest necessity.

In 1975, the U.S. Supreme Court reemphasized and restated the reasoning for authorizing an arrest without a warrant:

> Maximum protection of individual rights could be assured by requiring a magistrate's review of the factual justification prior to any arrest, but such a requirement would constitute an intolerable handicap for legitimate law enforcement. Thus, while the court has expressed a preference for the use of arrest warrants when feasible . . . it has never invalidated an arrest supported by probable cause solely because the officer failed to secure a warrant.[39]

---

[38]   *Steagald v. United States*, 451 U.S. 204 (1981).
[39]   *Gerstein v. Pugh*, 420 U.S. 103 (1975).

In seeking to strike a balance between the interests of the community and the rights of the citizens, legislatures and courts have distinguished between an arrest for a felony and an arrest for a misdemeanor. Because a felony constitutes a more serious threat to public safety, it was believed by most legislators that greater latitude in making warrantless arrests in felony cases was justified. Although some states have abolished this distinction, either in whole or in part, most states still make the distinction, and therefore it is necessary to discuss felony and misdemeanor arrest powers separately.

A. *Arrest without a Warrant in Felony Cases*

1   Definition of a Felony

Generally, a felony is defined as any crime that is punishable by death or imprisonment in a state prison. Because the laws in most states do not provide for imprisonment in a state institution unless the term is at least one year, in most instances an offense is a felony if the penalty is at least one year and the incarceration is in a state institution rather than a local jail. However, an offense may be designated a felony by statute even though it does not carry one year's incarceration. Some states have designated the specific crimes that are felonies and those that are misdemeanors by statute. To summarize, an offense is considered a felony when:

1. A statute designates it as a felony, or
2. There is no such designation, but the offense is punishable by imprisonment in a state prison, for a period of at least one year.

2   Grounds for Warrantless Felony Arrests

The states are uniform in authorizing a law enforcement officer to arrest without a warrant when he or she has reasonable grounds to believe that a felony has been committed and that the person to be arrested has committed it. A few states add a third requirement that limits the warrantless felony arrest to situations in which it is impractical to obtain a warrant before making an arrest.[40]

Two important requirements must be fully understood: (1) there must be reasonable grounds to believe that a felony has been committed; and (2) there must be reasonable grounds to believe that the person arrested committed that felony. An all-inclusive definition of reasonable grounds is difficult to establish. It lies

---

[40] For example, see TEX. CODE CRIM. PRO. ANN. art. 14.04 (Vernon 2005).

somewhere on the evidentiary scale between "good faith suspicion" and "proof beyond a reasonable doubt." To make an arrest in a felony situation, the officer must have *at least* as much evidence as he or she would have had if an arrest warrant was sought.

There is often confusion concerning the use of the terms "reasonable grounds to believe" and "probable cause." Although the terms are used interchangeably, there is a technical difference. "Probable cause" is the term used in the Fourth Amendment when discussing search and arrest warrants; "reasonable grounds" is not used in the Fourth Amendment and is a term used when referring to the knowledge an officer must possess prior to making an arrest without a warrant. However, many decisions regarding the amount of information the officer must have in order to make a warrantless arrest revolve around this quantum of evidence in terms of "probable cause" rather than "reasonable grounds."

In determining reasonable grounds, the Constitution does not demand infallibility. At the same time, the Constitution and court interpretations attempt to safeguard citizens from unfounded charges as well as unjustified arrest. However, the standards are intended to be flexible enough to permit efficient law enforcement. Although there is no bright-line rule for determining probable cause or reasonable grounds to make an arrest without a warrant, a review of some of the decisions will help in developing a workable approach.

A federal court discussing probable cause repeated that probable cause for an arrest exists when the person could reasonably believe, in light of facts and circumstances within the knowledge of the arresting officer at the time of the arrest, that the suspect had committed or was committing an offense.[41]

A Louisiana court indicated that probable cause to arrest exists when the facts and circumstances within the officer's knowledge are sufficient to justify "a man of ordinary caution" in believing that the person to be arrested has committed a crime.[42] The court also noted that the determination of probable cause, although requiring something more than bare suspicion, does not require evidence sufficient to support a conviction; probable cause deals with probabilities. Also, the determination of probable cause involves factual and practical considerations of everyday life on which average people, and average police officers particularly, can be expected to act.

Using somewhat different terminology, a Minnesota court held that probable cause for an arrest exists when the facts would lead a person of ordinary care and prudence to entertain an honest and strong suspicion that the person under consideration is guilty of a crime; each case must be determined on its own facts and

---

[41]   *United States v. Kincaid,* 212 F.3d 1025 (7th Cir. 2000).
[42]   *State v. James,* 755 So. 2d 995 (La. 2000).

circumstances, and the facts must justify more than mere suspicion but less than a conviction.[43] Furthermore, the lawfulness of an arrest is determined by an objective standard that takes into account the totality of the circumstances.

There are two important principles to remember at this point. One is that an arrest cannot be justified by what a subsequent search or investigation produces, but must stand or fall solely *on the basis of the facts possessed by the officer at the precise moment of the arrest.*[44] Second, the fact that the person arrested has not actually committed a felony makes no difference, as long as a police officer reasonably concludes that a felony has been committed, and that the person he or she is about to arrest committed that felony.

The Eighth Circuit Court of Appeals held that an officer may draw upon his or her own experience in determining whether probable cause exists.[45] In *United States v. Segars,* the Court of Appeals held that in determining whether probable cause exists to make a warrantless arrest of the defendant, the court looks to the totality of circumstances to see whether a prudent person would believe that the individual committed a crime, and the police may draw reasonable inferences from circumstances that the general public may find innocuous.

3   Guidelines in Determining Reasonable Grounds

The best guidelines for police action are not found in legal definitions given by the courts, but in factual situations in which probable cause and reasonable grounds have been found to exist. A police officer making a felony arrest may rely on information from a variety of sources. In fact, the more sources the officer can use in developing the required reasonable grounds, the more likely it is that the warrantless arrest will be approved. Some sources from which information can be obtained are discussed in the following paragraphs.

a   Personal Observations

Police officers probably obtain information on which to base the belief that reasonable grounds exist more through personal observation than from any other source. The trained and experienced officer who observes suspicious acts may, after further

---

[43] *State v. Cook,* 610 N.W.2d 664 (Minn. 2000).

[44] See *Smith v. Tolley,* 960 F. Supp. 977 (E.D. Va. 1997), which held that probable cause to arrest exists if, at that moment, facts and circumstances within the officers' knowledge and of which they had reasonable trustworthy information were sufficient to warrant a prudent man in believing that the suspect had committed or was committing an offense.

[45] *United States v. Segars,* 31 F.3d 655 (8th Cir. 1994).

inquiry, produce sufficient additional information to justify an arrest. When the totality of the circumstances—which could include the time of the day or night, the area,
attempted flight by the suspect, the known record of the suspect, and other factors
known to the officer—collectively lead the officer, in light of his or her experience,
to believe that a felony has been committed, the arrest is justified.

In explaining this concept, a Florida court noted that an offense is committed in
the presence or view of the officer, within the meaning of the rule authorizing an
arrest without a warrant, when the officer receives knowledge of the commission of
an offense in his or her presence through any of his or her senses, or by inferences
properly drawn from his or her senses, or when facts or circumstances occurring
within his or her observation, in connection with what, under the circumstances, may
be considered common knowledge, give him or her reasonable grounds to believe
that such is the case.[46]

An officer need not walk away when he or she observes a situation that plainly
indicates that a crime has been committed. For example, after officers received complaints about loud music, a chainsaw being operated, and shots being fired, they were
admitted into the defendant's apartment. They observed in plain view an empty holster and a chainsaw, which were objects of an investigation then being conducted.
The arrest of the defendant, based upon information within the officers' knowledge
and information they observed, was authorized.[47]

b Informants' Tips

Tips from informants are often a valuable source of pre-arrest information. However, the officer must be aware that he or she cannot *always* rely upon unconfirmed
informers' tips. When feasible, it is preferable to make an independent investigation
to substantiate the report before making an arrest.

Although it is preferable to obtain information from an informer who has given
accurate information in the past and to corroborate this information, there are times
when the arresting officer must rely, to a great extent, on the informant's information.
In *Illinois v. Gates*, discussed previously, the U.S. Supreme Court approved the use
of an informant's tip when obtaining an arrest warrant.[48] The rationale authorizing the
use of information from an undisclosed informant to obtain an arrest warrant is just
as valid when the arrest is made without a warrant.

Referring to the totality of circumstances approach discussed in *Gates*, an Illinois
court commented that in determining the existence of probable cause to arrest, it does

---

[46] *Steiner v. State*, 690 So. 2d 706 (Fla. 1997).
[47] *Latimore v. State*, 420 S.E.2d 91 (Ga. 1992).
[48] *Illinois v. Gates*, 462 U.S. 213 (1983).

not matter with what name the informant is labeled; the court looks to the informant's reliability as one of the factors considered in the totality of circumstances approach.[49] The court held that the rationale of protecting against unreasonable seizures by demanding reliable information from an informant is still relevant under the totality of circumstances test, and thus the basis of the informant's knowledge is relevant.

In a later case, a Minnesota court agreed that the police may rely on an informant's tip when making an arrest of a suspect if the tip has sufficient indicia of reliability and that when assessing the reliability of information provided by the informant, the courts examine the credibility of the informant and the basis of the informant's knowledge in light of all the circumstances.[50] The court noted that the assessment of a credible, reliable informant's basis of knowledge involves consideration of the quantity and quality of detail, and whether the police independently verified the important details of the informant's report.

If an officer uses information from an undisclosed informant in making a warrantless felony arrest, he or she must be prepared to articulate in court that the information received from the informant justified his or her conclusion that reasonable grounds for the arrest existed. There must be at least as much information to constitute reasonable grounds to make an arrest without a warrant as would be required to show probable cause for an arrest warrant.

The officer is not justified in creating a phantom informer in order to make an arrest, even if he or she is sure in his or her own mind that the person he or she has arrested has committed the offense. This conduct will not only invalidate the arrest, but will cause the officer to be subjected to criminal and civil liability.[51] However, if an informant gives erroneous information or makes untrue statements to the police officer, the arrest will not be invalidated, absent a showing of fraud or deceit on the part of the law enforcement officer or officials involved.[52]

c   Information from Other Officers or Agencies

The Constitution does not require the arresting officer to have personal knowledge of all the facts necessary to constitute probable cause. The arresting officer may use information furnished by members of his or her department or other agencies. In such circumstances, however, he or she must evaluate this on the basis of the collective information and the source of the information.

The officer receiving information by police radio or telephone has no more arrest authority than that of the officer who made the information available. A contrary rule

---

[49]   *People v. Kidd,* 675 N.E.2d 910 (Ill. 1996).
[50]   *State v. Cook,* 610 N.W.2d 664 (Minn. 2000).
[51]   *Oglesby v. Commonwealth,* 191 S.E.2d 216 (Ga. 1972).
[52]   *United States v. Garofalo,* 496 F.2d 510 (8th Cir. 1974).

would permit the police to do indirectly what the Constitution forbids them from doing directly, merely by publishing a report on a police radio. This rule was explained in *Whiteley v. Warden*,[53] in which an arrest warrant that was issued without probable cause was the basis for a bulletin sent to an officer in another county. The officer in the receiving county, relying upon the radio message that a warrant was outstanding, made the arrest and searched the suspect incident to the arrest. The state claimed that even though the warrant was invalid, because it was not supported by probable cause, the police officer who relied upon the bulletin in making the arrest nevertheless made a legal arrest and a legal search. The U.S. Supreme Court explained that if the initial warrant is defective, an arrest made by another officer, solely on the basis of a radio message stating that the warrant has been issued, is also defective. If the officer receiving the message had additional information on which he or she could base probable cause, this would add to his or her chances of having a valid arrest based upon probable cause.

An additional significant point in the *Whiteley* case was that the arresting officer, who relied on information received over a police radio, was protected from civil and criminal liability. The Court explained:

> Police officers called upon to aid other officers in executing arrest warrants are entitled to assume that the officers requesting aid offered the magistrate the information requisite to support a judicial assessment of probable cause.

As a general rule, when one officer asks another to take action but does not inform him or her of the underlying facts, the knowledge of the first officer is imputed to the second, and a valid seizure may be made.[54] The Court in *People v. Barros* was clear in stating that determining probable cause to arrest is based upon information that the arresting officer possesses at the time of arrest, either through personal observation or information relayed to him or her by fellow officers.[55] The Court made this even more certain by stating that to find probable cause for arrest, a request by one officer that another officer arrest the suspect can be conclusory, and there are no "magic words" that must pass from officer to officer.

The courts have been consistent in authorizing warrantless arrests in felony cases in which probable cause is based on information from a police dispatcher. In an Illinois case, the court stated that the arresting officer may rely upon dispatchers to establish probable cause for arrest, even if they are unaware of specific facts establishing such probable cause.[56] The court commented that in such a case, however, the

---

state must demonstrate that the officer directing the issuance of the dispatch possessed facts sufficient to establish probable cause for arrest. And in an Alabama case, the court held that probable cause existed for a warrantless arrest of the defendants when the arresting officer relied on a BOLO (be on the lookout) radio dispatch for which probable cause existed.[57]

A caveat is in order here, however. If the receiving officer has reason to doubt the authenticity of the message, the officer should investigate further before making the arrest.

d   Past Criminal Record

A police officer may use the prior criminal record of a suspect in conjunction with other information in deciding whether there are adequate grounds for arrest. It should be kept in mind, however, that the prior criminal record of a suspect, *standing alone*, can never constitute probable cause for an arrest.[58]

e   Physical Evidence Found at the Scene

Another source of evidence that can furnish probable cause to an officer in making a warrantless felony arrest is evidence found at the scene of the crime. It is quite common for an officer to locate fingerprints, a wallet, or other physical evidence at the scene of the crime that leads him or her to believe that a certain person committed the act. This, of course, must be weighed like any other evidence to determine whether, in fact, there is sufficient evidence to furnish reasonable cause for a felony arrest.

f   Report of the Victim or Eyewitness

The experienced investigator will certainly ask questions of eyewitnesses or victims of crimes. For example, an officer may obtain the license number of a car used in a holdup, the physical description of an assailant, or even the actual identity of a person observed at the scene. This information may be considered alone or in conjunction with other evidence in determining whether there are reasonable grounds to make the arrest.

In making the point that the police may rely upon information from private citizens, a New York court held that police officers may rely on information furnished

---

[57] *Ex parte Knotts,* 686 So. 2d 486 (Ala. 1995).
[58] *Beck v. Ohio,* 379 U.S. 89 (1964).

by private citizens who report crimes they have witnessed or that were perpetrated against them.[59]

The listing of the above sources of information is not exhaustive. Reliable information may be obtained from many other sources and may be used to determine whether there is probable cause for the officer to make a warrantless felony arrest. The more information obtained, from whatever sources, the better the chances of proving that reasonable grounds existed for the felony arrest.

B. Arrest without a Warrant in Misdemeanor Cases

In distinguishing between an arrest in a misdemeanor case and an arrest in a felony case, a federal court held that, under common law, a police officer did not need a warrant to make an arrest if he or she had probable cause to believe that a felony had been committed, but probable cause is not enough to authorize a warrantless arrest for a misdemeanor. A misdemeanor must also have been committed in the officer's presence.[60]

The authority of a police officer to arrest without a warrant for a minor criminal offense such as a failure to wear a seat belt as required by statute was considered by the U.S. Supreme Court in 2001.[61] In Texas, as in most states, passengers must wear seat belts and the driver must secure any small child. A violation is a misdemeanor punishable by a fine of not more than $50. Texas law also expressly authorizes any police officer to arrest without a warrant a person found committing a violation of the seat belt laws.[62] In *Atwater v. City of Lago Vista*, a motorist brought a § 1983 action against the city, the police chief, and the arresting officer after the motorist had been arrested, handcuffed, and taken to jail for failing to wear her seat belt and failing to fasten her children in seat belts. After a comprehensive review of common law cases, the Supreme Court held that: (1) the officer's authority to make warrantless arrests for misdemeanors was not restricted at common law to cases of "breach of the peace"; and (2) the arrest did not violate the motorist's Fourth Amendment rights.

The statutes in most states leave no room for a reasonable mistake on the part of an officer who makes a warrantless arrest for a misdemeanor. State statutes generally provide that a peace officer may arrest, without a warrant, a person who has committed a misdemeanor in his or her presence. A growing number of states

---

[59] *People v. Rutkoski,* 615 N.Y.S.2d 635 (1994).
[60] *Smith v. Tolley,* 960 F. Supp. 977 (E.D. Va. 1997).
[61] *Atwater v. City of Lago Vista,* 532 U.S. 318 (2001).
[62] TEX. CODE ANN. § 545.413 (2005).

have enlarged the power of police officers to make arrests without warrants for misdemeanors not committed in their presence. For example, some states provide that a peace officer may make an arrest when he or she has reasonable grounds to believe that the person is committing or has committed an *offense*.[63] These statutes make it possible for police officers to make arrests for misdemeanors based on reasonable grounds or probable cause even if the misdemeanor is not committed in their presence.[64]

Some states authorize police officers to make warrantless arrests for misdemeanors not committed in their presence under certain special conditions, such as: "The offender will flee if not immediately apprehended"; "he will destroy or conceal evidence of the commission of the offense if not apprehended immediately"; or "he may cause injury to himself or others or damage to property if not apprehended."[65]

In addition, some states authorize a warrantless arrest for a misdemeanor not committed in the officer's presence only for certain specified misdemeanors or classes of misdemeanors.[66] An example is the Oregon statute, which authorizes an arrest on probable cause for a Class A misdemeanor.[67]

Although there is a clear trend toward broadening the peace officer's misdemeanor arrest powers, most states still require that the misdemeanor be committed in the officer's presence and that the arrest take place immediately or shortly thereafter. Any deviation must be by statutory enactment. For this reason, it is necessary that the term *misdemeanor* be clearly defined and that cases be studied to determine what is meant by "in the officer's presence."

1 Misdemeanor Defined

Unless the offense is defined as a felony or unless it is punishable by at least one year in a state penitentiary, the offense is usually considered a misdemeanor. Many states specify which crimes are felonies so that there will be no doubt as to the procedure to be followed. However, in many instances, the officer must determine on the spot whether the offense for which the arrest is being made is a felony or a misdemeanor. If there is doubt, it should be treated as a misdemeanor for purposes of arrest and search.

---

[63] ILL. COMP. STAT. ANN. 72.5/107-2 (2004).
[64] These are among the state statutes authorizing a misdemeanor arrest even if the offense is not committed in the officer's presence: Arizona, Hawaii, Iowa, Louisiana, New York, and Wisconsin. (The list is not exhaustive.)
[65] Kansas, Nebraska, North Carolina, Utah, and Wyoming.
[66] District of Columbia, Maryland, and Washington.
[67] OR. REV. STAT. § 133.310(1)(a) (2005).

2   "In the Officer's Presence" Defined

In most states, the phrase "in the officer's presence" is crucial when determining whether a misdemeanor arrest is justified. An offense is deemed to have occurred in an officer's presence when any of his or her five senses (sight, smell, hearing, taste, or touch) gives him or her the knowledge that an offense is being committed. The officer must perceive the acts that make up the offense when they take place and not merely learn of the event at a later date.

An officer need not witness the entire misdemeanor; however, some part of the offense must be in progress when the officer reaches the scene. If not, the offense is not considered to have taken place "in the officer's presence." If the entire offense is committed before the police officer arrives on the scene and order has been restored, there can be no misdemeanor arrest unless state law has extended the authority to arrest.

3   Necessity of Quick Action

Although the rule has been criticized, the fact remains that, in a majority of states, an arrest must take place immediately after pursuit. If the officer delays in making a misdemeanor arrest, even though it has been committed in his or her presence, he or she must obtain a warrant. An example should clarify this point. If an officer, in carrying out his or her duties, observes a motorist speeding within his or her state or jurisdiction, the officer has the authority to arrest the motorist at that time because the offense occurred in his or her presence. On the other hand, if the officer does not make the arrest at that time and the speeder leaves the state, no arrest can be made if the violator returns at a later time, unless the officer has obtained a warrant or the speeder again violates the law in the officer's presence.

C.   Authority to Enter the Home to Make a Warrantless Arrest

For many years, there was disagreement among the states as to the authority of a police officer to enter a home to make a felony or misdemeanor arrest without a warrant. In some states, such as New York, the statute specifically provided that the officer could enter a home to make a routine felony arrest without a warrant if he or she had probable cause to believe that the suspect had committed a felony and was in the house. In 1980, when *Payton v. New York* was decided, 24 states permitted such warrantless, nonconsensual entries into a suspect's home in order to make a routine felony arrest. The remainder of the states had either prohibited such entry or had taken no position on the question.

In *Payton*, New York detectives, having probable cause to believe that Payton had murdered the manager of a gas station, went to Payton's apartment without an arrest warrant, intending to arrest him.[68] Receiving no response to their knock on the metal door, the officers used crowbars to break open the door and enter the apartment. Even though there was no one in the apartment, the officers observed, in plain view, a .30 caliber shell casing that was later admitted into evidence at Payton's murder trial.

The New York courts approved the entry into Payton's home, finding that the officers had reasonable grounds to believe that Payton had committed a felony and that he could be found in the apartment. On review, the U.S. Supreme Court determined that the New York statute authorizing such entry violated the Fourth Amendment to the Constitution. The Court held that absent exigent circumstances or consent, officers may not enter the home of the suspect or a third party's home to make a routine felony arrest without an arrest warrant. The Court noted that "an arrest warrant, founded on probable cause, implicitly carries with it the limited authority to enter a dwelling in which the suspect lives when there is reason to believe that the suspect is within."

Although *Payton* did not discuss a definition of "exigent circumstances," some light was cast on this by *Welch v. Wisconsin* in 1984.[69] In this misdemeanor case, the officers, without obtaining an arrest warrant, went to the home of the suspect to arrest him for operating a motor vehicle under the influence of alcohol. The Wisconsin Supreme Court upheld the action of the officers, indicating that there were exigent circumstances, that the officers were in "hot pursuit," that there was a need to prevent physical harm to the suspect, and that the need to prevent destruction of evidence of intoxication justified the entry.

The U.S. Supreme Court pointed out that there was no immediate pursuit of the defendant from the accident scene, nor was there a need to protect either the public or the defendant, inasmuch as he had abandoned the vehicle and was at home sleeping. The Court explained that the need to protect evidence does not justify the warrantless intrusion, and that there were no exigent circumstances as required in *Payton*. The Court again cautioned that before government agents may invade a home, the burden is on the government to demonstrate exigent circumstances that overcome the presumption of unreasonableness that attaches to all warrantless home searches.

Although the Court did not define "exigent circumstances," it did shed some light as to what factors are considered in determining exigent circumstances. The Court mentioned these examples: (1) hot pursuit of a fleeing felon; (2) possible destruction

---

68   *Payton v. New York*, 445 U.S. 573 (1980).
69   *Welch v. Wisconsin*, 466 U.S. 740 (1984).

of evidence; and (3) potential further criminal activity. The Court also indicated that, in determining exigency, one must consider the gravity of the underlying offense in progress, whether life or security is endangered, the time of the offense, the time of the arrest, and whether there is a threat to public safety.

Referring to *Payton v. New York* and *Welch v. Wisconsin*, the U.S. Supreme Court in 1990 held that the Minnesota Supreme Court applied the correct standard in determining "exigent circumstances."[70] In *Minnesota v. Olson*, police officers, without seeking permission and without an arrest or a search warrant, entered the home of a third party to arrest a suspect. Shortly after the police officers entered the home, the suspect made an inculpatory statement that the trial court refused to suppress. The defendant was convicted of first-degree murder. On review, the Minnesota Supreme Court ruled that the arrest was illegal because there were no exigent circumstances to justify the warrantless entry, that the defendant's statement was tainted, and that the statement should have been suppressed at the trial.

The U.S. Supreme Court agreed with the Minnesota Supreme Court that exigent circumstances did not exist and included this statement:

> The Minnesota Supreme Court applied essentially the correct standard in determining whether exigent circumstances existed. The court observed that a "warrantless intrusion may be justified by hot pursuit of a fleeing felon, or imminent destruction of evidence or the need to prevent a suspect's escape, or the risk of danger to the police or other persons inside or outside the dwelling."

Even though the U.S. Supreme Court made it clear that the police must have an arrest warrant to effect the nonemergency arrest of an individual in his or her own home, it is apparent from the cases that reach the review stage that law enforcement personnel are not following these rules. For example, in a Georgia case, the court held that the warrantless arrest of the defendant was invalid because the defendant was arrested inside his home and there was no evidence of exigent circumstances or of the defendant's consent to let the officers enter his home to arrest him.[71]

A federal court decided that a warrantless threshold arrest of the defendant violated the Fourth Amendment where no exigent circumstances existed.[72] The court explained that the defendant's door was closed when the officers approached, causing the officers to knock with guns drawn and instruct the defendant to exit his apartment, and consequently the defendant's arrest was not set in motion in a public place but in his apartment, a private and protected place, so that there was no "hot pursuit."

---

[70] *Minnesota v. Olson,* 495 U.S. 91 (1990).

[71] *Boatright v. State,* 483 S.E.2d 659 (Ga. 1997).

[72] *United States v. Saari,* 88 F. Supp. 2d 835 (W.D. Tenn. 1999).

Discussing the "consent" exception, a federal court ruled that the Fourth Amendment generally prohibits entering a person's home without a warrant, whether to make an arrest or to search for specific objects; however, the prohibition does not apply to situations in which voluntary consent has been obtained, either from the individual whose property is searched or from a third person who possesses common authority over the premises.[73]

To summarize the decisions relating to the entry into a home to make an arrest without a warrant, this is the current rule: without an arrest warrant, an officer may not enter the home of a suspect to make an arrest, even on probable cause, unless there are exigent circumstances or consent is given to enter the home by someone in authority. Also, without an arrest warrant, the officer may not legally enter the home of a third party to make an arrest of the suspect unless a search warrant for the home of the third party has been issued, consent is given to enter by one in charge of the premises, or exigent circumstances exist.

§ 5.6   Post-Arrest Probable Cause Determination

As indicated previously, constitutions, statutes, and case decisions require that the rights of the accused be protected prior to and during an arrest. The U.S. Constitution, the constitutions of the various states, and statutes and codes also safeguard the arrestee's post-arrest rights.

All state statutes and the federal code require that the person arrested be taken before a magistrate or commissioner "without unnecessary delay" or "forthwith." In *Gerstein v. Pugh*, the U.S. Supreme Court held that the Fourth Amendment requires a judicial determination of probable cause as a prerequisite to an extended restraint of liberty following arrest.[74] This determination must be made by someone independent of the police and the prosecutor.

In 1991, in *County of Riverside v. McLaughlin*, the U.S. Supreme Court held that a jurisdiction that chooses to combine the probable cause determination with other pretrial proceedings must do so as soon as is reasonably feasible, but in no event later than 48 hours after arrest.[75] But even with this specific statement, some questions were left unanswered. What if the arrested individual does not receive a probable cause determination within the 48-hour period? Recognizing that the standard established by *Gerstein* had not provided significant guidance and that the vague standard had led to a flurry of challenges, the Court set a more definite standard that must now be followed.

---

[73]   *United States v. Sculco,* 82 F. Supp. 2d 410 (E.D. Pa. 2000).

[74]   *Gerstein v. Pugh,* 420 U.S. 103 (1975).

[75]   *County of Riverside v. McLaughlin,* 500 U.S. 44 (1991). (Quote from syllabus.)

This wording indicates that the probable cause determination may be delayed, but the burden of proof is on the government to demonstrate that an emergency existed or that there were other extraordinary circumstances. The Court also warned, however, that holding an arrestee during an intervening weekend, as was the practice in some localities, is not considered a bona fide emergency or extraordinary circumstance. In other words, the probable cause determination must be made by a judicial officer within 48 hours, regardless of whether the arrest takes place during a weekend or at some other time.

In spite of the requirement that the probable cause determination take place within the 48-hour period, as a general matter, this leaves the door open to challenges even if the probable cause determination is made by the judicial officer within the 48-hour period, if the arrested individual can prove that his or her probable cause determination was delayed unreasonably.

The Court further explained that jurisdictions are not constitutionally compelled to provide a probable cause hearing *immediately* upon taking a suspect into custody and completing booking procedures, and the states are not required to establish a rigid procedural framework.

To summarize, the Fourth Amendment does not impose on individual jurisdictions a rigid procedural framework for making the required prompt determinations of probable cause after a warrantless arrest. The probable cause determination must be made as soon as reasonably feasible, but in the usual case no later than 48 hours after arrest. If the arrested individual does not receive a probable cause determination within the 48-hour period, the burden of proof is on the government to demonstrate the existence of a bona fide emergency or other extraordinary circumstance that prevented the probable cause determination from taking place. And even if the hearing is held within the 48-hour period, the procedure may still violate the *Gerstein* rule if the arrested individual can prove the probable cause determination was delayed unreasonably. In evaluating the reasonableness of the delay, the courts must allow a substantial degree of flexibility, taking into account the practical realities of pretrial procedures. Applying the rule established in *County of Riverside v. McLaughlin*, the U.S. Supreme Court held that a four-day delay between a warrantless arrest and a judicial probable cause determination was presumptively unreasonable.[76]

A federal court has reiterated that the arrestee has a constitutional right to have a judicial determination within the first 48 hours after arrest to determine whether probable cause exists for continued detention. Therefore, an arrestee's due process rights were violated when he was detained for 30 days without a judicial determination of probable cause following his arrest.[77] A second federal court pointed out that

---

[76] *Powell v. Nevada,* 511 U.S. 79 (1994).
[77] *Blumel v. Mylander,* 954 F. Supp. 1547 (M.D. Fla. 1997).

a detention of 61 hours between the arrest and appearance before the judge was not justified where there was no evidence of an "emergency" or "extraordinary circumstances."[78] However, when a suspect was detained for four days over a weekend without a determination of probable cause by a judicial officer, the detention was not wrongful as the delay was at least in part attributable to the fact that the defendant's attorney requested a polygraph examination and the examination could not be performed until the following Monday.[79]

§ 5.7   Use of Force in Making an Arrest

Police officers are responsible for apprehending individuals who violate the law. On the other hand, officers are subject to civil, and possibly criminal, liability if they use more force than is necessary in making an arrest. The officer making an arrest must decide on the spur of the moment what force can be used in effecting the arrest. Some discussion and guidelines will assist officers in making these difficult decisions.

The general rule is that an officer who is making a lawful arrest, or who has made an arrest, is justified in using such force as is *reasonably necessary* to secure and detain the offender, overcome his or her resistance, prevent his or her escape, recapture the offender if he or she escapes, and protect him- or herself from bodily harm.[80] The officer, however, is never justified in using unnecessary force or using or resorting to dangerous means when the arrest could be effected by less dangerous means.

Prior to 1985, state statutes were inconsistent concerning the use of deadly force in making an arrest. Some states followed the common law rule that authorized the use of deadly force to effect the arrest of a fleeing felon when all other means had failed. Some states followed a modified common law rule that generally allowed the use of deadly force to make an arrest for a felony only if the suspect was attempting to escape by the use of deadly weapons, had indicated that he or she would endanger a human life if not apprehended, or had committed a dangerous or atrocious felony. A third group of states followed the Model Penal Code, which justified the use of deadly force to effect a felony arrest only when the officer believed that: (1) the force employed would not create a substantial risk of injury to innocent persons; (2) the crime for which the arrest was made involved conduct that included the threatened

---

[78] *Kyle v. Patterson,* 757 F. Supp. 1031 (N.D. Ill. 1997).

[79] *Cornish v. Papis,* 962 F. Supp. 1103 (C.D. Ill. 1997).

[80] 6A C.J.S. *Arrest* § 49 (1975). See also *Rhodes v. State,* 945 S.W.2d 115 (Tex. 1997), in which the court held that an officer may use such force as is reasonably necessary to effect the goal of a stop, investigation, maintenance of status quo, or officer safety.

use of deadly force; or (3) there was a substantial risk that the person to be arrested would cause death or serious bodily harm if his or her apprehension were delayed.

The Supreme Court, in a landmark decision in 1985, handed down its own decision regarding the use of deadly force in making an arrest.[81] In *Tennessee v. Garner*, the state court found that the use of deadly force was justified under the Tennessee statute, which followed the common law rule. The state statute provided that "if, after notice of the intention to arrest the defendant, he either flees or forcibly resists, the officer may use all of the necessary means to effect the arrest." Both the Tennessee statute and the departmental policy allowed the use of deadly force in making a burglary arrest.

The facts of *Garner* indicate that a Memphis police officer shot and killed Garner after he was told to halt and after Garner, at night, climbed over a fence in the backyard of a house he was suspected of burglarizing. The officer testified that he saw no signs of a weapon and, although not certain, was "reasonably sure" and "figured" that Garner was unarmed. There was little doubt that a burglary actually occurred, because a purse taken from the house was found on Garner's body. However, there was also no indication that the officer's or anyone else's life was in danger.

In rejecting the reasoning that the common law rule should still apply, the Supreme Court stated:

> The use of deadly force to prevent escape of all felony suspects, whatever the circumstances, is constitutionally unreasonable. It is not better that all felony suspects die than that they escape. When a suspect poses no immediate threat to the officer and no threat to others, the harm resulting from failing to apprehend him does not justify the use of deadly force to do so. It is no doubt unfortunate when a suspect who is in sight escapes, but the fact that the police arrive a little late or are a little slower afoot does not always justify killing the suspect. A police officer may not seize an unarmed, nondangerous suspect by shooting him dead.

The Court did not hold the Tennessee statute unconstitutional as *written*, but unconstitutional *as applied* in that case. In affirmatively stating that deadly force may still be used in some instances, the Court noted:

> Thus, if the suspect threatens the officer with a weapon, or there is probable cause to believe he has committed a crime involving the infliction or threatened infliction of serious physical harm, deadly force may be used, if necessary, to prevent escape and if, where feasible, some warning has been given.

In a case before the U.S. Supreme Court in 1989, the Court phrased the use-of-force question in this manner: "This case requires us to decide what constitutional

---

[81]   *Tennessee v. Garner*, 471 U.S. 1 (1985).

standard governs a free citizen's claim that law enforcement officials used excessive force in the course of making an arrest, investigatory stop, or other 'seizure' of his person."[82] In this case, Graham, a diabetic, had asked his friend to drive him to a convenience store to purchase orange juice to counteract the onset of an insulin reaction. Upon entering the store and seeing the number of people ahead of him, the petitioner hurried out and asked his friend to drive him to the friend's house. Connor, a police officer, became suspicious after seeing Graham hastily enter and leave the store, followed the car, and made an investigatory stop, ordering the pair to wait while he found out what had happened in the store. Meanwhile, backup officers arrived on the scene, handcuffed Graham, and ignored or rebuffed Graham's attempts to explain, and failed to treat his condition. During the encounter Graham sustained multiple injuries. He brought a § 1983 action against the police officers, seeking to recover damages for the injuries he allegedly sustained when the officers used physical force against him during the course of the investigatory stop.

After applying factors that are to be considered in determining whether the excessive use of force gives rise to a cause of action under § 1983, the trial court granted the officer's motion for a directed verdict. The court of appeals ruled that the district court had applied the correct legal standard in addressing Graham's excessive force claim and Graham appealed to the U.S. Supreme Court.

In reviewing the lower court's decision, the Supreme Court noted that an excessive force claim arising from either an arrest or *Terry* stop implicates the Fourth Amendment protection against unreasonable searches and seizures. Determining whether the force used to effect a particular seizure is "reasonable" under the Fourth Amendment requires a careful balancing of the "nature and quality of the intrusion on the individual's Fourth Amendment interest" against the countervailing government interest. The opinion in *Graham v. Connor* included this reasoning:

> Our Fourth Amendment jurisprudence has long recognized that the right to make an arrest or investigatory stop necessarily carries with it the right to use some degree of physical coercion or threat thereof to effect it . . . however, its proper application requires careful attention to the facts and circumstances of each particular case, including the severity of the crime at issue, whether the suspect poses an immediate threat to the officers or others, and whether he is actively resisting arrest or attempting to evade arrest by flight.

The Court recognized that "the calculus of reasonableness in making an arrest must embody allowance for the fact that the police officers are often forced to make split-second judgments—in circumstances that are tense, uncertain, and rapidly evolving—about the amount of force that is necessary in a particular situation." The

---

[82] *Graham v. Connor,* 490 U.S. 386 (1989).

question in each case is whether the officers' actions are objectively reasonable in light of the facts and circumstances confronting them, without regard to their underlying intent or motivation. An officer's evil intentions will not make a Fourth Amendment violation out of an objectively reasonable use of force; nor will an officer's good intentions make an objectively unreasonable use of force constitutional.

Lower courts have held that the test for determining whether unreasonable or excessive force was used in making an arrest is not what in hindsight seems prudent, but is what a reasonable officer would do in the heat of the moment.[83] A New York court held that, in making its determination as to the reasonableness of force, the court must judge the officer's actions from the perspective of a reasonable officer on the scene and must take into account such factors as the severity of the crime at issue, whether the suspect poses an immediate threat to the safety of the officer or others, and whether he or she is actively resisting arrest or attempting to evade arrest by flight.[84]

After a comprehensive review of the law relating to the use of force, a federal court held that in determining whether an officer's use of force is objectively reasonable under the Fourth Amendment, the court considers factors such as the need for application of force, the relationship between the need and amount of force used, the extent of the injury inflicted, and whether force was applied in good faith or maliciously and sadistically.[85] The court further explained that in making this objective assessment, the court may consider, in addition to physical injury, other relevant factors, including the possibility that persons subject to police action are themselves violent or dangerous, the duration of the action, whether the action takes place in the context of effecting an arrest, the possibility that the suspect may be armed, the number of persons with whom the police officers must contend at one time, the severity of the crime, whether the suspect posed an immediate threat, and whether the suspect was resisting or fleeing.

§ 5.8   The Citation and Summons in Law Enforcement

Most state statutes include provisions for the issuance of a citation or summons instead of making a physical arrest of the person. A citation is a written notice to appear in court at a stated time and place to answer for an offense charged.[86]

---

[83]   *Swanson v. Fields,* 814 F. Supp. 1007 (D. Kan. 1993).

[84]   *Thornton v. City of Albany,* 831 F. Supp. 970 (N.D.N.Y. 1993).

[85]   *Jackson v. Sauls,* 206 F.3d 1156 (11th Cir. 2000). See also *Headwaters Forest Defense v. County of Humboldt,* 211 F.3d 1121 (9th Cir. 2000), which listed factors to be weighed in determining whether the force used to effect was reasonable.

[86]   § 15A-302 (2004) of the General Statutes of North Carolina provides that a citation is a directive, issued by a law enforcement officer or other person authorized by statute, that a person appear in court and answer a misdemeanor or infraction or charges.

Does the issuance of a citation constitute an arrest? The person who is cited may or may not be arrested at the time the citation is issued, depending on the wording of the statute that permits issuance of the citation. These statutes are generally of two types. Under the first type, the citation is issued *instead* of making a physical arrest. For example, the Ohio Revised Code provides:

> 2935.26   When citation must be used rather than arrest; exceptions; procedures
> (A) any other provision of the Revised Code, when a law enforcement officer is otherwise authorized to arrest a person for the commission of a minor misdemeanor, the officer shall not arrest the person, but shall issue a citation, unless one of the following applies:
>   (1) The offender requires medical care or is unable to provide for his own safety.
>   (2) The offender cannot or will not offer satisfactory evidence of his identity.
>   (3) The offender refuses to sign the citation.
>   (4) The offender has previously been issued a citation for the commission of that misdemeanor and has failed to do one of the following:
>   (a) Appear at the time and place stated in the citation;
>   (b) Comply with division (C) of this section . . .[87]

The Ohio statute includes some instances in which a citation may not be issued and provides what information the citation must contain. It is obvious from the wording of the statute that a citation is used *in place of* an arrest.[88]

Some of the statutes refer to the issuance of a *citation*, some refer to the issuance of a *summons*, and some use the phrase *notice to appear*. Regardless of the wording under these statutes, a person who has been cited is not under arrest, because the statute specifically indicates that the citation is issued instead of an arrest.

Some statutes establish the procedure for issuance of a summons or a citation *after* an arrest. For example, the California Penal Code provides:

> (a) In any case in which a person is *arrested* for an offense declared to be a misdemeanor, including violation of any city or county ordinance, and does not demand to be taken before a magistrate, that person shall, instead of being taken before a magistrate, be released according to the procedures set forth by this chapter. If a person is released, the officer or superior shall prepare in duplicate a written notice to

---

[87]   OHIO REV. CODE ANN. § 2935.26 (Anderson 2000).

[88]   Other statutes that authorize the issuance of a citation in place of an arrest are: DEL. CODE ANN. II, § 1907 (2005) (summons method of arrest); Ill. L.C.S. 5/107-11 (II) (2004) (notice to appear instead of arrest); IOWA CODE ANN. § 805.1 (2004) (citation issued as alternative to making an arrest); KAN. STAT. ANN. § 22-2408 (2004) (notice to appear); LA. CODE CRIM. PROC. ANN. Art. 211 (2005) (summons instead of arrest); N.Y. CRIM. PROC. § 150.20 (2005) (officer issues an "appearance ticket" instead of arrest).

appear in court, containing the name and address of the person, the offense charged, and the time and place where and when the person shall appear in court. If, pursuant to subdivision (i), the person is not released prior to being booked and the officer in charge of the booking or his or her superior determines that the person should be released, the officer or superior shall prepare a written notice to appear in court.[89]

As a general rule, the use of the citation does not enlarge an officer's authority to make an arrest without a warrant. For example, the Ohio statute provides that an officer may issue a citation when he or she is otherwise authorized to arrest a person for the commission of a misdemeanor. However, in some states, the statute provides for the issuance of a citation when a physical arrest would not be authorized. In fact, in North Carolina, "failure of the person cited to sign the citation shall not constitute grounds for arrest or the requirement that he post a bond."[90]

Because the issuance of a citation is not generally an arrest in itself, warrantless searches of vehicles are not permitted under the "search incident to arrest" exception when a driver receives a traffic citation but is not placed under arrest.[91] However, if the circumstances indicate that the officer is in danger, a self-protective search or "frisk" would be in order under the rule established in *Terry v. Ohio.*[92]

§ 5.9   Arrest after Fresh Pursuit

Fresh pursuit has been defined as "pursuit without unreasonable interruption" or "the immediate pursuit of a person who is endeavoring to avoid arrest." At common law, the doctrine of fresh pursuit applied only in felony cases. Although a few states retain this common law limitation, the majority of the states recognize the right of a peace officer to pursue a person who has committed any offense, including a misdemeanor, across corporate lines or county lines, anywhere *within* the state if the pursuit is immediate and continuous. Although some states authorize police officers to pursue a suspected misdemeanant within the state but outside the officer's geographical jurisdiction only if there is express statutory authorization,[93] the general rule is that officers may make extraterritorial (outside their jurisdiction) arrests for misdemeanors if the acts that gave the officer reasonable grounds to believe the suspect committed the offense occurred while the officer was still in his or her own jurisdiction.[94]

---

[89] CAL. PENAL CODE § 853.6 (2004).
[90] N.C. GEN. STAT. § 15A-302 (2004).
[91] *State v. Pallone,* 613 N.W.2d 568 (Wis. 2000).
[92] See § 7.11 for a discussion of stop-and-frisk seizures and searches.
[93] *State v. Frieze,* 525 N.W.2d 646 (Neb. 1994).
[94] *People v. Leinwever,* 600 N.E.2d 901 (Ill. 1992).

No state can confer upon its officers any power that is effective in another state. Before a police officer can act as an officer of another state, there must be a statute in the second state that confers authority on an officer entering that state in fresh pursuit. In recent years, there has been a trend among the states toward increased cooperation in the area of law enforcement.

Many states have adopted the Uniform Fresh Pursuit Act or similar legislation permitting law enforcement officers from other states to enter their state in fresh pursuit to make an arrest. For example, the North Carolina statute provides that a law enforcement officer of a state contiguous to the state of North Carolina, who enters North Carolina in fresh pursuit of a person who is in immediate and contiguous flight from the commission of a criminal offense, has the same authority to arrest as a law enforcement officer of the state of North Carolina.[95]

The North Carolina statute uses the term *criminal offense*, whereas some statutes authorize fresh pursuit into their state only when a *felony* has been committed. Most states that have adopted the Uniform Fresh Pursuit Act provide that this applies only to law enforcement officers of a state that, by its laws, has made similar provisions for the arrest and custody of persons closely pursued within its territory. A few states, such as Illinois, authorize a peace officer from another state who enters the state of Illinois in fresh pursuit to arrest the person the officer is pursuing if that person has committed an offense in the other state. Illinois does not require that adjoining states have reciprocal provisions authorizing Illinois officers to enter in fresh pursuit.[96]

Failure to follow the provisions of the "fresh pursuit" statute makes a stop and arrest invalid. In a Pennsylvania case, the court held that the extraterritorial arrest of the defendant in Delaware, after Pennsylvania troopers stopped the defendant's vehicle and the defendant failed a sobriety test, was not in accordance with Delaware's "fresh pursuit" statute, and thus the arrest was unlawful when the officers did not bring the defendant to a Delaware justice of the peace to determine the lawfulness of the arrest.[97]

Because of the difference in the laws of the various states, an officer who might have occasion to follow a suspect into another state in fresh pursuit must know the laws of the surrounding states. The fact that the officer's own state authorizes agents from other states to come into that state in fresh pursuit to make either a felony or a misdemeanor arrest does not mean that the bordering states reciprocate. For example, a peace officer from Kentucky may enter Illinois and make an arrest as an officer of the state of Illinois for a misdemeanor. But officers from Illinois do not have the same privilege in Kentucky, as that state has not adopted the Uniform Fresh Pursuit Act and has no other statutory provisions extending out-of-state authority.

---

[95] N.C. GEN. STAT. § 15A-403 (2004).

[96] 725 ILL. L.C.S. 5/107-4 (2004).

[97] *Commonwealth v. Sadvari,* 752 A.2d 393 (Pa. 2000).

§ 5.10 Summary

The Fourth Amendment to the U.S. Constitution, as interpreted by the U.S. Supreme Court, forms the basis for constitutional standards concerning detention and arrest. State statutes define the authority of officers to arrest with or without warrants, but these statutes cannot grant authority that conflicts with the rights guaranteed by the Constitution.

One definition of an arrest is the taking, seizing, or detaining of another either by touching or putting hands on him or her, or by any act that indicates an intention to take him or her into custody and subjects the person arrested to the actual control and will of the person making the arrest. A person may come within the custody and control of the law by submission or by manual caption as evidenced by some touching of the body.

Statutes in all states provide that a peace officer may make an arrest under an arrest warrant. However, in order for the arrest warrant to be valid, it must, among other things: (1) be supported by probable cause; (2) be supported by oath or affirmation; (3) particularly describe the person who is to be arrested; (4) state the nature of the offense; (5) designate the officer or class of officers authorized to execute the warrant; (6) be issued in the name of a state or the United States; and (7) be signed by a neutral and detached judicial officer. Even if an arrest warrant is valid on its face, the officer must still execute it properly.

In addition to arrest with a warrant, an officer is entitled to make an arrest without a warrant in certain instances. As a general rule, an officer can arrest a person without a warrant in felony cases when he or she has reasonable grounds to believe that a felony has been committed and reasonable grounds to believe that the person to be arrested has committed that felony.

In misdemeanor cases, the general rule is that an officer may arrest for a misdemeanor only if it is committed in his or her presence. There are some exceptions to this rule, and the trend is to extend this authority to apply the rule concerning felony cases. However, unless the authority is extended by statute, the officer must make the misdemeanor arrest at the time of the misdemeanor or immediately thereafter.

The courts have placed tight restrictions on the authority of a police officer to enter the home of a suspect in order to make an arrest. The current rule is that *with* an arrest warrant, the officer may enter the home of the person named in the warrant and execute the warrant. An officer may not execute the warrant in the home of a third party without consent of the third party, a search warrant for the third party's home, or exigent circumstances. Without an arrest warrant, an officer may not enter the home of the suspect, even on probable cause, unless there are exigent circumstances or consent is given to enter the home. Without an arrest warrant, the officer may not enter the home of a third party to make an arrest of the suspect unless there is a search warrant for the home of the third party, the officer has the consent of someone in charge of the premises, or exigent circumstances exist.

Several Supreme Court decisions have also placed limits on the use of deadly force in making an arrest. The current rule is that an officer may not use deadly force to seize an unarmed, non-dangerous suspect. However, if the suspect threatens the officers with a weapon or there is probable cause to believe that he or she has committed a crime that has involved the infliction or threatened infliction of serious physical harm, then deadly force may be used, if necessary, to prevent escape and if, where feasible, some warning has been given.

To save the time of the officer and for the convenience of the arrestee, a citation or summons may be issued in certain instances. There are several types of statutes that authorize the use of the citation or summons, but in any event the issuance of the citation is not an arrest but rather is an alternative procedure applied in lieu of a physical arrest or as a substitute for taking the arrestee before a magistrate.

Of necessity, courts have had to recognize the authority of police officers to pursue individuals who have committed violations if the pursuit is without unreasonable interruption. Although generally this fresh pursuit may be continued outside the officers' jurisdiction within the state, it may not continue outside the state unless the pursuit is authorized by a statute of the other state.

Chapter 6
Search and Seizure with a Warrant

In Jones v. United States, this Court, strongly supporting the preferences to be accorded searches under a warrant, indicated that in a doubtful or marginal case a search under a warrant may be sustainable where without one it would fail . . .

The fact that exceptions to the requirement that searches and seizures be undertaken only after obtaining a warrant are limited underscores the preference accorded police action taken under a warrant against searches and seizures without one.

United States v. Ventresca, 380 U.S. 102 (1965)

§ 6.1   General Considerations

Possibly more evidence is excluded in criminal cases because of violation of the Fourth Amendment than for any other reason. The law relating to search and seizure is complex, but not impossible to understand. If officers are to carry out their responsibilities, it is an absolute necessity that they understand the law relating to the seizure of evidence.

Before *Mapp v. Ohio*[1] was decided by the U.S. Supreme Court in 1961, the validity of the search was not critical in some states because evidence was admitted even though it was seized illegally. The Supreme Court had ruled years earlier that federal officers could not conduct a search in violation of the Fourth Amendment;[2] however, this right was not extended to actions of police at the state and local levels until *Mapp*. The Court's ruling in *Mapp* meant that evidence obtained by illegal searches would be inadmissible in state as well as federal courts.

This means that officers must determine, at the time a search is conducted, the grounds on which they can justify the search in court. The requirement of the Fourth Amendment for searches to be valid is that they must be conducted pursuant to a search warrant authorized by a magistrate. Searches with a valid warrant are the subject of this chapter. However, there are at least nine exceptions to the warrant requirement that have been authorized by the Supreme Court. Most warrantless searches are valid because they are made incident to a lawful arrest or with consent. If an officer is aware of all the technical grounds on which a search and seizure may be validated, he or she can make the determination at the time of the search—not after it has begun. On the other hand, if the officer cannot base his or her search on one of the legal justifications, it is better to not make the search at all. Once the evidence has been contaminated by an illegal search, it cannot be used in court. The exclusion of evidence because of an illegal search was covered in Chapter 2, and is applied in this chapter and Chapter 7. The law relating to searches under valid search warrants is covered in this chapter. In Chapter 7, exceptions to searches with a warrant are discussed.

§ 6.2   Constitutional Provisions

The Fourth Amendment protects a person's right to be free of unreasonable searches and seizures. It states:

> The right of the people to be secure in their persons, houses, papers, and effects against unreasonable searches and seizures, shall not be violated, and no Warrants

---

[1]   *Mapp v. Ohio*, 367 U.S. 643 (1961).
[2]   *Weeks v. United States*, 232 U.S. 383 (1914).

shall issue, but upon probable cause, supported by Oath or affirmation, and particularly describing the place to be searched, and the persons or things to be seized.

The first part of this Amendment is the general protection from unreasonable searches and seizures (the basis of the exclusionary rule in Chapter 2). The focus of this chapter begins with ". . . and no Warrants shall issue . . ." This is the beginning of the requirement that a valid search should be based on a proper warrant (unless it falls within one of the exceptions in the next chapter). The clauses that follow this statement are the particular requirements for a search warrant to be valid. These are the subjects of the sections below.

As in the case of the other provisions of the Bill of Rights, the Fourth Amendment would mean little without judicial interpretation. Many of the words and phrases are not defined; therefore, it is necessary to look to the courts for definitions and interpretations.

State constitutions often impose similar restraints on state and local officials. The wording of state constitutions may differ slightly from one another or from the federal Constitution, and there will occasionally be a behavior not protected in a state constitution that is protected by federal law, or vice versa.

§ 6.3   Seizure with a Valid Search Warrant—General

The preferred way to conduct a legal search, and one that is universally recognized, is a search with a valid search warrant. Both the U.S. Constitution and the constitutions of the various states describe the circumstances under which warrants may be issued. They generally provide that: (1) a warrant shall not be issued unless there is probable cause; (2) the warrant must be supported by oath or affirmation; and (3) the place to be searched and the things to be seized must be particularly described. In addition to these requirements, others have been added either by legislation or by court interpretation.

A search warrant has been defined as an order, in writing, in the name of a state, signed by a judicial officer in the proper exercise of his or her authority, directing a law enforcement officer to search for personal property and to bring it before the court. From this definition, it is clear that the officer, in executing the warrant, is merely carrying out the instructions of a judicial officer.

For a search warrant to be valid, it must meet certain requirements. Also, even though the warrant has been issued correctly, the evidence can be made inadmissible by improper execution of the warrant. The requirements for valid issuance and execution are discussed in the following sections.

§ 6.4   The Warrant Must Be Issued on Probable Cause

The Fourth Amendment to the Constitution and state constitutions provide that no warrants shall issue but upon probable cause. This is a constitutional requirement and is binding on all state and federal courts. In discussing probable cause for the issuance of a search warrant, the U.S. Supreme Court made this statement:

> If the apparent facts set out in the affidavit are such that a reasonably discreet and prudent man would be led to believe that there was a commission of the offense charged, there is probable cause justifying the issuance of a warrant.[3]

There is no requirement that the affiant furnishes proof beyond a reasonable doubt, but he or she must show more than "mere suspicion." In 1986, the U.S. Supreme Court explained the probable cause standard.[4] The Court noted:

> The term "probable cause" . . . means less than evidence which would justify condemnation . . . It imports a seizure made under circumstances which warrant suspicion . . . Finely tuned standards such as beyond a reasonable doubt or by the preponderance of the evidence, useful in formal trials, have no place in the magistrate's decision.

In its concluding comment, the Court reiterated that "probable cause requires only a probability or substantial chance of criminal activity, not an actual showing of such activity."

Using different terms, a California court, in defining the probable cause standard, commented that probable cause to issue a search warrant need not be tantamount to proof beyond a reasonable doubt; probability is the touchstone.[5] The court continued by indicating that the probable cause standard for issuing search warrants does not require a showing of an officer's belief that evidence will be found in the searched premises is correct or more likely true than false; rather, probable cause to search a home exists as long as the underlying affidavit contained information showing a fair probability that evidence of a crime would be found there.

The facts to support probable cause must be obtained legally. If information to be included in the affidavit for a search warrant is obtained in violation of the Fourth Amendment, the issuance of the warrant will not cure the illegality. That is, if

---

[3]   *Dumbra v. United States*, 268 U.S. 435 (1925).

[4]   *New York v. P.J. Video, Inc.*, 475 U.S. 868 (1986).

[5]   *United States v. Grant*, 218 F.3d 72 (1st Cir. 2000).

evidence is obtained by an illegal entry into a protected area, and that evidence is used for probable cause for a warrant, the general rule is that the warrant will not be enforceable. If the search warrant is based on information totally unconnected with an illegal entry, however, the search warrant may be executed lawfully.

This rule was tested in *Murray v. United States*.[6] The Supreme Court again considered the application of the "independent source" doctrine. In this case, agents forced their way into a warehouse and observed in plain view numerous burlap-wrapped bales that they suspected were narcotics. Prior to this illegal entry, the agents had observed suspects driving vehicles and had lawfully seized marijuana. Without disturbing the bales that they discovered in the warehouse, the officers applied for a warrant for a search of the warehouse, giving to the magistrate only the evidence they had obtained independently of that located during the illegal entry. Upon issuance of the warrant, they reentered the warehouse and seized 270 bales of marijuana and other evidence of drug crimes. The defendants argued that the warrant was tainted by the first illegal entry. On review, the Supreme Court explained the "independent source" doctrine, which permits the introduction of evidence initially discovered during, or as a consequence of, an unlawful search but later obtained independently from lawful activities untainted by the initial illegality. The Court then ruled that, even if the police illegally enter private property, evidence discovered during that illegal entry may be admissible in court if it is later discovered during a valid search that was wholly unrelated to the illegal entry.

This doctrine is also tested when police may use technology to gather information. In a case decided by the United States Supreme Court in 2001, agents, suspicious that marijuana was being grown in Kyllo's home, used a thermal imaging device to scan the triplex to determine whether the amount of heat emanating from it was consistent with the high-intensity lamps typically used for indoor marijuana growth. The scan showed that the garage roof and a side wall were relatively hot compared to the rest of the home, and substantially warmer than the neighboring units. Based in part on the thermal imaging, a federal magistrate issued a warrant to search the home, where the agents found marijuana growing. Kyllo moved to suppress the evidence seized from the home. The United States Supreme Court reversed lower court rulings and held the search was invalid.[7] The Supreme Court summarized that:

> Where, as here, the government uses a device that is not in general public use, to explore details of a private home that would previously have been unknowable without physical intrusion, the surveillance is a Fourth Amendment "search" and is presumptively unreasonable without a warrant.

---

[6] *Murray v. United States*, 487 U.S. 533 (1988).
[7] *Kyllo v. United States*, 533 U.S. 27 (2001).

Danny Lee Kyllo stands in front of the house in Florence, Oregon, where narcotics agents, using a thermal imaging device, burst in on him in the early morning to find 100 marijuana plants growing in the attic. In *Kyllo v. United States*, the Court conceded that the degree of intrusion was such as to make the search contrary to the Fourth Amendment. (*AP Photo/ Don Ryan*)

The Court conceded that there was no compromise of Kyllo's privacy in his home, but the degree of intrusion was such as to make the search contrary to the Fourth Amendment.

The Fourth Amendment requires that law enforcement officers submit sufficient evidence about probable cause to a neutral magistrate before a search warrant may be issued.[8] The courts have recognized that an affidavit in support of a search warrant is not to be read hypertechnically, but in light of everyday experience, and the affidavit is to be read in favor of the warrant.[9] In *People v. Galimulla*, the Court concluded that the warrant is to be read in a "commonsense and realistic fashion," and "in the clear light of everyday experience and accorded all reasonable inferences." In a 1997 case, a state court used almost the same language in stating that affidavits for search

8   *People v. Collazo*, 12 Cal. Rptr. 2d 842 (1992).
9   *People v. Galimulla*, 588 N.Y. Supp. 2d 110 (1992).

warrants should not be reviewed and tested in a hypertechnical manner, but must be tested and interpreted by both magistrates and the reviewing appellate courts in a commonsense and realistic fashion, and the magistrate is entitled to draw reasonable inferences from the evidence presented.[10]

Two important points should be reemphasized here: (1) probable cause cannot be justified by what the subsequent search discloses; and (2) the facts to determine probable cause must be provided in full to the proper official. From a legal standpoint, it makes no difference whether the officer locates the described property. The probable cause for the warrant must be apparent at the time a judicial officer issues that warrant. If those facts are not available, the warrant is invalid even though the articles authorized and described by the warrant are located. On the other hand, the warrant does not become invalid (thereby making the officer liable) even if no evidence whatsoever is located. Concerning the second point, the facts available to the affiant (usually the police officer) must be made known to the magistrate so the magistrate may then make an intelligent and independent decision. The fact that an officer or others have information that would support a finding of probable cause is of no legal value if this probable cause is not made available to the issuing official.

In a Florida case, the reviewing court noted that the existence of probable cause for issuance of a search warrant must be determined solely from affidavits submitted.[11] Another court, however, ruled that a magistrate who is asked to issue the search warrant is entitled to draw reasonable inferences from the facts and circumstances recited in the affidavit.[12]

An affidavit for a search warrant need not include extrinsic corroboration of the informant's veracity when such information is provided orally to the magistrate.[13] The court explained that this information may be conveyed orally by police officers seeking a warrant or through the magistrate's direct examination of the informer while under oath.

An issue related to probable cause concerns the use of undisclosed informants to establish probable cause for a search warrant. In a series of earlier cases, the Supreme Court indicated that information from an undisclosed informant may be used in establishing probable cause. However, in two cases decided in 1964 and 1969,[14] the Supreme Court established standards for establishing the credibility of the informant. The Court warned that an informant's tip must be corroborated, and the issuing

---

10 *State v. Wilson*, 938 P.2d 1251 (Idaho 1997).

11 *State v. Badgett*, 695 So. 2d 468 (Fla. 1997).

12 *State v. Geboroff*, 939 P.2d 706 (Wash. 1997).

13 *Polston v. Commonwealth*, 485 S.E.2d 632 (Va. Ct. App. 1997).

14 *Aguilar v. Texas*, 378 U.S. 108 (1964); *Spinelli v. United States*, 393 U.S. 410 (1969).

official must be given sufficient information to reach an independent conclusion that the informant was credible and the information reliable. In these cases, the Court established what became known as the "two-pronged test," which mandated that: (1) the magistrate be given some of the underlying circumstances from which the affiant concluded that the informant was credible or the information reliable; and (2) the magistrate be given some of the underlying circumstances from which the informant reached the conclusion conveyed in the tip.

After much confusion in attempting to determine the scope of this requirement, the Supreme Court in 1983 clarified its decision in *Illinois v. Gates*.[15] In this case, a police officer received an anonymous letter indicating that an individual and his wife were engaged in selling drugs, that the wife would be driving a car loaded with drugs on a certain day, and that the suspect had more than $100,000 worth of drugs in his basement. Acting on this information, a police officer, with assistance from the Drug Enforcement Administration, verified that the husband, Gates, took a flight as stated in the anonymous letter, met a woman in an automobile bearing Illinois license plates issued to the husband, and the two of them drove north to the area where the narcotics were alleged to have been stored. Based on this information, a search warrant was issued for the residence and for the automobile.

The question before the Supreme Court was whether the two-pronged test established by *Aguilar* and *Spinelli* had to be met—which it could not because the credibility of the informant could not be verified because it was an anonymous letter. The U.S. Supreme Court decided that despite the fact that the judge was not given the underlying circumstances from which the affiant concluded that the informant was credible and his information reliable, the issuing judge did have a substantial basis for concluding that probable cause to search the subject's car and home existed. The Court indicated that the informant's reliability and basis of knowledge are relevant in determining probable cause, but that the Court should consider the "totality of circumstances."

In hundreds of cases, the courts have been asked to determine whether an informant's allegations are sufficient to support a finding of probable cause for the issuance of a search warrant. In many of these cases, the outcome is determined by the validity of the search warrant. The courts have been consistent in holding that an affidavit to support the issuance of a search warrant must include more than bare conclusions of the confidential informant. It must demonstrate corroboration of the information from the confidential informant and contain verifiable facts.[16]

---

[15]   462 U.S. 213 (1983). See also *Stubblefield v. State*, 645 So. 2d 320 (Ala. 1994), which held that probable cause to support a search warrant must be determined by examining the totality of circumstances.

[16]   *Lee v. State*, 2 P.3d 517 (Wyo. 2000).

Corroboration through other sources is often sufficient to provide a substantial basis for believing the informant's statement in an affidavit in support of a search warrant.[17]

§ 6.5   The Proper Official Must Issue the Warrant

In most instances, state statute designates the officials who may issue a search warrant. This is a function of the judicial officer, and if issued by a nonjudicial officer, it is not valid even though authorized by statute. The Supreme Court in 1971 made it clear that neither prosecutors nor police officers can be asked to maintain the requisite neutrality when deciding whether a search warrant should be issued.[18]

State courts have recited this rule in state decisions. For example, an Oklahoma court held that the purpose of the warrant is to allow a neutral judicial officer to assess whether the police have probable cause to make an arrest or conduct a search.[19] A New Jersey court opined that searches and seizures may be lawfully undertaken in many circumstances, and one such circumstance is when the search warrant is obtained from a neutral judicial officer.[20]

One other caution: the warrant must be signed by the magistrate who issues it, but it must be signed *after* it has been written and *before* it is executed. The magistrate cannot legalize the search by signing the warrant after it has been executed. Likewise, the magistrate cannot authorize the warrant before it is written and then simply "rubber stamp" it when presented by the police.

§ 6.6   The Warrant Must Be Supported by Oath or Affirmation

The Constitution requires that a warrant be supported by an oath or affirmation. Although the responsibility for requiring the oath is that of the issuing official, it is often necessary that the official be reminded of this requirement. If the oath or affirmation is not administered as required by the Constitution, the evidence obtained under the warrant will be inadmissible. Not only the police officer but the prosecutor should make certain this provision is carried out.

---

[17] *State v. Mitchell*, 20 S.W.3d 546 (Mo. 2000). Some states, however, have maintained the two-pronged *Spinelli-Aguilar* test. See, for example, *State v. Smith*, 756 P.2d 722 (Wash. 1988).

[18] *Coolidge v. New Hampshire*, 403 U.S. 443 (1971).

[19] *Mollett v. State*, 939 P.2d 1 (Okla. 1997).

[20] *State v. Ravotto*, 755 A.2d 602 (N.J. 2000).

There is a presumption that the warrant is supported by oath or affirmation; however, this is a rebuttable presumption, and the defense may introduce evidence, including statements from the officer, indicating that no oath was in fact administered.[21] Also, although there is a presumption that a warrant is valid, the defense may introduce evidence to establish by a preponderance of the evidence that the person who made the affidavit gave false statements, knowingly or with a reckless disregard for the truth.[22] If the defense can show that the affiant, such as a police officer, made false statements or recklessly disregarded the truth, the search warrant will be declared invalid and all evidence obtained under it will be inadmissible.

§ 6.7   The Place to Be Searched and the Things to Be Seized Must Be Particularly Described

Another constitutional provision is that the place to be searched, as well as the things to be seized, must be particularly described in the warrant. The Constitution does not define the word "particular," but many cases have been decided on this issue.[23]

A. *The Place to be Searched*

It is not necessary to have a legal description, such as would appear on a deed. The Constitution only requires that the premises be defined with practical accuracy. Two phrases have been used in defining what is meant by "particularly described." One is that the description of the place to be searched must be sufficiently definite so as to clearly distinguish the premises from all others. The second guideline is that the description must be such that the officer executing the warrant can, with reasonable effort and certainty, identify the exact place to the exclusion of all others.[24]

In defining the place to be searched, it is necessary to keep in mind that it must be a "particular" place. If the description can fit many places, it is not particular and, therefore, the search will be illegal. On the other hand, it is not necessary to have the house number or other formal description if the description is such that it leaves no doubt as to the place to be searched.

---

21   *Lee v. State*, 2 P.3d 517 (Wyo. 2000).

22   *Franks v. Delaware*, 438 U.S. 154 (1978).

23   *United States v. Layne*, 43 F.3d 127 (1995).

24   *Commonwealth v. Rodriguez*, 732 N.E.2d 906 (Mass. 2000).

In a Supreme Court decision in 1987, some allowance was made for mistakes by the police in describing the place to be searched. In *Maryland v. Garrison*,[25] police officers, in seeking a warrant to search an apartment for controlled substances and related paraphernalia, believed that there was only one apartment on the third floor of the premises. It was later determined that the third floor was divided into two apartments. Before they became aware that they were in the wrong apartment, the officers discovered contraband that provided evidence for conviction under Maryland's Controlled Substance Act. The Supreme Court, agreeing that the officers made a reasonable effort to ascertain the identity of the place intended to be searched, reasoned that the discovery of the later facts demonstrating that the warrant was unnecessarily broad does not retroactively invalidate the warrant. Reiterating that the warrant clause of the Fourth Amendment prohibits the issuance of a warrant except when it "particularly describes the place to be searched and things to be seized," the Court nevertheless acknowledged that it must judge the constitutionality of officers' conduct in light of the information available to them at the time they acted.

B. The Things to be Seized

Not only must the place to be searched be particularly described, but the things to be seized must also be described with reasonable accuracy and certainty. That purpose was stated in one case as follows:

> The purpose of the particularity requirement of the Fourth Amendment is to avoid general and exploratory searches by requiring a particular description of items to be seized.[26]

For the search warrant to be sufficiently particular, the searcher must be able to reasonably ascertain and identify the things authorized to be seized.[27]

If the description of the things to be seized is too broad or too sweeping, it is not "particular" within the meaning of the Fourth Amendment. For example, a description that described property sought as "books, records, pamphlets, cards, receipts, lists, memoranda, pictures, and recordings and other written instruments concerning the Communist Party" was too broad.[28] On the other hand, where the description is specific as to certain items, adding the phrase, "together with other fruits, instrumentalities, and evidence of crime" does not invalidate the warrant if this follows a detailed specific list of items.[29]

---

[25] *Maryland v. Garrison*, 480 U.S. 79 (1987).

[26] *People v. Bradford*, 65 Cal. Rptr. 2d 145, 939 P.2d 259 (1997).

[27] *United States v. Abbell*, 963 F. Supp. 1178 (S.D. Fla. 1997).

[28] *Stanford v. Texas*, 379 U.S. 476 (1985).

[29] *Andresen v. Maryland*, 427 U.S. 463 (1976).

The search warrant authorizes only the seizure of objects described in the warrant. In executing the warrant, however, the officer is often in a position to seize articles not described in the warrant under one of the exceptions to the warrant requirement. For example, one court held that items discovered during the execution of a search pursuant to a valid warrant may be seized if: (1) they are observed in plain view while the officer is in a place where he or she has a right to be; (2) the discovery is inadvertent; and (3) it is apparent to the officer that he or she is viewing evidence.[30]

C A Warrant May Be Issued Only for Authorized Objects

Generally, the object of a search warrant is clear: it is something related to a crime such as drugs, a body, or a weapon used in a crime. These are simple matters for a search warrant. But not all things to be seized are that clear. An early case decided by the U.S. Supreme Court adopted what became known as the "mere evidence" rule.[31] In this case, the Court distinguished among stolen or embezzled evidence, property used to commit a crime, or contraband goods and "mere evidence." "Mere evidence" is something that is related to the case but is not, by itself the object of a crime, such as bank statements for a drug dealer that might show relevance in court but has no direct connection to the illegal enterprise. The Court held that searches for and seizure of items to be used as "mere evidence" of a crime could not be authorized unless the government could assert a right to the property.

The "mere evidence" rule was overruled in *Warden v. Hayden*,[32] which held that a seizure was justified in spite of the fact that the evidence constituted "mere evidence" of a violation. In this case, the court rejected the distinction between the seizure of items of evidentiary value only and the seizure of an instrumentality, fruits of a crime, or contraband.

Following this decision, Congress amended the federal code by providing that a warrant may be issued to search for and seize any property that constitutes evidence of a criminal offense in violation of the laws of the United States.[33] Many state legislatures, recognizing the arbitrary distinction of types of evidence that could be seized, broadened the authority by statute. For example, an Illinois statute provides that a search warrant may be issued for seizure of "any instruments, articles, or things

---

[30] *State v. Mitchell*, 20 S.W.3d 546 (Mo. 2000). See Chapter 6 for a discussion of recognized exceptions that specifically authorize a search without a warrant.

[31] *Gouled v. United States*, 255 U.S. 298 (1921).

[32] *Warden v. Hayden*, 387 U.S. 294 (1967).

[33] 18 U.S.C. § 3103 (1970).

which have been used in the commission of, or which may constitute evidence of, the offense in connection with which the warrant is issued."[34]

Although the courts have indicated that there is nothing in the Constitution limiting the type of evidence that can be seized under a warrant, some states still have provisions limiting evidence that can be seized. It is therefore necessary to check state statutes to determine whether there is limiting language concerning the issuance of a search warrant.

§ 6.8 Execution of the Search Warrant

Once the warrant has been properly issued by the judicial official, a law enforcement officer is charged with executing the warrant and, in the absence of statutory authority, cannot refuse to do so. In executing the warrant and in proceeding in the manner in which the warrant directs, the officer is carrying out the orders of the court. As a general rule, if the warrant is valid on its face, has been issued by the proper official, and is executed properly, the officer is protected from civil liability. However, if the officer's activity in obtaining the warrant indicates gross negligence or neglect of duty in presenting supporting affidavits to justify the issuance of the warrant, he or she is not entitled to rely on a judicial officer's judgment in issuing the warrant.[35] The police cannot avoid civil liability for causing an unconstitutional arrest or search by presenting the judicial officer with a complaint in a supporting affidavit, which, because of his or her gross incompetence, fails to establish probable cause. This makes it necessary for the officer to be trained in the legal aspects of search and seizure and particularly the requirements necessary to obtain and execute a valid search warrant.

A police officer may not automatically assume that a search warrant is valid because a reviewing magistrate has executed it. The officer must read the affidavit and warrant carefully and must be objectively persuaded that the warrant is sufficient.[36] In executing the warrant, an officer must follow a number of guidelines. These are discussed in the remainder of this section.

A. The Warrant Must Be Executed by an Officer or Officers So Commanded

The warrant may be directed to an officer or several officers, or a class of officers. Under most statutes today, the warrant is issued to a class of officers; that is,

---

[34] ILL. REV. STAT. CH. 38, § 108-3 (1988).
[35] *Malley v. Briggs*, 475 U.S. 335 (1986).
[36] *People v. Randolph*, 4 P.3d 477 (Colo. 2000).

"any officer in the Commonwealth of Kentucky." If the warrant is issued to a class of officers, any officer within that class may legally execute it. If it is to a named officer, only that officer or those with him or her may execute the warrant.[37]

B. The Warrant Must Be Executed within Certain Time Limitations

Some states by statute provide the period within which the warrant must be executed. For example, the Illinois code provides that the warrant shall be executed within 96 hours of the time of issuance. If there is no provision in the statute concerning the execution of the warrant, it must be executed within a "reasonable" time. The warrant must be executed while there is still probable cause to believe the items sought are on the described premises. If there is evidence that the described property has been removed from the premises, then the search may not be used as a weapon or form of coercion upon the person or premises against whom it is directed. In some states, the warrant must be executed in the daytime unless there is a provision authorizing execution after dusk. On the other hand, a federal court has held that a search initiated in the daytime under a daytime search warrant may continue into the night for so long as is reasonably necessary for completion.[38]

In 2006, the U.S. Supreme Court heard a case in which a search warrant was issued for evidence that was not yet at the place to be searched.[39] This revolves around a police practice called "anticipatory warrant." An anticipatory warrant is "a warrant based upon an affidavit showing probable cause that at some future time (but not presently) certain evidence of a crime will be located at a specified place." In this case, Grubbs purchased child pornography from a web site controlled by Postal Inspectors. After shipping the child pornography in a controlled delivery, the postal inspectors applied for a warrant to search Grubbs' house once the item was delivered. However, the items were not at Grubbs' house when the warrant was applied for or issued. Once the warrant was approved, agents waited until the package was delivered, then executed the search warrant. At trial, Grubbs sought to suppress the evidence, reasoning there was no probable cause of criminality when the warrant was applied for. The Supreme Court disagreed, stating, "when an anticipatory warrant is issued, the fact that the contraband is not presently at the place described is immaterial, so long as there is probable cause to believe it will be there when the warrant is executed."

---

[37]   *United States v. Abbell*, 963 F. Supp. 1178 (S.D. Fla. 1997).

[38]   *United States v. Joseph*, 278 F.2d 504 (3d Cir. 1960).

[39]   *United States v. Grubbs*, 547 U.S. 90 (2006).

C. Only Necessary Force May Be Used in Executing the Warrant

By common law and under the statutes in all states, a law enforcement officer is justified in using necessary force to execute the warrant.[40] Deadly force or force that may cause serious bodily injury should not be used and is generally not authorized unless the officer is protecting him- or herself.

The United States Code provides that, in executing a warrant, an officer has the authority to break both outer and inner doors if, after giving notice of his or her authority and purpose and demanding entrance, he or she is refused admittance.[41] A denial of admittance does not have to be specific, but may be inferred from the surrounding circumstances; for example, when a person known to be inside refuses to open the door.

The degree of force justified in entering a dwelling to execute a search warrant depends upon the situation. For example, in view of the fact that the defendant's apartment was protected by a heavy wood and metal door that opened out, officers were justified in using force to pry the door open to prevent disposal of narcotics.[42] In this case, the court found that exigent circumstances existed and that the officers did not violate state or federal knock-and-announce statutes (see below).

If no one is in charge of the premises, the officer nevertheless may use reasonable force to carry out the instructions of the court in searching the premises described. If there is no need for prompt action, it is advisable to seek entrance from a neighbor or delay until the legal occupant of the premises can admit the officers. If the force used is unreasonable, it will not pass constitutional muster. For example, using a battering ram in broad daylight to execute a search warrant, when the officer admitted that he and other officers had no specific information about anyone in the residence being armed, no indication that anyone in the residence could have destroyed evidence, and no indication that anyone was in a position to warn the occupants of the officers' approach, was unreasonable and in violation of the Constitution.[43]

---

[40] *Gates v. Langford*, 729 P.2d 822 (Cal.). See also *Jacobs v. City of Chicago*, 215 F.3d 758 (7th Cir. 2000), which held that a warrant to search for contraband founded on probable cause implicitly carries with it the limited authority to detain the occupants of the premises while a proper search is conducted; and *Illinois v. McArthur*, 531 U.S. 326 (2001), which held that where there is a need to preserve evidence until the police can obtain a warrant, they may temporarily prevent a person from entering his or her house.

[41] 18 U.S.C. § 3109 (1995).

[42] *United States v. Johnson*, 643 F. Supp. 1465 (D. Or.).

[43] *State v. Thompson*, 693 So. 2d 282 (La. 1997).

D. *Prior Notice and Demand Should Usually Precede Forcible Entry*

One of the most complex requirements regarding execution is that notice be given prior to forcible entry. The purpose of the knock-and-announce rule is to protect the privacy of the individual, to avoid needless destruction of property, and to shield the police from attack by surprised residents. On the other hand, officers recognize what the courts call the "anarchism of the notice rule" in an era when the suspect often has the opportunity to injure the officer or to dispose of evidence.[44]

Notwithstanding the statutes requiring notice of intention to enter the premises, the courts have recognized an exception for exigent circumstances, such as immediate physical danger, flight, or destruction of evidence.[45] In 1974, the Court of Appeals for the Second Circuit listed three exceptions to the requirement that the officer must knock, announce his or her authority and purpose, and be refused admittance before he or she can enter.[46] These are: (1) when the persons within already know of the officer's authority and purpose; (2) when the officers are justified in the belief that the persons within are in imminent danger of bodily harm; or (3) when those within, made aware of the presence of someone outside, are then engaged in activity that justifies the officer in the belief that an escape or the destruction of evidence is taking place.

Questions concerning the knock-and-announce principle reached the U.S. Supreme Court in 1995.[47] In this case, Wilson claimed that the police had violated the common law principle requiring them to announce their presence and authority before entering her house and that the search of the house was invalid. The Supreme Court unanimously held that the common law knock-and-announce principle forms a part of the Fourth Amendment reasonableness inquiry. The Court noted that "this Court has little doubt that the Amendment's framers thought that whether the officers announced their presence and authority before entering a dwelling was among the factors to be considered in assessing a search's reasonableness." The Court added, however, that there are exceptions to the rule. The Court explained that countervailing law enforcement interests, including the threat of physical harm to the police, the fact that an officer is pursuing a recently escaped arrestee, or the existence of a reason to believe that evidence would likely be destroyed if advance notice were given, may establish the reasonableness of an unannounced entry. The Court then said that, for now, it would leave to the lower courts the task of determining such relevant factors.

---

[44] *Jackson v. United States*, 354 F.2d 980 (3d Cir. 1965).
[45] *United States v. Miller*, 357 U.S. 301 (1958).
[46] *United States v. Artieri*, 491 F.2d 440 (2d Cir. 1974).
[47] *Wilson v. Arkansas*, 514 U.S. 927 (1995).

Some states have enacted statutes that authorize the issuing officials to provide for an entry by officers without the normally required warnings. In view of the holdings by the Supreme Court in *Wilson* that the common law knock-and-announce principle forms a part of the Fourth Amendment reasonableness inquiry, these state statutes must be carefully reviewed.

The *Wilson* decision was examined and clarified by the U.S. Supreme Court in *Richards v. Wisconsin*.[48] In this case, an officer armed with a search warrant but without authorization for a "no-knock" entry kicked down a door and found cash and cocaine in the bathroom. The government in this case attempted to get the courts to impose a blanket rule that all drug warrants should be "no-knock" because of the likelihood of danger to officers or destruction of evidence. The U.S. Supreme Court held that the Fourth Amendment does not permit a blanket exception to the knock-and-announce requirement for felony drug investigations. The Court explained that if a *per se* exception were allowed for each criminal activity category that included a considerable risk of danger to officers or destruction of evidence, the knock-and-announce requirement would be meaningless.

An Idaho state court pointed out that the knock-and-announce statute in that state is designed to prevent surprise entries by police officers. In interpreting that statute, the court cautioned that the knock-and-announce statute prohibits a peace officer from making a forcible entry by breaking through a door or window of a house unless the officer has first demanded admittance and explained the reason for the entry.[49] Further, a federal court determined that police officers may effect no-knock entries based on exigent circumstances only as they exist at the time of the entry, as opposed to the time that the search warrant was issued.[50]

In *United States v. Ramirez*,[51] the Court addressed the amount of force that may be used during a seizure and whether an entry that destroys property requires a different rationale for knock-and-announce. In this case, officers obtained a no-knock warrant. During execution of the warrant, officers broke a window and pointed a weapon through it to prevent anyone from obtaining weapons in a garage (where weapons were thought to be stored). Over Ramirez's objection, the Court ruled that there is no higher standard for no-knock searches when officers destroy property in the process of executing the warrant.

In another case, a federal court held that, in determining whether the amount of force used during a seizure is excessive in violation of the Fourth Amendment, the court's inquiry is whether the force used to seize the suspect was excessive in relation

---

48 *Richards v. Wisconsin*, 520 U.S. 385 (1997).
49 *State v. Gregory*, 936 P.2d 1340 (Idaho 1997).
50 *United States v. Beckford*, 962 F. Supp. 767 (E.D. Va. 1997).
51 *United States v. Ramirez*, 523 U.S. 65 (1998).

to the danger posed to the community or the arresting officers.[52] The court held that police officers' alleged conduct of breaking down a door to the resident's apartment, entering the apartment without warning, and pointing a gun at the resident's head for more than 10 minutes constituted "excessive force" in violation of the Fourth Amendment. In this case, the officers were attempting to execute a search warrant that incorrectly described the building as a single-family residence, they had no probable cause to believe the resident was involved in criminal activity, and the resident did not engage in any threatening conduct.

States may add provisions that are more restrictive than federal law. For example, Hawaii has a statute that authorizes police officers to forcibly enter the home while executing a search warrant, but provides that three steps are required before the officer may physically break into the place to be searched: the officer must state his or her office, must state his or her business, and must demand entrance.[53]

In 2003, the Supreme Court held in *United States v. Banks* that police need wait only a "reasonable" period before breaking down the door when they give notice and there is no response. In this case, the Court held that a 20-second wait was sufficient.[54]

An issue left open in knock-and-announce cases is the remedy for improperly knocking and announcing. One of these issues was answered in *Hudson v. Michigan*.[55] In this case, Michigan police executed a search warrant where officers entered Hudson's home after a three- to five-second delay after knocking. There they found drugs and a weapon in the chair where Hudson was sitting. At trial, Michigan authorities admitted that they violated the knock-and-announce rule, so the period of delay was not at issue in this case. The U.S. Supreme Court decided in this case the issue of whether the exclusionary rule was appropriate for violation of knock-and-announce requirements. The Court recognized the exceptions they had authorized for knock-and-announce, including: (1) a threat of physical violence against officers; (2) destruction of evidence; and (3) when knocking and announcing would be futile. They also stated that police are only required to have reasonable suspicion one of these exists to forgo the requirement. The Court also seemed to rely on the fact that knock-and-announce cases always included a warrant that had been signed by a magistrate, and were therefore different from warrantless entries. Based on this, the Court held that violation of the knock-and-announce rule does not require suppression of evidence found in a search. As a result, it would seem there is no longer value in knocking and announcing prior to executing a search warrant.

---

[52] *Jacobs v. City of Chicago*, 215 F.3d 758 (7th Cir. 2000).
[53] *State v. Garcia*, 887 P.2d 671 (Haw. 1995).
[54] *United States v. Banks*, 540 U.S. 31 (2003).
[55] *Hudson v. Michigan*, 547 U.S. 1096 (2006).

The U.S. Supreme Court decided an interesting aspect of the knock-and-announce rule in *Brigham City, Utah v. Stuart et al.*[56] In this case, officers responded to a loud party call. Once there, they heard shouting inside and saw through a screen door and window an altercation taking place inside. The officers knocked on the screen door and announced themselves, which went unnoticed. The officers then went into the house and announced themselves again, finally quelling the fight. The occupants were arrested for liquor violations and contributing to the delinquency of a minor. The defendant sought to suppress the arrest based on violations of the requirement to knock and announce and because, they argued, the officers entered to make an arrest, not to prevent further violence. The court held:

> Under these circumstances, there was no violation of the Fourth Amendment's knock-and-announce rule. Furthermore, once the announcement was made, the officers were free to enter; it would serve no purpose to require them to stand dumbly at the door awaiting a response while those within brawled on, oblivious to their presence.

Thus, the Court ruled that "police may enter a home without a warrant when they have an objectively reasonable basis for believing that an occupant is seriously injured or imminently threatened with such injury."

E. Only the Property Described May Be Seized under the Warrant

It is fundamental that only the property particularly described in the warrant may be seized under the warrant. If other property is seized, it must be seized under separate legal authority such as the plain view doctrine. This will be discussed in the next chapter.

In addition to the requirements discussed previously, other requirements may be included in the state statute or code. Therefore, officers should be acquainted with all the statutory provisions in their state concerning the execution of warrants.

§ 6.9   Search of a Person on the Premises

If the officer is aware that a person will be on the premises and the described property is such that it can be secreted on that person, the warrant should include a description of the person to be searched, as well as the place to be searched. In some

---

[56] *Brigham City, Utah v. Stuart et al.*, 547 U.S. 8 (2006).

instances, however, the officer does not know who will be on the premises and cannot describe them in the warrant. Failing to search the person on the premises could place the officer's personal safety in jeopardy or result in the concealment of the items sought. To give some protection to officers in these situations, the Supreme Court has decided cases providing that the person executing the warrant may reasonably detain and search a person on the premises when executing a warrant.

In *Michigan v. Summers*, officers went to a home to conduct a search warrant for drugs when they encountered Summers on the front steps of the house.[57] Officers requested his assistance in gaining entry to the house. Summers replied that he did not live there but that he would get someone from inside. When the person answered the door and refused entry to the officers, the officers forced their way into the house and detained Summers and eight others. The Supreme Court ruled that detention is allowed without probable cause to arrest for a crime while a search is conducted, even when there is no particular suspicion that an individual is involved in criminal activity or poses a specific danger to the officers. This was based on three rationales. The first is officer safety, which may include detaining current occupants so the officers can search without fear that the occupants will become disruptive, dangerous, or otherwise frustrate the search. This would also apply to occupants of the residence who return to the premises after the search begins. The second law enforcement interest is the facilitation of the completion of the search. Unrestrained occupants could hide or destroy evidence, seek to distract the officers, or simply get in the way. Alternatively, detained occupants could assist officers in opening locked doors or containers to avoid using force. The final interest is the interest in preventing flight. The Court reasoned that, if officers are concerned about the flight of a person in the event incriminating evidence is found, they might rush the search, causing unnecessary damage or compromising its careful execution. Taken in the total, the Supreme Court reasoned that if these rationales apply to persons inside the premises during a search, they would also apply to persons in the immediate vicinity of the premises. The Supreme Court expanded the ruling in *Summers* to allow officers to handcuff the occupants they detain for the duration of the search.[58]

The question of what the Court meant by immediate vicinity of the premises was answered in *Bailey v. United States*.[59] In this case, based on information from an informant that the owner of the house was in possession of a handgun, police obtained a search warrant. While undercover officers were watching the house prior to the execution of the search, they saw two men, one of whom fit the description of the owner provided by the informant, leave the apartment and get in a car. Officers

---

[57] *Michigan v. Summers,* 452 U.S. 692 (1981).
[58] *Muehler v. Mena,* 544 U.S. 93 (2004).
[59] *Bailey v. United States,* 568 U.S. ___, No. 11-770 (2013).

followed the two and stopped them while other officers began the search. During a pat-down search of Bailey, officers found a key that would ultimately be determined to fit a lock at the apartment. Both men were handcuffed and driven in a patrol car to the apartment, where the search team had found a gun and illicit drugs in plain view inside the apartment. In deciding this case, the Court ruled: "The rule in *Summers* is limited to the immediate vicinity of the premises to be searched and does not apply here, where Bailey was detained at a point beyond any reasonable understanding of the immediate vicinity of the premises in question." The significance for law enforcement, then, is that persons in the premises and in the immediate vicinity of the premises (where they may return) may be detained. But those who are sufficiently far away as to not represent a threat to the officers or search cannot be detained.

In discussing these cases, it is important to understand the ruling of the courts related to the *seizure* of persons related to execution of a search warrant (in the cases above) and the *search* of persons related to a search warrant. The authority to search persons on the premises who are not described in the warrant was addressed in *Ybarra v. Illinois*.[60] In this case, police officers obtained a search warrant authorizing the search of a tavern and the person of the bartender for "evidence of the offense of possession of a controlled substance." Upon entering the tavern to execute the warrant, the officers announced their purpose to conduct a search of the customers present in the tavern. As a part of executing the warrant, officers searched all of the customers who happened to be present. In conducting a search of one of the patrons (Ybarra), an officer felt what he described as a cigarette pack with an object in it. Inside the packet he found six tinfoil packets containing a brown powdery substance that was later determined to be heroin.

The Supreme Court determined that the search of Ybarra was unconstitutional and, therefore, the seizure of narcotics should have been excluded. The reasoning of the majority was:

> Where the standard is probable cause, a search or seizure of a person must be supported by probable cause particularized with respect to that person. This requirement cannot be undercut or avoided by simply pointing to the fact that coincidentally there exists probable cause to search or seize another or to search the premises where the person may happen to be. The Fourth and Fourteenth Amendments protect the legitimate expectation of privacy.

In essence, the Court ruled that the search of Ybarra was invalid because the police had no reason to believe he had any special connections with the premises and there was no basis to believe he was armed.

---

[60] *Ybarra v. Illinois*, 444 U.S. 85 (1979).

The decision in *Ybarra* means that a warrant describing a premises only does not justify the search of a person on the premises *under the warrant*. However, some courts have ruled that police have the authority pursuant to the search warrant authorizing the search of the premises and "any persons on the premises at the time of the service" to search individuals who are on the premises at the time the search is conducted.[61] An Alaska court reasoned that a search warrant authorizing the police to search any persons who were present on the premises at the time the warrant was served was valid and that the defendants were on the premises named in the warrant when they walked into the residence's enclosed vestibule leading into the residence's interior front door.[62] Even if the search of a person is not authorized, the frisk or search of persons on the premises may be justified even if they are not named in the warrant if there are grounds to believe criminal activities are afoot, or if, during the execution of the warrant, officers determine there is probable cause to make an arrest of the person(s).

§ 6.10 Return of the Warrant

The final step for the officer in carrying out the orders of the court is to return the warrant, with the results of its execution, to the court or to a designated agency. The return should list the items particularly described in the search warrant, and indicate when and where these items were seized. Generally, a copy of the inventory is forwarded to the warrant applicant and the person from whose premises the instruments, articles, or things were taken.

Some statutes contain provisions that indicate the amount of time the officer has before the warrant must be returned. In other states, the provisions state that the return shall be made without unnecessary delay. Although there is some indication that failure to strictly comply with the statute will not void the warrant, good procedure would indicate that the requirement be followed.

As stated above, a copy of the warrant and an inventory of items seized are often provided to the person whose property is taken. This may be provided by the court, or it may be a state law or departmental policy that the officer is to leave these documents at the location of the search. This is not a constitutional requirement, however. The Supreme Court ruled in *City of West Covina v. Perkins*[63] that the due process clause of the Constitution does not require officers to leave detailed notice of the

---

[61] *United States v. Graham*, 563 F. Supp. 149 (W.D.N.Y. 1983).

[62] *Davis v. State*, 938 P.2d 1076 (Alaska 1997).

[63] *City of West Covina v. Perkins*, 525 U.S. 234 (1999).

procedures for the return of the property and the information needed to use those procedures.

§ 6.11 Summary

The Fourth Amendment to the U.S. Constitution was added in 1791 to "protect persons, houses, papers, and effects against unreasonable searches and seizures." This amendment also provides that "no warrant shall issue but upon probable cause, supported by oath or affirmation, and particularly describing the place to be searched, and the persons or things to be seized."

The preferred means of making a search is with a search warrant. For a search warrant to be valid, the following requirements must be met: (1) the warrant must be issued on probable cause; (2) a proper official must issue the warrant; (3) the warrant must be supported by oath or affirmation; and (4) the place to be searched and the things to be seized must be particularly described. Some states add other requirements.

In establishing probable cause, an informant's tip may be used without disclosing the name of the informant. However, sufficient information must be given to the issuing official so that, considering the totality of circumstances, the official can make a decision from the circumstances that contraband or evidence of the crime will be in a particular place.

If the search is to be legal and the evidence admissible, the officer must follow certain rules when executing a warrant. These include: (1) the warrant must be executed by the officer or officers so commanded or be within the class designated; (2) the warrant must be executed within certain time limitations; (3) only necessary force may be used when executing the warrant; (4) usually, prior notice and demand of entry should precede entry; and (5) only the property described in the warrant may be seized under the warrant.

In executing the warrant, only the premises and persons described in the warrant may be searched under the authority of the warrant. However, a search of persons on the premises may be justified under exceptions that are described in the following chapter.

Chapter 7
Search and Seizure without a Warrant

It is unreasonable searches that are prohibited by the Fourth Amendment. It was recognized by the framers of the Constitution that there were reasonable searches for which no warrant was required. . . . The right to search a person incident to the arrest always has been recognized in this country and in England.

United States v. Rabinowitz, 339 U.S. 56 (1950)

§ 7.1   General Considerations

There are no provisions in the Fourth Amendment specifically authorizing a search without a warrant. However, courts have long recognized exceptions and have, out of necessity, approved searches without a warrant. If a warrantless search does not fall within one of the specific exceptions, the search probably will be considered illegal and evidence obtained thereby will be inadmissible for most evidentiary purposes.

Although states may recognize and adopt the exceptions approved by the U.S. Supreme Court, the states generally may not, by court action or legislation, add exceptions that have not been recognized by the Supreme Court. On the other hand, state courts or legislatures may limit the number of exceptions. For example, all state courts have recognized the exception for the search of a person incident to a lawful arrest. Some state courts, however, limit the search to a search for weapons or fruits of the crime for which the arrest was made, even though this limitation has not been required by the U.S. Supreme Court.[1]

§ 7.2   Search Incident to a Lawful Arrest

A. Rationale for Exception

A search incident to a lawful arrest was one of the earliest recognized exceptions to the rule that a search must be made with a search warrant. In practice, more searches are carried out under this exception than under a warrant. It is obvious that the authority to search incident to a lawful arrest is necessary because it is impractical to obtain warrants in all instances. A search incident to a lawful arrest is permitted for two reasons: (1) to protect the arresting officer; and (2) to avoid destruction of evidence by the arrested person. When conducting a search incident to an arrest, officers may search the person and/or may search the area within the immediate control of the person. The rationales for the search and who/what may be searched are explained below.

The authority to search a person incident to an arrest was established in *U.S. v Robinson*.[2] Prior to *Robinson*, officers were allowed to frisk a person if he or she

---

[1]   *State v. Kaluna*, 520 P.2d 51 (Haw. 1974). See also *People v. Bresendine*, 119 Cal. Rptr. 315, 531 P.2d 1099 (1975), in which the court noted that California citizens are entitled to greater protection under the California Constitution against unreasonable searches and seizures than that required by the U.S. Constitution. In *People v. Hamilton*, 710 P.2d 937 (1985), the California court discussed the fact that the state may add limitations to search and seizure that exceed the U.S. Supreme Court's limitations.

[2]   *U.S. v. Robinson*, 414 U.S. 218 (1973).

suspected the suspect was armed or there was a threat to the officer's safety. *Robinson* allowed a full body search of a person incident to an arrest, allowing the arresting officer to search for and seize any evidence on the arrested person to prevent its concealment or destruction. Searches incident to an arrest often occur in vehicle stops. This issue is introduced in the sections below and addressed in more detail in Chapter 7.

B. Requirements

Before a search incident to a lawful arrest can be made, certain requirements must be met. These requirements include making a lawful arrest and conducting the search at the time of the arrest. There is also a limit on what can be seized incident to an arrest. These are discussed in this section.

1   The Arrest Must Be Lawful

At one time, there was the requirement that the arrest itself be lawful. It makes sense that if the arrest is not lawful, all that follows, including the search, is unlawful, and evidence obtained thereby is inadmissible except in the rare cases discussed in previous chapters.[3] That is still the prevailing rule; however, it has been somewhat diminished.

As stated in Chapter 2, in *Herring v. United States*,[4] officers made an arrest based on a warrant that was later determined to have been withdrawn. Incident to the arrest, Herring and his automobile were searched and drugs were discovered. As such, the arrest of Herring was unlawful. The Supreme Court ruled, however, that the officers were relying in good faith on the warrant; therefore, the search incident to the arrest was constitutional even though the arrest was not.

Recently, the issue of lawful arrest has become more important and more pervasive, especially as it relates to detention of illegal (or potentially illegal) aliens. As would be expected, the greater part of this issue revolves around the legality of arrest. This is covered in more detail in Chapter 5. Another issue for the Fourth Amendment, however, is whether fingerprints can be taken if it is determined that the arrest was unlawful.

In *Davis v. Mississippi*,[5] the Supreme Court ruled that fingerprints taken from a person who was illegally arrested for the sole purpose of collecting fingerprints to compare to crime scene prints were inadmissible. The Court conceded, however, that

---

[3]   See *State v. Pallone, supra,* in which the court explained the "bright-line rule" that for the search incident to a lawful arrest exception to the warrant requirement to apply, there must be an arrest.

[4]   *Herring v. United States,* 555 U.S. 135 (2009).

[5]   *Davis v. Mississippi,* 394 U.S. 721 (1969).

there could be situations in which fingerprints could be admitted even if the arrest was illegal. This was somewhat contrary to the Court's holding in *Frisbie v. Collins*,[6] in which it stated that an illegal arrest did not prevent a person from being tried in court. The distinction here was based on whether the issue was jurisdictional (i.e., related to whether a court had jurisdiction to try a person) or evidentiary (whether actions/evidence violated the Fourth Amendment).

This became an immigration issue when an illegal alien was detained and where the arrest was subsequently suppressed.[7] In *United States v. Guevara-Martinez*,[8] Guevara-Martinez was arrested during a vehicle stop where methamphetamine was discovered. Because there was a question regarding Guevara-Martinez's identity and whether he was in the United States legally, INS agents interviewed him. Officers fingerprinted Guevara-Martinez. Based on those fingerprints, his identity as a person of interest for INS was established and deportation proceedings began. The stop was subsequently held to be illegal and Guevara-Martinez sought to suppress the fingerprints as fruits of the illegal arrest. The court ruled to suppress the fingerprints based on three issues that are important for law enforcement officers. First, the fingerprints were not taken as a standard booking procedure—which quite probably would have resolved this issue entirely.[9] Second, Guevara-Martinez did not consent to the taking of fingerprints, which the courts have ruled is often a way to purge the taint of activities (such as an arrest) later determined to be inadmissible. Finally, the fingerprints were taken during the unlawful detention and not as part of a subsequent investigation (similar to *Davis*).

These cases illustrate the issue of requiring the arrest to be lawful for the search to be admissible. Even if the arrest is later declared to be unlawful, evidence obtained from the arrest may be admitted at trial; but officers must follow procedures carefully so evidence is not tainted by the unlawful arrest.

2   Only Certain Articles May Be Seized

The U.S. Supreme Court, in a 1967 opinion, made it clear that there is no constitutional demand that the seizure be limited to certain articles.[10] In that case, the majority overruled previous decisions and held that there was no constitutional prohibition concerning the seizure of "mere evidence."

---

[6] *Frisbie v. Collins*, 342 U.S. 519 (1952).

[7] *United States v. Guevara-Martinez*, 262 F.2d 751 (2001).

[8] *Id.*

[9] See, for example, *Paulson v. State*, 257 So. 2d 303 (Fla. Dist. Ct. App. 1972) (holding that fingerprints routinely taken after illegal arrest could be used in a subsequent prosecution for another crime).

[10] *Warden v. Hayden*, 387 U.S. 294 (1967).

Although the U.S. Congress has modified the federal statute concerning the seizure of any evidence, some state legislatures have not done so. Therefore, state officers must consult state statutes and state court decisions to determine whether there are any restrictions relating to articles that can be seized incident to a lawful arrest.

3   The Search Must Be Made Contemporaneously with the Arrest

The rationale for authorizing a search incident to a lawful arrest is that it is necessary to protect the officer and avoid destruction of evidence. It follows, then, that the search should be made contemporaneously with the arrest. The importance of conducting a search at the time and place of arrest somewhat depends on whether it is a search of the arrested person or a search of the area surrounding the arrest. As discussed below, an arrested person can be searched later if justified at the time of the arrest. For the most part, if the arrestee is in custody, or is unable to destroy evidence or attack the arresting officer, the necessity justifying the incidental search no longer exists (although see *Arizona v. Gant* below for an exception to this rule).

The federal courts and some state courts, especially in recent years, have struggled with the term "contemporaneous." A strict interpretation would require that the search be made at the same time as the arrest. However, in recognizing the practicalities, courts have not required such strict compliance. For example, in *United States v. Edwards*,[11] the court held that a search of the suspect's clothing for paint chips was valid even though Edwards was in jail and not in possession of his clothes because the search would have been justified incident to the original arrest. The Supreme Court also held that a search incident to an arrest could occur as a normal part of the booking and/or jailing of a suspect.[12] In *State v. Williams*, the court held that "contemporaneous" is not the same as "simultaneous."[13] All that is required, according to the court, is that the search takes place during the "same time period" as the arrest. The time period is measured by the time reasonably necessary to perform a law enforcement officer's duties attendant upon arrest.

In determining what is contemporaneous, the courts consider the place of arrest, the time of arrest, the circumstances surrounding the arrest, and the degree of custodial control. At least in one state, however, the officer cannot make an arrest and transport the suspect to jail and then return to search the area as incident to a lawful arrest.[14]

---

[11]   *United States v. Edwards*, 415 U.S. 800 (1974).

[12]   *Illinois v. Lafayette*, 462 U.S. 640 (1982).

[13]   *State v. Williams*, 516 So. 2d 1081 (Fla. Dist. Ct. App. 1987). See also *United States v. McKibben*, 928 F. Supp. 1479 (D.S.D. 1996).

[14]   *Dixon v. State*, 327 A.2d 516 (Md. Ct. App. 1974).

In *Arizona v. Gant*,[15] many of these issues were examined by the U.S. Supreme Court. In this case, acting on an anonymous tip that a residence was being used to sell drugs, police officers went to the residence. Gant answered the door and stated that he expected the owner to return later. The officers asked for his name, then left. They conducted a records check of Gant, which revealed that Gant's driver's license was suspended and there was an outstanding warrant for his arrest for driving with a suspended license. Officers later returned to the house and arrested two people, handcuffed them, and secured them in separate patrol cars. When Gant arrived, officers recognized his car and confirmed Gant was the driver by shining a flashlight into the car. Gant parked at the end of the driveway, got out of his car, and shut the door. Gant was arrested about 10 feet from his car, handcuffed, and placed in the back of a third patrol car. Two officers then searched his car, finding a gun and a bag of cocaine in the pocket of a jacket on the backseat. The Supreme Court ruled that "police may search the passenger compartment of a vehicle incident to a recent occupant's arrest only if it is reasonable to believe that the arrestee might access the vehicle at the time of the search or that the vehicle contains evidence of the offense of arrest." In this case, Gant was handcuffed in the back of a patrol car, where he could not gain access to his vehicle. In addition, there was no way for police to find evidence in the search related to him driving under a suspended license.

Although the U.S. Supreme Court has ruled that the search of a person incident to an arrest may occur *before* the suspect is advised that he or she is under arrest if the arrest occurs contemporaneously with the search, it is preferable to advise the person apprehended that he or she is being arrested as soon as practicable.[16] In *Smith v. Ohio*,[17] the U.S. Supreme Court was asked to answer the question of "whether a warrantless search that provides probable cause for an arrest can nonetheless be justified as an incident of that arrest." In this case, Smith, when asked by an officer to "come here a minute," threw onto the hood of the car a paper grocery sack that he was carrying. The officer, *before* making an arrest, pushed the defendant's hand away and opened the bag, which contained drug paraphernalia. Because the defendant was not arrested until *after* the contraband was discovered, the contraband could not serve as part of his justification. The Court concluded that:

> The exception for searches incident to arrest permits the police to search a lawfully arrested person and areas within his immediate control . . . it does not permit police to search any citizen without a warrant or probable cause so long as an arrest immediately follows.

---

[15] *Arizona v. Gant*, 556 U.S. 332 (2009).
[16] *Rawlings v. Kentucky*, 448 U.S. 98 (1980). See also *State v. Moultrie*, 451 S.E.2d 34 (S.C. 1994), which held that a police officer's search of the defendant qualified as a search incident to the defendant's arrest, as the defendant was arrested almost immediately after the challenged search.
[17] *Smith v. Ohio*, 594 U.S. 541 (1990).

The courts have been in general agreement, however, with the fact that the challenged search occurred immediately prior to the defendant's arrest does not prevent the search from being considered incidental to a lawful arrest, as long as the fruits of the search incidental to the arrest were unnecessary to support probable cause for the arrest.[18] As an example of the application of this concept, an Ohio court held that where a police officer has probable cause to arrest independent of the items obtained in the warrantless search, but does not arrest until shortly after the search, the search is valid under the Fourth Amendment as a search incident to arrest; but where there is no probable cause to arrest, the arrest is invalid, and any evidence seized during the search is inadmissible.[19]

4   The Arrest Must Be in Good Faith

If the arrest is a sham or subterfuge, even though it is supported by probable cause, the incidental search will not be upheld. For example, if an officer stops a car ostensibly to arrest the person for driving with a burned-out headlight, but in fact for the purpose of searching the driver, the search may not be admissible in court. If the court is convinced that the arrest was a hoax or a subterfuge to make the search, the use of evidence obtained as a result of this search will generally be inadmissible.[20] This is especially true if the minor charge on which the arrest was made is later dropped.[21] The caveat to this is that officers can make a warrantless arrest (and conduct a search incident to the arrest) for a misdemeanor crime even if state law prohibits the arrest if there is probable cause to do so.[22] In determining whether an arrest constitutes subterfuge, the courts assess the officer's actions in terms of whether the officer was objectively authorized and legally permitted to make the arrest he did.[23]

C. Area of Search

Even if the arrest is lawful, the incidental search is limited in geographic scope. After more than 40 years of indecision concerning the scope of the search incident to a lawful arrest, the U.S. Supreme Court in 1969 finally defined the scope with reasonable accuracy. In *Chimel v. California*,[24] the Supreme Court held that a search incident to a lawful arrest is limited to the arrestee's person and to the area from which he or

---

[18] *United States v. Ho*, 94 F.3d 932 (5th Cir. 1996); *State v. Valdez*, 562 N.W.2d 64 (Neb. Ct. App. 1997). See also *State v. Sullivan*, 16 S.W.2d 551 (Ark. 2000).

[19] *State v. Bing*, 731 N.E.2d 266 (Ohio Ct. App. 1999).

[20] *State v. Sullivan*, 16 S.W.3d 551 (Ark. 2000).

[21] *United States v. Pampinella*, 131 F. Supp. 595 (N.D. Ill. 1955).

[22] *Virginia v. Moore*, 553 U.S. 164 (2008)

[23] *State v. David*, 13 S.W.3d 308 (Mo. 2001).

[24] *Chimel v. California*, 395 U.S. 752 (1969).

she might obtain either a weapon or something that could be used as evidence against him or her. The facts of the case are not unusual. Police officers arrested Chimel with an arrest warrant and, incident to the arrest for burglary, made a physical search of the entire premises. The Court specifically reaffirmed the authority of an officer to conduct a search incident to a lawful arrest, but limited the scope of such a search. The Court, in establishing the proper extent of a search incident to a lawful arrest, noted:

> There is ample justification, therefore, for a search of the arrestee's person and the area within his immediate control—construing that phrase to mean the area from which he might gain possession of a weapon or destructible evidence.

Even with this definition of scope, some questions are left unanswered. For example, what is meant by the terms "reach" or "gain possession"? Some terms that have been used by courts in discussing the area of search are "wingspan" and "within the lunge area."[25]

In applying the rules established in *Chimel*, many factors will be considered by the reviewing courts. For example, if the arrestee is handcuffed, the reach or lunge area is more limited than if he or she is not handcuffed. Also, it is reasonable to consider the type of evidence to be seized and even the physical agility of the arrestee. If the reason for the rule is considered, application will be less difficult. To more fully explain the geographic parameters of a search incident to a lawful arrest, specific situations will be discussed in the sections that follow.

1   Search of the Person Arrested

In *Chimel*, the Court clearly indicated that the arresting officer may search for and seize any evidence on the arrestee's person to prevent its concealment or destruction. In *United States v. Robinson*,[26] the question presented was whether a full search could legitimately follow an arrest for a traffic violation. In rejecting the argument that a search incident to a lawful arrest depends on the probability of discovering fruits or further evidence of the particular crime for which the arrest is made, the Supreme Court upheld the full search of the person arrested. The Court explained that the justification for the authority to search incident to a lawful arrest rests as much on the need to disarm the suspect to take him or her into custody as it does on the need to preserve evidence on his or her person for later use at trial.

Although there are some state decisions limiting the scope of a search under the circumstances described in *Robinson*, the current rule is that an officer who has proper authority to make an arrest may make a full search of the arrestee and seize

---

[25] *Scott v. State*, 256 A.2d 384 (Md. Ct. App. 1969).
[26] *United States v. Robinson*, 414 U.S. 218 (1973). See also *Gustafson v. Florida*, 414 U.S. 260 (1973).

evidence from the person of the arrestee, even though such evidence has no direct connection with the arrest.[27]

The authority to search a person incident to a lawful arrest necessarily includes the right to search the arrestee's clothing and, in some instances (where justified), the seizure of the clothing. For example, in a Nebraska case, the court held that the warrantless seizure of the defendant's cash, jacket, sweater, cap, and a saliva sample was valid when made incident to a lawful arrest.[28]

2   Search of Arrestee's Clothing

A practical question that often confronts an arresting officer is whether he or she can search the clothing of an arrestee after the arrestee has been jailed. In a 1974 case, the U.S. Supreme Court again expressed the view that the Fourth Amendment prohibits only unreasonable searches, and approved the search of the clothing of the person after he had been arrested and placed in jail. In upholding the examination of the arrestee's clothing, the Court stated:

> Once an accused is lawfully arrested and in custody, the effects in his possession at the place of detention that were subject to search at the time and place of his arrest may lawfully be searched and seized without a warrant even though a substantial period of time has elapsed between the arrest and the subsequent administrative processing, on the one hand, and the taking of property for use as evidence on the other.[29]

The Court cautioned that the decision was limited to the facts of that case and that there is a time when the Fourth Amendment would prohibit post-arrest seizure of the effects of an arrestee. In this case, however, the Court held that the seizure of the clothes was reasonable under the circumstances. Typically, a search such as this will be made as an inventory search exception to the warrant requirement rather than search incident to arrest (see below).

3   Search of Premises Where the Arrest Was Made

Although cases prior to 1969 held that a search of an entire dwelling place was justified as incident to a lawful arrest where the arrest was made in the living room, the *Chimel* ruling overturned that reasoning. In some instances, other evidence may be seized or other parts of the house searched, but not as incident to that lawful arrest.

---

[27] Some states do not follow the Robinson rule; see *State v. Kaluna*, 520 P.2d 51 (Haw. 1974) and *State v. Florence*, 527 P.2d 1202 (Or. 1974).

[28] *State v. Buckman*, 613 N.W.2d 463 (Neb. 2000).

[29] *United States v. Edwards*, 415 U.S. 800 (1974).

The U.S. Supreme Court in 1978 and again in 1984 reiterated the rule that an arrest in an apartment does not justify a search of the entire apartment incident to that arrest.[30] In *Mincey v. Arizona*, an undercover officer was shot and killed during a narcotics raid on Mincey's apartment. The investigating officers arrested Mincey and searched the apartment for four days, during which time the entire apartment was searched, photographed, and diagrammed. The officers opened drawers, closets, and cupboards, and inspected their contents. They even pulled up sections of the carpet and removed them for examination. No warrant was obtained, but the evidence, including the bullets and shell casings, guns, narcotics, and narcotics paraphernalia, was used at the trial in which Mincey was found guilty of murder, assault, and narcotics violations.

The Supreme Court refused to justify this search as incident to a lawful arrest and refused to add a "murder exception" to the list of searches justified without a warrant. The Court indicated that there was no objection to warrantless entries when officers believe that a person within the premises is in need of immediate aid. Also, when police officers come upon the scene of a homicide, they may make a prompt, warrantless search of the premises to see whether there are other victims or if the killer is still on the premises. While searching for victims or other persons involved, the police may seize evidence that is in plain view. The Court insisted, however, that there was no indication in this case that evidence would be lost, destroyed, or removed during the time required to obtain a search warrant, and there was no suggestion that a search warrant could not have been obtained easily and conveniently. In *Thompson v. Louisiana* the Court again refused to add another exception, and held that there can be no murder scene exception to the rule even if the search lasts two hours rather than four days.

In 1990, the U.S. Supreme Court, in examining the search area issue, held that the Fourth Amendment permits a properly limited protective sweep of an apartment in conjunction with an in-home arrest, when the searching officer has a reasonable belief, based on specific and articulable facts, that the area to be searched harbors an individual posing a danger to those on the arrest scene.[31] Such searches, however, are limited to a "cursory inspection" of spaces in which a suspect may be found. Even though a sweep of the area to locate individuals posing a danger to those on the arrest scene is justified, this authorization does not extend to searches of such areas as desk drawers or other closed or concealed areas (not in plain view) in parts of the premises that are not within the reach or lunge area of the arrestee.[32]

To summarize, when a legal arrest is made on the premises, officers may, incident to the arrest, search the person of the arrestee for weapons or evidence and, in

30 *Mincey v. Arizona*, 437 U.S. 385 (1978); *Thompson v. Louisiana*, 469 U.S. 17 (1984).
31 *Maryland v. Buie*, 494 U.S. 325 (1990).
32 *United States v. Melgar*, 927 F. Supp. 939 (E.D. Va. 1996).

addition, may search the area in which the arrestee might reach to obtain a weapon or destroy evidence. But a thorough search of the whole premises incident to an arrest is not authorized on "incident to arrest" grounds.

4   Search of Premises Outside of Buildings

When an arrest is made outside of the residence or other building described in the warrant, a search of the person is authorized to protect the officer and to prevent concealment or destruction of evidence. In addition, the search may extend to areas into which the arrestee might reach. However, a search of outbuildings not described in the warrant as an incident to an arrest made in the residence would not be justified unless the contents came within the immediate reach of the arrestee.[33]

5   Search of Automobiles Incident to Arrest

The discussion here concerns the search of an automobile as incident to a lawful arrest, not a search under the automobile exception to the warrant requirement. The *Chimel* rule applies to automobiles just as it does to fixed premises; that is, the arresting officer may search the person arrested and the immediate area to protect him- or herself or to prevent the destruction or concealment of evidence.

The scope of the search of an automobile incident to a lawful arrest has been the topic of many court cases. For example, whether an officer may search the entire passenger compartment as incident to the arrest, when the arrest is made just outside the automobile, or whether packages found in the passenger compartment of an automobile can be opened when the search is incident to a lawful arrest.

In *New York v. Belton*,[34] the Supreme Court established what has become known as the *Belton* rule. In this case, an automobile in which Belton was a passenger was stopped for speeding. After stopping the car, the officer smelled marijuana and saw an envelope that he suspected contained marijuana on the floor of the car. He directed the occupants to get out of the car and arrested them for unlawful possession of marijuana. After searching each of the occupants, he searched the passenger compartment of the car, where he found a jacket belonging to Belton. He unzipped the pockets and discovered cocaine inside. The U.S. Supreme Court ruled that the search was justified, stating:

> Accordingly, we hold that when a policeman has made a lawful custodial arrest of the occupant of an automobile, he may, as a contemporaneous incident of that arrest, search the passenger compartment of the automobile.

---

[33]   *Vale v. Louisiana*, 399 U.S. 30 (1970).
[34]   *New York v. Belton*, 453 U.S. 454 (1981).

As to the contents of containers found in the passenger compartment, the Court continued:

> The police may also examine the contents of any containers found within the passenger compartment, for if the passenger compartment is within reach of the arrestee, so also will containers within it be within his reach.

The *Belton* rule states that police may search the passenger compartment of an automobile as incident to arrest, and may examine the contents of any containers found in the passenger compartment, whether they are open or closed. It *does not* justify a search of the trunk of the car as incident to a lawful arrest. As stated above in *Gant*, however, for a search incident to an arrest to be valid, there has to be a belief the offender could gain access to the vehicle. If the offender is handcuffed in the back of a patrol car, officers would be pressed to apply *Belton* for a search.

At one point, the *Belton* rule only applied to occupants who had reasonable access to their vehicle (for example, they were in the vehicle or could perhaps return to the vehicle as in *Belton*). Under this rationale, if a person had been immobilized and taken into custody, the *Belton* rule would no longer apply (see for example *United States v. Vassey*[35]). This rationale was upheld in *Gant*, as discussed above. Also under this old rationale, the Florida Supreme Court ruled that *Belton* did not cover searches of a vehicle incident to arrest of a defendant with whom the police initiated contact only after he had exited the vehicle.[36] The rationale of a suspect having to be in the vehicle or exiting at the direction of police officers changed with the U.S. Supreme Court ruling in *Thornton v. U.S.*[37] In this case, an officer became suspicious of Thornton and pulled behind him to check his license plate. Before the officer could pull him over, Thornton pulled into a parking lot and the officer saw him exit the vehicle. The officer stopped Thornton outside his vehicle and questioned him about his license. When Thornton acted nervous, the officer asked him if he had any weapons or narcotics on him or in his vehicle. Thornton replied no and consented to a pat-down search. The officer discovered narcotics on Thornton, arrested him and placed him in the back seat of the police vehicle. The officer then searched his vehicle and found a gun. The Court reasoned that there are circumstances where an officer may not, or may not want to, encounter a person still in a vehicle. It is acceptable, therefore, for the officer to search the vehicle of a "recent occupant" even though the person is in custody and not in a position to return to the vehicle. The Court distinguished

---

[35] *United States v. Vassey*, 834 F.2d 782 (9th Cir. 1987); see also *People v. Nicodemus*, 669 N.Y.S.2d 98 (N.Y.A.D. 1998).

[36] *State v. Thomas*, 761 So. 2d 1010 (Fla. 2000).

[37] *Thornton v. United States*, 541 U.S. 615 (2004).

Thornton and *Gant* in two respects. First, the evidence discovered in *Thornton* was reasoned to be related to the original stop where it was not in *Gant*. Second, Thornton was reasoned to be physically close enough to the vehicle to return to it, where Gant was determined to be too far away from the vehicle to return to it when first contact with the police was made.

Based on these decisions, it is still constitutional for officers to search a vehicle incident to an arrest when the arrestee was in the vehicle at the time of arrest. It is also constitutional to conduct such a search if the arrestee is in very close proximity to the vehicle, especially if the search is related to the arrest. If the arrestee is physically removed from the vehicle, the only way to conduct the search seems to be if it is directly related to the arrest.

D. Seriousness of the Crime

Although not a requirement for a search incident to an arrest, the seriousness of the crime for which the arrest is made and the law governing the search is also important. Obviously, if an officer is making an arrest for a felony, a search incident to an arrest is justified, but it is not so clear from less serious offenses.

In *Knowles v. Iowa*,[38] police stopped Knowles for speeding and issued a traffic citation (although the officer had the authority to arrest him). The officer then conducted a search of Knowles' car and found marijuana. At trial, the officer admitted he had neither consent nor probable cause, but relied on a state law allowing "search incident to citation." The U.S. Supreme Court ruled that officers must have consent or probable cause to make an arrest incident to a traffic citation, otherwise the search is invalid. The court did not address whether the search would have been valid if the officer had arrested Knowles rather than issuing a citation.

In *Virginia v. Moore*,[39] the situation of *Knowles* was reversed. In this case, police officers stopped a car driven by Moore based on a police radio announcement that Moore was driving on a suspended license. The officers determined that Moore's license was in fact suspended. Under state law, officers should have issued Moore a summons because the crime was a misdemeanor. Acting on another part of the law that allowed officers to arrest in specific circumstances where the officer believes the person will disregard the summons, the officers arrested Moore. The officers subsequently searched Moore and found 16 grams of crack cocaine. A state court found the officers did not have justification to make the arrest. The U.S. Supreme Court ruled that the "police did not violate the Fourth Amendment when they made an arrest that

---

[38] *Knowles v. Iowa*, 525 U.S. 113 (1998).

[39] *Virginia v. Moore*, 553 U.S. 164 (2008).

was based on probable cause but prohibited by state law, or when they performed a search incident to the arrest."

Given the complexity of this issue, officers should seek advice from local counsel to ensure they are following policy and law. Otherwise, it is best to only search incident to arrest for a crime that state law clearly allows for arrest and the officer carries out the arrest.

§ 7.3   Search with a Valid Waiver (Consent Searches)

A favorite tool of police officers is the *consent search*. In accordance with the general principle that allows a person to waive other constitutional rights, rights protected under the Fourth Amendment may be waived. However, this and other constitutional rights are considered waived only after careful evaluation and only after compliance with certain requirements. As a rule of law, the courts have taken the approach that a person will be presumed *not* to have waived his or her rights. The burden of showing that the rights have been waived is on the prosecution.[40]

To determine whether rights have been waived, certain principles have been established by the courts. These principles are discussed in the following paragraphs.

A. The Consent Must Be Voluntary

To be constitutionally adequate, the consent must be given without force, duress, or compulsion of any kind. Submission to authority or acquiescence is not the specific consent that is required. On the other hand, a *Miranda* type of warning is not required to waive rights in a search and seizure situation. The U.S. Supreme Court, in upholding a consent search, included this comment:

> We hold only that when the subject is not in custody and the state attempts to justify a search on the basis of his consent, the Fourth and Fourteenth Amendments require that it demonstrate that the consent was in fact voluntarily given, and not the result of duress or coercion, express or implied. Voluntariness is a question of fact to be determined from all of the circumstances, and while the subject's knowledge of the right to refuse is a factor to be taken into account, the prosecution is not required to demonstrate such knowledge as a prerequisite to establishing voluntary consent.[41]

---

[40] *In the Interest of Thomas B.D.*, 486 S.E.2d 498 (S.C. Ct. App. 1997). See also *Schneckloth v. Bustamonte*, below.

[41] *Schneckloth v. Bustamonte*, 412 U.S. 218 (1973).

In determining whether the consent to a search is in fact voluntary or is the product of duress or coercion, the courts consider the "totality of circumstances." In *United States v. Mendenhall*,[42] police officers told the suspect she had a right to decline the search if she desired and she responded "go ahead." The court held that this was consent under the circumstances.

There is an additional issue in consent to search cases: whether the person believes he or she is free to leave or to end the encounter with the officer. The U.S. Supreme Court addressed the issue of whether a person thinks he or she is "free to go" in holding that the Fourth Amendment does not require a lawfully seized detainee to be advised that he or she is "free to go" before his or her consent to search will be recognized as voluntary. In *United States v. Robinette*,[43] after an Ohio deputy sheriff stopped Robinette for speeding, he gave him a verbal warning and returned his driver's license. The deputy then asked whether Robinette was carrying illegal contraband, weapons, or drugs in his car. Robinette answered, "No," and consented to a search of the car, which revealed a small amount of marijuana and a pill. Concluding that "it would be unrealistic to require the police to always inform detainees that they are free to go before consent to search may be deemed voluntary," the U.S. Supreme Court held that:

> The Fourth Amendment does not require that a lawfully seized defendant be advised that he is "free to go" before his consent to search will be recognized as voluntary.

Although the Court rejected a *per se* rule, it opined that the voluntariness of a consent to search is a question of fact to be determined from all of the circumstances. It is not necessary to advise the defendant that he or she is "free to go," but if the circumstances indicate that he or she is *not* free to go, the consent to search will probably not be recognized as voluntary.

Obviously, if the suspect is handcuffed before giving consent, it is unlikely that the consent will be considered voluntary. In a Tennessee case, the suspect opened his door after dark and was faced with at least four officers pointing guns in his direction. He was ordered out of his apartment and placed in handcuffs. He then consented to a search of his home.[44] The Court stated that for consent to enter the premises to be valid, the defendant must have the authority to consent and must consent freely and voluntarily. The Court held that, in this case, the consent did not meet this test. The Court further explained that even if the defendant, who was the subject of the arrest, actually gave the police consent to enter his apartment, his consent was not freely and voluntarily given, and therefore could not purge the taint of the illegal arrest.

---

[42] *United States v. Mendenhall*, 446 U.S. 544 (1980); *United States v. Watson*, 423 U.S. 411 (1976).

[43] *United States v. Robinette*, 519 U.S. 53 (1996).

[44] *State v. Saari*, 88 F. Supp. 2d 835 (W.D. Tenn. 1999).

Acquiescence is also not consent. The state's burden of proving consent to a warrantless search cannot be satisfied by showing nothing more than acquiescence to a claim of lawful authority.[45] Although consent to search may be given expressly by words or implied by conduct or gesture, the defendant's act of walking through a door to his apartment without shutting it behind him in response to a police officer's request for identification did not amount to implied consent for the officer's warrant-less entry.

It is also unlawful to obtain consent by claiming possession of a search warrant that officers will execute if the person in charge of the premises does not consent.[46] If the officer has a search warrant or indicates he or she will apply for a search warrant, this is apparently not considered coercive. This should be distinguished, however, from the situation in which the officer claims to have a warrant and will use it if consent to search is not given when, in fact, the officer does not have a warrant, or has a warrant that is unserveable.[47]

To avoid the risk of later challenge, an officer should not even comment concerning a search warrant unless he or she has a search warrant in his or her possession. In such a case, it is preferable to proceed under the warrant rather than under the waiver.

B. The Extent of the Search Is Limited to the Exact Words or Meaning of Consent

The consent to search must be such that it is clear that the person intends to give consent and the consent should be in specific terms. For example, if the person giving consent makes a comment such as, "Come with me and I will show you where the stolen property may be found," the consent is valid. The officer who conducts the search must carefully observe any geographic limitations placed on the consent, either directly or by inference. Consent to search one portion of the premises is not consent to search the other portions.

The authorization by a motorist to search his or her car gives the police permission to open closed containers found within the car.[48] The Court explained that, in this case, because the driver did not place any explicit limitations on the scope of the search, the search could extend beyond the car's interior surfaces.

A second limitation concerns the items that can be seized. For example, consent by a resident for officers to search his or her house for narcotics does not authorize

---

[45] *Turner v. State*, 754 A.2d 1074 (Md. Ct. App. 2000).

[46] *United States v. Faruolo*, 506 F.2d 490 (2d Cir. 1974). See also *Smiley v. State*, 606 So. 2d 213 (Ala. 1992).

[47] *Bumper v. North Carolina*, 391 U.S. 543 (1968).

[48] *Florida v. Jimeno*, 499 U.S. 934 (1991).

the seizure of other articles, such as ledgers. Other articles may be seized under the plain view doctrine, which will be discussed later, but they cannot be seized under the consent exception.[49]

C. Consent May Be Withdrawn

One danger of conducting a search under the consent rule is that the consent may be withdrawn at any time. If the person giving consent withdraws consent during the search, the officer must honor this and stop the search immediately.[50] In this situation, the officer may use any evidence obtained up to this point, or may seize other evidence within view if the circumstances justify.

D. The Person Giving Consent Must Have the Authority to Do So

The most serious problem confronting an officer who is contemplating a consent search is whether the person who gives consent is legally qualified to do so. This situation arises in the cases of landlords, joint tenants, partners, spouses, or agents. The general rule, as established by the U.S. Supreme Court, is that "[t]he consent of one who possesses common authority over the premises or effects is valid against the absent, non-consenting person with whom the authority is shared."[51]

Under this rule, valid consent to search the premises may be given by a person who has the *immediate and present right to possess those premises*. This third-party consent does not rest upon the law of property, but upon the reasonableness of recognizing that the absent party assumes the risk that a co-occupant might permit a search.[52]

Explaining the "common authority" principle, a Michigan court noted that the common authority justifying the third-party consent to search cannot be implied from a mere property interest of the third party; rather, such authority rests on mutual use of the property by persons generally having joint access or control for most purposes.[53] The court continued by indicating that it is reasonable to recognize that

---

[49] *United States v. Dichiarinte*, 445 F.2d 126 (7th Cir. 1971).

[50] *Strong v. United States*, 46 F.2d 257 (1st Cir. 1931). See also *State v. Samarghandi*, 680 N.E.2d 738 (Ohio 1997).

[51] *United States v. Matlock*, 415 U.S. 164 (1974).

[52] *Coolidge v. New Hampshire*, 403 U.S. 443 (1971).

[53] *People v. Goforth*, 564 N.W.2d 526 (Mich. Ct. App. 1997).

any of the co-inhabitants has the right to permit the inspection and that the others have assumed the risk that one of their number might permit the common areas to be searched.

Another issue that may face officers is where the person giving consent appears to have the legal authority to do so, but it is later discovered the person did not have that authority. In *Illinois v. Rodriguez*,[54] a woman told the police she had been beaten by Rodriguez. She referred to Rodriguez's apartment as "our apartment" and produced a key. After the police entered the apartment without a warrant and found drugs in plain view, Rodriguez was arrested and charged with possession of a controlled substance. At the trial, he moved to suppress all evidence seized at the time of the arrest, claiming that the woman who had given the consent had no authority to do so, as she had moved out of the apartment several weeks earlier. The Supreme Court stated that the warrantless entry into a private home by police is valid if based on consent from a person who the police may reasonably believe to have authority to grant consent, even if it is later determined that the person did not have such authority.

The rules laid out in *Rodriguez*, however, change if the other person is present and objects to the consent. In *Georgia v. Randolph*,[55] police went to the Randolphs' house to investigate a domestic dispute. While there, Janet Randolph indicated that her husband, Scott, was a drug user and that there was evidence of drug use in the house. Officers asked Scott Randolph for consent to search the house, which he unequivocally refused. The officers then asked Jane Randolph for consent, which she readily gave. She then led them into the house, where they recovered evidence of drug use. At trial, the government argued that Janet Randolph shared common access to the house and should be able to provide consent based on the rulings in *Matlock* and *Rodriguez*. While not overturning these cases, the U.S. Supreme Court ruled that consent by another person with common access to the area to be searched may only be given in the absence of the other party, and that the consent is not valid if the other party is present and objects. Further, the Court ruled that law enforcement officers could not effect the circumstances (such as removing the other party to a patrol car) to create a situation where only one party is asked for consent without objection by the other.

1   Consent by the Spouse

The general rule is that a spouse may give consent to search common areas shared with a spouse who is absent at the time of the search; however, he or she may not validly waive consent if the other spouse is on the premises at the time and refuses

---

[54] *Illinois v. Rodriguez*, 497 U.S. 177 (1990).
[55] *Georgia v. Randolph*, 547 U.S. 103 (2006), 126 S. Ct. 1515 (2006).

to authorize the search. One court, however, has held that a person who shares living space with others can authorize police to search the residence even over the objection of the other inhabitant.[56] Also, the courts are generally in agreement that one spouse cannot consent to a search of a part of the premises used exclusively by the other spouse.[57] As to the latter point, one court rendered a decision that invalidated the search of a rented garage that was leased entirely by the husband and not used at all by the wife who gave the consent.[58] But if the wife has access to a dresser drawer used by the husband, located in a room that is available to both, the wife's consent to take evidence from the dresser drawer is valid unless the facts indicate that one spouse has exclusive control over it.[59]

2   Consent by a Parent or Other Family Member

The general rule is that a minor child's possessory right in the family home is only that which he or she derives from the parent, and the parent may authorize a consent search that is valid against the child.[60] If an adult child has a room that he or she uses exclusively, allows no one else in the room, and the child is paying rent specifically for that room, the parent cannot legitimately consent to a search of that room. On the other hand, the Pennsylvania Supreme Court in 1982 reiterated that a parent may consent to the search of a child's room, even if the child is contributing toward his or her room and board, if the parent has access to the room.[61] In this case, the son lived at home with his parents and paid $100 a month for room and board. However, he never locked his bedroom door or forbade family members to enter the room. In approving the consent to the search by the mother, the justices considered several factors in reaching their decision. Among these were: (1) the son had access to the whole house, not just one room; (2) he never objectively manifested an expectation of privacy in his room; and (3) the son and the mother had joint access and control over the room.

Following the general rule that one who possesses the authority in the premises may consent to a search, a court ruled that a defendant's sister had authority to

---

[56]   *People v. Cosme*, 397 N.E.2d 1319 (N.Y. App. 1979). See also *United States v. Kerchurn*, 71 F. Supp. 2d 779 (N.D. Ohio 1999).

[57]   But see *United States v. Gevedon*, 214 F.3d 807 (7th Cir. 2000), in which the court held that the defendant's estranged wife had the authority to consent to a search of the garage and shop used only by the husband even though the wife was denied access to the shop by the husband when the wife no longer lived in the home but her name was still on the deed for the entire property.

[58]   *United States ex rel. Cabey v. Mazurkiewicz*, 312 F. Supp. 11 (E.D. Pa. 1969).

[59]   *People v. Stacey*, 317 N.E.2d 24 (Ill. 1974).

[60]   *United States v. Peterson*, 524 F.2d 167 (4th Cir. 1975).

[61]   *Commonwealth v. Lowery*, 451 A.2d 245 (Pa. 1982). See also *People v. Goforth*, 564 N.W.2d 526 (Mich. Ct. App. 1997).

consent to the search of the apartment that she had leased and allowed the defendant to live in.[62] Even though the sister had given her key to the defendant, and she stayed there only occasionally, the fact that she kept furniture and household possessions there, and had not subleased the apartment to the defendant, was sufficient to justify the court considering the sister as a tenant-in-common.

3   Consent by a Minor Child

It is risky to rely on the consent of a minor child. While several courts have held that minority status alone does not prevent one from giving consent, the prosecution must prove that the consent was given voluntarily, intelligently, and knowingly.[63] In determining whether the minor intelligently and knowingly consented to the search, the courts will take into consideration the age of the minor, the scope of the consent requested and given, and whether the consent to the search was unequivocal and specific.[64] Also, the availability or presence of the parent in the home is a factor to consider in determining the scope and validity of the minor's consent to search and seizure.

The age of the minor plays an important part in determining whether the consent is valid. An older child who has tenant-in-common status would probably be recognized as one who has the authority to consent.

4   Consent to Search for and Seize Articles
Left in Another's Care

If a person leaves an article in another's home or in another's care, the person who has custody of such article may consent to the search of that article. If, for example, the borrower of a car has legitimate possession and control of that vehicle, the owner cannot complain if the borrower consents to a search of the car unless the owner has specifically told him or her in the beginning that he or she could not give such consent.[65]

5   Consent by School Authorities

In *New Jersey v. T.L.O.*,[66] the U.S. Supreme Court considered the reasonableness of the search of a student's purse by a school official. In this case, the Court held that, under ordinary circumstances, the search of a student or a student's purse by a teacher

---

[62] *Smiley v. State*, 606 So. 2d 213 (Ala. 1992).

[63] *State v. Kriegh*, 937 P.2d 453 (Kan. 1997).

[64] *People v. Santiago*, 64 Cal. Rptr. 2d 794 (1997).

[65] *Marshall v. United States*, 352 F.2d 1013 (9th Cir. 1965).

[66] *New Jersey v. T.L.O.*, 469 U.S. 325 (1985).

or other school official will be justified if there are reasonable grounds for suspecting that the search will turn up evidence that the student has violated or is violating the law or rules of the school. The Supreme Court indicated that school authorities could make searches on reasonable grounds for suspecting that evidence would be found, and that the Fourth Amendment standard, which requires probable cause, should not be applied in school situations. A 2009 U.S. Supreme Court case made clear, however, that there are limits to what even a school authority can search.[67] School searches by law enforcement with the consent of school authorities should be carefully planned and based on the advice of local counsel.

The answer to the question of whether the principal or administrator of the school can consent to a search of a student's locker or personal belongings at the request of a law enforcement officer is still in doubt. If the principal or a person in charge has made it clear by written posters or rules and regulations that lockers are subject to inspection, then the student's expectation of privacy would be diminished and the courts would be more likely to recognize that the principal can consent to or make the search him- or herself. Another factor to consider is whether the lockers used by the students, as well as the locks used to secure them, are owned by a municipality or school board, or by a private individual.[68]

§ 7.4   Search of Movable Vehicles and Objects

The Supreme Court has recognized an important difference between the search of a dwelling house, for which a warrant may be readily obtained, and the search of a ship, boat, wagon, airplane, automobile, or other movable vehicle, for which it is not practical to secure a warrant because the object may quickly be moved out of the jurisdiction.[69] This exception to the warrant requirement was decided by the Supreme Court in 1925, when officers searched the vehicle of a known whiskey smuggler without a warrant and discovered illegal liquor.[70] The Court held that officers may search a vehicle without a warrant if there is probable cause that the vehicle contains contraband. The justification for this exception is that, because the vehicle is moving or could be moved from the officer's jurisdiction, there is no time to obtain a search warrant even if probable cause for the warrant exists. For the search to be valid, the officer must at least have facts or information that would authorize issuance of a search warrant had an application been made. The difference is that probable cause is

---

[67]   *Safford v. Redding*, 557 U.S. 2633 (2009).

[68]   *State v. Stein*, 456 P.2d 1 (Kan. 1969).

[69]   *Carroll v. United States*, 267 U.S. 132 (1925).

[70]   *Id.*

proved in court *after* the search rather than before a magistrate and before the search. The same rationale is applied when a search is made of a boat, plane, truck, trailer, or tractor-trailer.[71]

Carroll v. United States began a line of cases related to the Fourth Amendment that would produce perhaps more litigation at the Supreme Court level than any other issues affecting law enforcement. Searches related to vehicles also enjoy more freedom from Fourth Amendment restriction than any other type of search. A small portion of the most important cases related to vehicle searches are discussed in this section of the book.

In 1970, the Supreme Court approved the moving vehicle doctrine in *Chambers v. Maroney*,[72] and reaffirmed the right of police officers to search a vehicle even if they have taken possession of it, provided there is probable cause to believe that the vehicle contains articles the officers are entitled to seize. In *Chambers*, the Supreme Court held that a search warrant is unnecessary when there is probable cause to search an automobile, even if there is time to obtain a warrant.[73] This case differed from *Carroll*, in that *Carroll* dealt with a movable vehicle. Following *Carroll* there was the assumption that it applied only if there was no time to obtain a warrant; and if police took possession of a vehicle, a warrant was still necessary. *Chambers* removed this restriction, and held that if officers have probable cause to search a vehicle at the scene of a stop without a warrant, they can also do so after the vehicle arrives at a police facility under the same justification.

In recent years, lower courts have applied the *Carroll* doctrine to other movable objects. For example, the California Supreme Court found a degree of similarity between a motor vehicle and a package being sent by air freight. The Court concluded that the exception to the warrant requirements explained in *Carroll* applies to such a package.[74] And the Eighth Circuit Court of Appeals had no difficulty applying the rationale to the search of a duffel bag when probable cause existed and the item was about to be moved.[75] In other cases, both federal and state courts have approved searches of suitcases in transit where exigent circumstances justified such action.[76]

In 1982, the U.S. Supreme Court rendered a decision that clarified the rule relating to containers found in an automobile. The Court concluded that police, acting under the automobile exception to the Fourth Amendment warrant requirement, may search

---

[71]   *United States v. Bozada*, 473 F.2d 389 (8th Cir. 1973).

[72]   *Chambers v. Maroney*, 399 U.S. 42 (1970).

[73]   See also *Texas v. White*, 423 U.S. 67 (1975).

[74]   *People v. McKinnon*, 500 P.2d 1097 (Cal. 1972).

[75]   *United States v. Wilson*, 524 F.2d 595 (8th Cir. 1975). See also *People v. Santana*, 622 N.Y.S.2d 44, which held that the automobile exception authorized the search of the handlebar of a bicycle.

[76]   *People v. McKinnon*, 500 P.2d 1097 (Cal. 1972); *United States v. Mehciz*, 437 F.2d 145 (9th Cir. 1971).

every part of a vehicle, including closed containers that might conceal the contraband for which they are looking. In *United States v. Ross*,[77] the Court held, in effect, that if an officer has probable cause to search an occupied vehicle for a particular type of evidence, for example, contraband or stolen goods, he or she is entitled to conduct a warrantless search of all compartments or closed containers within the vehicle in which the evidence sought may reasonably be found.

The *Ross* decision made it clear that if an officer has probable cause to believe that an automobile contains contraband, he or she is entitled to conduct a warrantless search of the car as well as containers within the car in which evidence may reasonably be found. The decision did not overrule previous decisions, which held that if the search is directed toward a particular container in the automobile, it will be necessary to obtain a search warrant. Previous cases had drawn a line between the search of an automobile that coincidentally turns up a container and the search of a container that coincidentally turns up in an automobile.[78]

In *Arkansas v. Sanders*, the court decided that the automobile exception would not be extended to the warrantless search of personal luggage "merely because it was located in an automobile lawfully stopped by the police."

In 1991, the U.S. Supreme Court again considered the authority of police to search luggage or other containers that happened to be located in an automobile. Justice Blackmun, writing for the majority, noted that "[u]ntil today, this Court has drawn a curious line between the search of an automobile that coincidentally turns up a container and the search of a container that coincidentally turns up in an automobile . . . [t]he protections of the Fourth Amendment must not turn upon such coincidences."[79] According to this ruling, if an officer has probable cause to believe that a container in an automobile holds an object or objects that are contraband or otherwise illegally possessed, the officer may open the containers and seize the evidence if it is in fact contraband or otherwise held illegally. However, the fact that police have probable cause to believe the container placed in the vehicle contains contraband or illegally possessed evidence does not justify a search of the entire automobile. Explaining the rationale for the automobile exception, the Court noted:

> The scope of a warrantless search based on probable cause is no narrower—and no broader—than the scope of a search authorized by a warrant supported by probable cause. Only the prior approval of the magistrate is waived; the search otherwise is as the magistrate could authorize.

---

[77]   *United States v. Ross*, 456 U.S. 798 (1982).

[78]   *United States v. Chadwick*, 433 U.S. 1 (1977); *Arkansas v. Sanders*, 442 U.S. 753 (1979).

[79]   *California v. Acevedo*, 500 U.S. 565 (1991).

Courts have also ruled that the search does not have to take place at the scene. As interpreted by the Supreme Court, if an officer had probable cause to make a search at the time the car was stopped, he or she could conduct a warrantless search of the vehicle under the moving vehicle doctrine even if the car had been taken into police custody and returned to the station.[80] The rationale for this noncontemporaneous search is that once an officer has probable cause to conduct a search under the moving vehicle doctrine, he or she may act as if a warrant has been obtained. The legality of a search does not depend on whether the car has been immobilized, but on whether probable cause existed at the time the car was originally stopped.

In an Oregon decision, the court warned that the automobile exception to the search warrant requirement of the state constitution applies if the automobile is operable and constructively occupied; that is, someone is in a position to operate it and leave in it immediately at the time the police first encounter it.[81] If these conditions do not exist, the state must be able to justify a warrantless search by demonstrating the impracticality of obtaining a warrant.

The Supreme Court in 1985 considered the legality of the search of a motor home temporarily parked in a downtown parking lot. In *California v. Carney*,[82] officers had probable cause to believe that marijuana was possessed for sale from a motor home parked in a downtown lot in San Diego. The Supreme Court concluded that privacy expectations are reduced in automobiles not only because some parts of the vehicle are open to plain view, but also because motor vehicles are heavily regulated. The Court reasoned that because the vehicle is readily mobile and there is a reduced expectation of privacy stemming from its use as a licensed motor vehicle subject to regulation, it may be searched if located in a place not regularly used for residential purposes. If a motor home is permanently parked in a space designed for such vehicles and is not readily movable, it is a "home" protected by the Fourth Amendment. To justify the warrantless search or seizure of a motor home under the vehicle exception to the search warrant requirement, the government must establish that probable cause existed to believe that the vehicle contained contraband or other evidence that is subject to seizure under law, that the vehicle was readily mobile, and that it was located in a setting that objectively indicated that it was being used for transportation.[83]

Although not directly addressed in these cases, at issue when stopping a vehicle is that, under the law, any vehicle stopped by police officers represents a seizure, which is what makes it fall under Fourth Amendment requirements (see, for example,

---

[80]   *Michigan v. Thomas*, 458 U.S. 259 (1982).
[81]   *State v. Coleman*, 2 P.3d 399 (Or. Ct. App. 2000).
[82]   *California v. Carney*, 471 U.S. 386 (1985).
[83]   *United States v. Adams*, 845 F. Supp. 1531 (M.D. Fla. 1994). See also *United States v. Boettger*, 71 F.3d 1410 (8th Cir. 1995).

Brower v. County of Inyo in § 5.3). The courts have generally ruled the driver of the vehicle is also seized at this point, and may challenge the legality of the stop. In *Brendlin v. California*,[84] the U.S. Supreme Court was required to determine whether passengers in stopped vehicles had the same standing to challenge the legality of the stop. In this case, officers pulled over a vehicle in which Brendlin was a passenger, even though there was no reason to believe it was being operated illegally. Once stopped, officers recognized Brendlin as being a parole violator. Officers ultimately arrested Brendlin and searched the vehicle, finding evidence of methamphetamine manufacturing. The Court ruled that a stop of a vehicle is a seizure of a passenger as well as the driver. They based this on the fact that passengers surely would not feel free to leave once stopped by police, arguing:

> If the likely wrongdoing is not the driving, the passenger will reasonably feel subject to suspicion owing to close association; but even when the wrongdoing is only bad driving, the passenger will expect to be subject to some scrutiny, and his attempt to leave the scene would be so obviously likely to prompt an objection from the officers that no passenger would feel free to leave in the first place.

The Court did not decide the issue of whether the suppression of evidence should have been allowed; only that Brendlin had the right to argue for suppression as a result of the Fourth Amendment violation.

Somewhat extending *Brendlin*, the court held in *Arizona v. Johnson*[85] that officers may order passengers out of a lawfully stopped vehicle and pat them down if there is reasonable suspicion that they may be armed and dangerous. The Court reasoned that, if the vehicle is lawfully stopped, and as *Brendlin* held passengers are seized, the first element of *Terry v. Ohio* was met. It was reasonable, therefore, for the officer to conduct a pat-down of Johnson for officer protection (the second element of *Terry*).

As indicated by these cases, the issues related to automobile searches are complex and include many different aspects. At this point, it is reasonable that officers may do the following after legally stopping a vehicle:

1. Order the driver to exit the vehicle;
2. Order the passengers to exit the vehicle;
3. Ask the driver to produce a driver's license and other documents required by state law;
4. Ask questions of the driver and occupants;
5. Require drunken driving suspects to take a Breathalyzer test;
6. Locate and examine the vehicle identification number; and
7. Search the vehicle if probable cause develops.

---

[84] *Brendlin v. California*, 551 U.S. 1 (2007).
[85] *Arizona v. Johnson*, 555 U.S. 323 (2009).

If the circumstances are such that probable cause exists to search the vehicle, officers may do the following:

1. Conduct a search of the passenger compartment of a car and of the contents therein if it is incident to a lawful arrest;
2. Search the entire car and open the trunk and any packages or luggage found therein that could reasonably contain the items for which they are looking;
3. Search a container in a car if there is probable cause to believe that it holds contraband or seizable items, even in the absence of probable cause to search the car; and
4. If there is probable cause to search a vehicle, officers may also inspect the belongings of passengers in the vehicle as long as those belongings are capable of concealing the object of the search.

The Supreme Court has given the police extensive authority to search motor vehicles. Essentially, if there is probable cause of illegality, officers may search a vehicle without the requirement of a warrant.

§ 7.5 Search after Lawful Impoundment (Inventory Searches)

Often a police officer has the duty and responsibility, either by law or department regulation, to impound a car that has been abandoned, is blocking traffic, is illegally parked, or is in the officer's care for some other reason. The officer is often required to make an inventory of the contents of the vehicle before taking it to an impoundment lot. Generally, there is no legal prohibition on the use of evidence coming into his or her possession as a result of making such an inventory.

The rationale for the use of evidence obtained as a result of the "inventory search" is that an officer should not be required to close his or her eyes and not seize stolen or contraband evidence that he or she discovers during the inventory. As in the case of other legal tools, however, some law enforcement officers have overused and abused this "inventory seizure," in many instances carrying the search far beyond what is justifiable. As a result, as one court stated, there has been a "credibility gap" in Fourth Amendment rights wrought by inventory searches.[86]

The purpose of an inventory search is not to uncover criminal evidence; rather, it is designed to safeguard seized items to benefit both the police and the defendant. Inventory searches serve one or more of the following purposes: to protect the owner's property while it remains in police custody, to protect the police against claims or disputes over lost or stolen property, to protect the police from potential danger, and

---

[86] *Dixon v. State*, 327 A.2d 516 (Md. Ct. App. 1974).

to assist the police in determining whether the vehicle was stolen and then abandoned.[87] This would not justify a search into the parts of a car that are not normally searched when making an inventory. For example, a search into the hubcaps or into the area under the dashboard would not be a legitimate inventory search. If, therefore, the police officer's conduct indicates that the search is for exploratory rather than for inventory purposes, using the fruits of the search is forbidden.[88]

Partially as a result of abuses, some state courts have prohibited an inventory search of the entire automobile. For example, the Kentucky Court of Appeals held that officers may close and lock a car and seize whatever is in plain view in the process, but they may not open compartments or containers within the vehicle.[89] The Wisconsin Supreme Court, in suppressing evidence obtained after an inventory was made of an impounded car, acknowledged that cases from other jurisdictions are divided on the question of whether making an inventory of the contents of an impounded car is actually a search, but concluded that protecting the police from false claims of theft or "safeguarding" the defendant's property does not justify an inspection of closed suitcases and containers.[90]

Because of the widely differing opinions of lower courts concerning the seizure of articles from impounded cars, the U.S. Supreme Court in 1976 gave limited approval on this procedure. In *South Dakota v. Opperman*,[91] an automobile was towed to the city impound lot after it had been illegally parked overnight. From outside the car, a police officer observed a watch on the dashboard and some items of personal property located on the backseat. At his direction, the car was unlocked and a standard inventory form was used to inventory the contents. Marijuana was found in the unlocked glove compartment. It was seized and used as evidence. The U.S. Supreme Court held that the evidence was properly admitted. The Court, in approving this procedure in limited circumstances, first distinguished between automobiles and homes or offices in relation to Fourth Amendment protections, and then, under the facts of the individual case, approved the seizure of evidence from the impounded car. The Court pointed out that the police were indisputably engaged in a "caretaker" search of the lawfully impounded automobile and that there was no suggestion of investigatory motive on the part of the officers.

Citing the *Opperman* case, the Supreme Court in 1987 reaffirmed the use of evidence obtained during the lawful inventory of an automobile. In *Colorado v. Bertine*,[92] an officer arrested a motorist for driving his van while under the influence of alcohol.

---

[87] *Commonwealth v. Hennigan*, 753 A.2d 245 (Pa. 2000).
[88] *State v. Wallen*, 173 N.W.2d 372 (Neb. 1970).
[89] *City of Danville v. Dawson*, 528 S.W.2d 687 (Ky. 1975); *Wagner v. Commonwealth*, 581 S.W.2d 352 (Ky. 1979).
[90] *State v. McDougal*, 228 N.W.2d 671 (1975).
[91] *South Dakota v. Opperman*, 428 U.S. 364 (1976).
[92] *Colorado v. Bertine*, 479 U.S. 367 (1987).

A Chelan County (Washington) Sheriff's deputy and a drug-sniffing dog search an impounded car for drugs. The Supreme Court has emphasized that the inventory search serves a governmental interest in protecting the owner's property while it is in police custody; ensuring against claims of lost, stolen, or vandalized property; and guarding the police from danger. (*AP Photo/WENACHEE WORLD, Kelly Gillin*)

After he was taken into custody and before a tow truck arrived to take the van to an impoundment lot, another officer, acting in accordance with local police procedures, inventoried the van's contents, opening a closed backpack in which he found various containers holding controlled substances, cocaine paraphernalia, and a large amount of cash. The U.S. Supreme Court held that there was no showing that the police acted in bad faith or for the sole purpose of conducting an investigatory search. The Court, in approving the use of the evidence, emphasized that the inventory search serves a governmental interest in protecting the owner's property while it is in police custody; ensuring against claims of lost, stolen, or vandalized property; and guarding the police from danger.

Referring to language used in the *Bertine* case, the Florida Supreme Court in 1990 decided that because the highway patrol had no policy on the opening of closed containers found during inventory searches, a search by an officer without such policy was insufficiently regulated to satisfy the Fourth Amendment.[93] The U.S. Supreme Court, although disagreeing with the Supreme Court of Florida that *Bertine* required

---

[93]   *Wells v. State*, 539 So. 2d 464 (Fla. 1989).

a policy to justify an inventory search, did agree that standardized criteria or an established routine must regulate the opening of containers found during inventory searches.[94] The Court explained that an inventory search must not be a ruse for general rummaging to discover incriminating evidence. The Court continued by stating that:

> The policy or practice governing inventory searches should be designed to produce an inventory. The individual police officer must not be allowed so much latitude that inventory searches are turned into a purposeful and general means of discovering evidence of crime.

The Court noted, however, that a police officer may be allowed sufficient latitude to determine whether a particular container should or should not be opened in light of the nature of the search and characteristics of the container itself. After noting that the Florida Highway Patrol had no policy whatsoever with respect to the opening of closed containers encountered during inventory searches, the Court concluded "that absent such a policy, the instant search was not sufficiently regulated to satisfy the Fourth Amendment and that the marijuana which was found in the suitcase, therefore, was properly suppressed by the Supreme Court of Florida."

Following the *Wells* decision, departments that did not have a policy concerning the inventory of impounded automobiles added instructions to guide officers in conducting inventories after the automobiles were lawfully impounded. With such policies, inventory searches are generally upheld. For example, in a federal case, the reviewing court agreed that if an inventory search is part of a bona fide, routine, administrative, caretaking function of the police and not a pretext to disguise impermissible searches for evidence, probable cause is not required.[95] A federal court in Missouri held that, having conducted a search of the defendant's van according to standardized inventory procedures, the officers' suspicions that incriminating evidence might be discovered did not invalidate the search.[96]

In 1996, the Ninth Circuit Court of Appeals was asked to determine whether the rules concerning the inventory of automobiles that were developed in earlier cases applied if the inventory occurred at the police station rather than at the arrest scene.[97] The court, after first reiterating that an inventory search exception to the warrant requirement is premised on the individual's diminished expectation of privacy in an automobile and governmental interests in inventorying the automobiles—that is, to protect the owner's property while the automobile is in police custody, to ensure

---

[94] *Florida v. Wells*, 495 U.S. 1 (1990).
[95] *United States v. Doe*, 801 F. Supp. 1562 (E.D. Tex. 1992).
[96] *United States v. Lewis*, 3 F.3d 252 (8th Cir. 1993).
[97] *United States v. Lomeli*, 76 F.3d 146 (9th Cir. 1996).

against claims of loss, and to guard police from danger—agreed that if the department had a general policy that sufficiently regulated inventory searches, the inventory could be conducted at the police station rather than at the scene of the arrest.

§ 7.6   Exigent Circumstances Exception to the Warrant Requirement

It is a basic principle of Fourth Amendment law that searches and seizures inside a home without a warrant are *per se* unreasonable in the absence of one of a number of well-defined exigent circumstances.[98] Accordingly, the Supreme Court has empha-sized that exceptions to the warrant requirement are "'few in number and carefully delineated' and that the police bear a heavy burden when attempting to demonstrate an urgent need to justify a warrantless search."[99]

In *United States v. Dawkins*,[100] the District of Columbia Circuit examined the exigent circumstances exception and listed guidelines that had been established in previous cases. This case held that: (1) the government must demonstrate that prob-able cause exists; and (2) the government must demonstrate that its failure to procure a warrant was justifiable in light of circumstantial exigencies. The probable cause is that which would justify the issuance of a warrant had there been an opportunity to obtain a warrant. The existence of probable cause does not in itself immunize the officers' conduct. There is a heavy burden on the police to show that a warrant could not be obtained without a delay.

The courts have been reluctant to approve the entry of a home under the exigent circumstances exception. For example, an officer's belief that the suspect might have been alerted to the officers' presence in the neighborhood, or that their presence was arousing suspicion, was not sufficient to constitute exigent circumstances justifying a warrantless entry into the suspect's apartment.[101]

One court, in discussing the exigent circumstances exception, noted that the factors relevant in determining whether exigent circumstances exist, justifying a warrantless and nonconsensual search of someone's home or hotel room, include: (1) the degree of urgency involved and the amount of time necessary to obtain a warrant; (2) the reasonable belief that contraband is about to be removed; (3) the possibility of danger to police officers guarding the site of the contraband while the search warrant is sought; (4) information indicating that the possessors of the contraband are aware that the police are on their trail; and (5) ready destructibility of the contraband.[102]

---

[98] *Coolidge v. New Hampshire*, 403 U.S. 443 (1971).
[99] *Welsh v. Wisconsin*, 466 U.S. 740 (1984).
[100] *United States v. Dawkins*, 17 F.2d 399 (D.C. Cir. 1994).
[101] *United States v. Cabassa*, 782 F. Supp. 226 (S.D.N.Y. 1992).
[102] *United States v. Richard*, 994 F.2d 244 (5th Cir. 1993).

Much of the issue of exigency to search surrounds the issue of whether officers must knock on the door and announce their presences before entering a home. This issue was covered in the previous chapter. The combining of these two issues was addressed in 2013 by the Supreme Court. In *Kentucky v. King*,[103] officers executed a controlled buy of drugs outside of an apartment complex. An officer watched the buy and radioed other officers to apprehend the suspect. Before officers could reach the person, he entered into a breezeway of the apartment complex and shut the door. There were two apartments at the end of the breezeway, and officers did not see which door he entered; but they smelled burning marijuana coming from the left door. Officers knocked on the door and announced their presence. When they heard movement inside that was consistent with destruction of evidence, they broke the door and entered. King and another person were arrested for possession of drugs, paraphernalia, and cash. The Court ruled that the officers did not "create" the exigency in this case by knocking on the door; and that the suspects were the ones who created the exigency to enter by attempting to destroy evidence. The Court warned, however, that officers cannot create an exigency by engaging in or threatening to engage in contact that violates the Fourth Amendment, such as threatening to enter when there is no legal justification to do so.

The courts have generally been consistent in holding that officers may enter a home if a delay in procuring a warrant would gravely endanger the life of the officer or others. For example, exigent circumstances existed to justify police officers' warrantless search of the defendant's apartment to search for individuals who had shot at the officers as well as for weapons involved in the shooting, because the police did not know the whereabouts of the armed individual who had just shot at officers from the immediate vicinity of the defendant's apartment, and there was a risk of bodily harm or death to both police officers and civilians.[104] Officers can also enter a home if they have an objectively reasonable basis for believing that an occupant is injured or imminently threatened with injury.[105] In this case, officers responded to a disturbance call; and once arriving at the home could see through a screen door that a fight was taking place. The officers announced their presence and entered the home to break up the fight and avoid injury.

§ 7.7   Plain View Searches

The Fourth Amendment, as well as provisions of state constitutions, protects individuals against unreasonable *searches* and *seizures*. Where there is no *search* required, the constitutional guarantee does not apply. In *Minnesota v. Dickerson*,[106]

---

[103] *Kentucky v. King*, 561 U.S. ___, No. 09-1272 (2011).

[104] *Robinson v. State*, 730 N.E.2d 185 (Ind. 2000).

[105] *Brigham City, Utah v. Stuart, et al.*, 547 U.S. 47 (2006).

[106] *Minnesota v. Dickerson*, 508 U.S. 366 (1993).

the Supreme Court noted that the rationale for the plain view doctrine is that if contraband is left in the open and is observed by a police officer from a lawful vantage point, there is no invasion of a legitimate expectation of privacy and thus no "search" within the meaning of the Fourth Amendment. In other words, if an officer is in a place where he or she has a right to be and recognizes contraband, instrumentalities of crime, or other evidence that he or she has a right to seize, the officer may seize the evidence that is in plain view. The Supreme Court has explained that the police are not required to close their eyes and need not walk out and leave an article where they saw it. Any other principle might lead to an absurd result and at times perhaps even defeat the ends of justice.[107] There are two legal conditions that must be met before this doctrine will apply: (1) the officer must be lawfully present when he or she views the object; and (2) the officer must recognize the article as contraband, illegally possessed property, stolen property, or otherwise subject to seizure.[108]

Officers may be lawfully present under many circumstances. They may be in a part of a business establishment that is open to the public; they may see something through an open door or window; they may be on the premises to conduct an investigation; or, in the most common situation, they may be on the premises to execute a search warrant. In any event, they must come upon the article to be seized without making a search. If the officers become trespassers on property that is under the protection of the Fourth Amendment, their actions then amount to an illegal search and seizure. They cannot use information so obtained to procure a warrant, nor can they seize the evidence without a warrant.

In *Washington v. Chrisman*,[109] the Supreme Court agreed that a police officer was properly in a position to observe contraband from a doorway when he accompanied a student to his room to obtain identification. A more common situation is when officers have responded to a call and find evidence as a part of their investigation into the call. This issue is illustrated in a case in which officers received a 911 call of shots fired and arguing.[110] When police arrived at the scene, they encountered three people who they handcuffed, separated, and detained. Officers then approached the residence to search for potential victims and weapons. The officers found a shotgun and expended and live shotgun shells. The court ruled in this case that "when exigent circumstances demand an immediate response, particularly where there is danger to human life, protection of the public becomes paramount and can justify a limited, warrantless intrusion into the home. Once in the home, officers may seize any evidence found within plain view."[111]

---

[107] *Washington v. Chrisman*, 455 U.S. 1 (1982).
[108] *United States v. Blair*, 214 F.3d 690 (6th Cir. 2000).
[109] *Washington v. Chrisman*, 455 U.S. 1 (1982).
[110] *United States v. Holloway*, 290 F.3d 1331 (2002).
[111] 290 F.3d at 1332.

The Supreme Court also held that an aerial surveillance by officers in a plane (or helicopter) of marijuana growing in a backyard does not violate the Fourth Amendment.[112] This case was decided in favor of the officers even though the Court admitted that the backyard was part of the curtilage of the house (which usually enjoys great protection by the Fourth Amendment). Similar cases have also held that officers may use binoculars to aid their observation.[113] This includes the use of binoculars or a telescope either from the ground or from the air, and it includes the use of a flashlight to illuminate the area being observed.

The second requirement—that the officer recognize the article as contraband, illegally possessed property, stolen property, or otherwise subject to seizure—is somewhat more difficult to comply with. The general rule is that the officer must recognize the article without further search. In the 1983 case of *Texas v. Brown*,[114] the Court, in clarifying past decisions, indicated that the officer need not "know" that certain items are contraband or incident to the crime before the seizure is justified under the plain view approach; all that is necessary is that he or she have "probable cause" to believe that the evidence is subject to seizure. In that case, the Court agreed that the officer possessed probable cause to believe that opaque green party balloons in a car occupied by the defendant were subject to seizure where the officer's experience led him to believe that narcotics were frequently packaged in such balloons.

In another case, however, the Court indicated that the search was invalid where the police had only reasonable suspicion (less than probable cause) to believe that stereo equipment was stolen.[115] The officer, who was on the property legally, had to move a turntable to check the serial numbers. This amounted to a "search" without probable cause.

Two other cases indicate the expanding use of the plain view search in seizing evidence. Using this doctrine, the Supreme Court in 1986 announced that officers were justified in seizing a gun observed under the seat of a car while attempting to obtain the vehicle identification number (VIN).[116] In this case, a police officer, after stopping the car, attempted to see the VIN but was unable to do so because some papers obscured the area on the dashboard where the number was located. In attempting to see the number, the officer reached into the interior of the car to remove the papers. In doing so, he saw the handle of a gun protruding from underneath the driver's seat and seized the gun. The Supreme Court indicated that because the officer was legally in the vehicle to observe the VIN and saw the gun in plain view, he had the authority to seize it.

---

[112] *California v. Ciraolo*, 476 U.S. 207 (1986).

[113] *Texas v. Brown*, 460 U.S. 730 (1983).

[114] *Id.*

[115] *Arizona v. Hicks*, 480 U.S. 321 (1987).

[116] *New York v. Class*, 475 U.S. 106 (1986).

Despite the many cases that have considered the plain view doctrine, questions still arise. In a District of Columbia case, officers on a drug interdiction patrol stopped Whren and others for a traffic violation, even though the department regulations instructed undercover officers not to conduct traffic stops.[117] The officers observed drugs in plain view, and the occupants of the vehicle were convicted on the basis of drugs discovered during the traffic stop. On appeal, Whren claimed that the traffic stop was just a pretext to search for drugs and that such "pretextual" stops constituted an unreasonable search for purposes of the Fourth Amendment. The U.S. Supreme Court held that the police officers' subjective motivation for making a traffic stop is irrelevant as long as there is probable cause to justify a traffic stop. The test is not whether an officer "would have" made the traffic stop but whether an officer "could have" made the traffic stop.

When *Coolidge v. New Hampshire*[118] was decided in 1971, the Court indicated that the seizure of items discovered in plain view was valid only if the discovery was *inadvertent*. Since that decision, the courts have attempted to define what is meant by an inadvertent discovery.

In 1990, the Supreme Court held that the inadvertency requirement would no longer apply.[119] In this case, a police officer obtained a warrant to search an apartment for stolen goods. The warrant specifically authorized the search for the proceeds of a robbery, but did not mention weapons that had been described in the warrant affidavit filed with the court. In the apartment, while searching for the stolen goods described in the warrant, the officer found weapons that fit the description on the affidavit and seized them. Horton sought to overturn the verdict on appeal on the grounds that the seizure of the items discovered in plain view was not an "inadvertent" seizure because the officer admitted that he was interested in finding incriminating evidence other than that described in the warrant. The court reiterated that a warrantless seizure of an object in plain view is valid if these conditions are met: (1) the officer did not violate the Fourth Amendment in entering the place where the object was seen; (2) the object's incriminating character was immediately apparent; and (3) the officer had lawful access to the object itself. The Supreme Court pointed out that the "inadvertency" prong of the test was never a part of the holding in *Coolidge*.

Since this decision, the seizure of evidence in plain view is no longer subject to the inadvertency requirement if the search is properly confined to the described area. Nevertheless, the plain view exception to the warrant requirement does not apply if a separate search is required to locate the object sought.[120]

---

[117] *Whren v. United States*, 517 U.S. 806 (1996).
[118] *Coolidge v. New Hampshire*, 403 U.S. 433 (1971).
[119] *Horton v. California*, 496 U.S. 128 (1990).
[120] *Id.*

§ 7.8   Search of Premises Not Protected by the Fourth Amendment (Open Fields)

Not all property is protected by the Fourth Amendment, and searches of unprotected property will not be considered unreasonable. Other property is not protected by the Constitution, although it may be protected by trespass laws. The term "houses" has been interpreted very broadly to include any dwelling, whether it be a mansion, a small house, an apartment, a hotel room, or even a tent. The house is protected even if it is temporarily occupied, as in the case of a summer or weekend home. However, once a dwelling has been vacated, such as when a tenant checks out of a hotel, it is no longer protected.

The wording of the Constitution has been interpreted to also protect the *curtilage* surrounding the home.[121] Curtilage has been defined as the open space situated within a common enclosure and belonging to the dwelling house. It is that place that is habitually used for family purposes, including a yard, a garden, or even a field that is nearby and used in connection with the dwelling.

Although the provisions of the Constitution have been applied broadly, certain areas and effects are not protected. A common exception is the *open fields* exception. In one case, an area 50 to 100 yards from the defendant's residence was held to be an open field and not protected by the Constitution.[122] Other examples of unprotected areas are a cave, a shack located a mile from the premises, and a field approximately 75 feet behind a house.

The rationale for the open fields doctrine is that open fields do not provide the setting for those intimate activities that the Fourth Amendment is intended to shelter from government interference or surveillance; therefore, there is no societal interest in protecting the privacy of activities that occur in open fields.[123] An individual may not legitimately demand privacy for activities conducted outdoors in fields, except in the area immediately surrounding the home. If the area is intimately tied to the home itself, it is a part of the curtilage and placed under the home's "umbrella" of Fourth Amendment protection.[124]

In *Oliver v. United States*,[125] the Supreme Court more accurately defined what is included in the curtilage, and offered some guidelines in determining when the open fields exception applies. Here, officers drove past the Olivers' house to a locked gate with a no trespassing sign but with a footpath around one side of the gate. Officers

---

[121] *United States v. Rabinowitz*, 339 U.S. 56 (1950).
[122] *Hester v. United States*, 265 U.S. 57 (1924).
[123] *Mauk v. State*, 529 S.E.2d 197 (Ga. Ct. App. 2000).
[124] *State v. Ross*, 4 P.3d 130 (Wash. 2000).
[125] *Oliver v. United States*, 466 U.S. 170 (1984).

followed the footpath around the gate and found a marijuana field approximately one mile from the Olivers' house. In this case, the Court determined that the "open fields" doctrine applied and explained that the special sanction accorded to persons, houses, papers, and effects does not extend to open fields, such as existed in this case. The reason is because there is no, or at least a reduced, expectation of privacy in these places. Even the no trespassing sign did not increase the expectation of privacy because, as the Court reasoned, the public routinely ignores such signs.

Applying this reasoning, the Supreme Court in 1986 held that a 200-acre chemical plant operated by Dow Chemical Company was an open area of an industrial complex and comparable to an open field. In that case, aerial photography of the chemical company's industrial complex was not a "search" for Fourth Amendment purposes.[126]

Similarly, the Court ruled that a barn 60 yards from a house was not a part of the curtilage for Fourth Amendment purposes. In *United States v. Dunn*,[127] agents crossed several interior fences and approached the barn, located 50 yards from a fence surrounding the family residence. From this vantage point, and using a flashlight, they observed what appeared to be a drug laboratory and obtained a warrant to search the entire ranch. The U.S. Supreme Court upheld the search and provided some guidelines. The Court indicated that extent-of-curtilage questions should be resolved with particular reference to the following four factors: (1) the proximity of the area to the home; (2) whether the area is within an enclosure surrounding the home; (3) the nature and uses to which the area is put; and (4) the steps taken by the resident to protect the area from observation by others. Applying these four criteria, the Court decided that the barn in this case was not within the curtilage and therefore not within the protection of the Fourth Amendment.

The open fields exception to the warrant requirement results from a legitimate interpretation of the scope of the Fourth Amendment. However, it should be kept in mind that even though the evidence might be admissible as an exception, the officer who enters private property could be trespassing if entry is prohibited by a statute of that state.[128]

After a long debate by lower courts, the U.S. Supreme Court in 1988 concluded that the Fourth Amendment does not prohibit the warrantless search and seizure of garbage left for collection outside the curtilage of the home.[129] In this case, investigators obtained evidence of narcotics violations from garbage bags left on the curb in front

---

[126] *Dow Chemical Co. v. United States*, 476 U.S. 227 (1986).

[127] *United States v. Dunn*, 480 U.S. 294 (1987).

[128] *United States v. Pinter*, 984 F.2d 376 (10th Cir. 1993).

[129] *California v. Greenwood*, 486 U.S. 55 (1988). See also *United States v. Bowman*, 215 F.3d 951 (9th Cir. 2000), which held that a homeowner did not have a legitimate expectation of privacy in a garbage can left at curbside for a pick up, even though the garbage was sealed.

of the defendant's house. The Court first found that the curb was not part of the curtilage, and second, that residents of the house could have no reasonable expectation of privacy in the inculpatory items that they discarded. Applying this logic, a federal court of appeals also approved the warrantless search of trash in a plastic garbage bag that was on top of a garbage can.[130]

§ 7.9   Search by a Private Individual

Constitutional prohibitions against unreasonable searches and seizures operate only against official action. Where evidence is seized by a private person, therefore, even though it is seized unlawfully, it may be used in evidence. A private person who unlawfully enters the premises of another may be subject to a civil suit or even criminal action, but this does not contaminate the evidence he or she makes available to authorities. Such a search and seizure is outside the scope of constitutional protection. If a government agent is involved, however, either directly as a participant or indirectly as an encourager of the private citizen's actions, those actions are brought within the purview of the Fourth Amendment and the evidence would not be admissible. In analyzing whether the person conducting the search is acting as a government agent, two critical factors are to be considered: (1) the government's knowledge and acquiescence; and (2) the private party's intent in making the search.[131]

In interpreting this exception to the warrant rule, the Supreme Court agreed that employers of private freight carriers were not government agents and that seizure of a white powdery substance from damaged baggage did not constitute a search within the meaning of the Fourth Amendment.[132] In this case, private freight carrier employees found an opened package and suspected that it contained narcotics. The agents contacted Drug Enforcement Administration (DEA) agents, who made a field test of the powdery substance and determined it was contraband. The U.S. Supreme Court admitted the evidence even though DEA agents had advised earlier that the carrier employees should be on the alert for narcotics.

Action by school officials was held to be "state action," rendering the Fourth Amendment applicable, when marijuana was seized from a high school student.[133] The Court compromised, however, in establishing standards to be applied and agreed that although school officials were not private individuals but public officials for purposes of the Fourth Amendment, they would not be held to the same probable

---

[130]   *United States v. Comeaux*, 955 F.2d 586 (8th Cir. 1992).
[131]   *State v. Kopsa*, 887 P.2d 57 (Idaho 1994).
[132]   *United States v. Jacobsen*, 466 U.S. 109 (1984).
[133]   *New Jersey v. T.L.O.*, 469 U.S. 325 (1985).

cause standards as law enforcement agents. The legality of the search of the student simply depends on the reasonableness of the circumstances of the search. In defining this, the Court commented:

> Under ordinary circumstances, the search of a student by a school official will be justified at its inception when there are *reasonable grounds for suspecting* the student has violated or is violating either the law or rules of the school. (Emphasis added.)

An issue that is becoming of greater concern is whether the exclusionary rule should apply to private security personnel, private contract police, private investigators, and railroad police. If personnel who make such investigations and seize property are licensed by the state, there is a good chance that such licensed personnel will be considered "official" and the exclusionary rule will apply. For example, a housing authority police officer was acting in his official capacity, under color of state law, not as a private citizen, when he arrested a driver for a motor vehicle code violation.[134] However, a Federal Express agent was not a government agent when he opened a damaged package.[135]

In *Griffin v. Wisconsin*,[136] the U.S. Supreme Court held that probation and parole officers are government agents; however, this does not necessarily mean that a probation officer must follow the same probable cause requirements that apply to police officers. According to a majority of the members of the Supreme Court, supervision of probationers is a "special need" of the state that may justify departure from the usual warrant and probable cause requirements for police officers. This provision was extended to police officers in *Samson v. California*[137] in 2006. Based on the arguments in *Griffin* that parolees have a reduced expectation of privacy and may be required to agree to suspicionless searches as a condition of parole, the Court found that officers could conduct a suspicionless search of a parolee without violating his or her Fourth Amendment rights.

§ 7.10 Standing to Challenge the Search

The Court in *Mapp* indicated that the only door remaining open to evidence secured by an illegal search was closed. Yet evidence may be admitted even if the search violates the Fourth Amendment, if it is used against one who has no standing to challenge the search. As one court explained, "It is not enough for a defendant to

---

[134] *Commonwealth v. Brandt*, 691 A.2d 934 (Pa. 1997).

[135] *United States v. Barry*, 693 F.2d 912 (6th Cir. 1982).

[136] *Griffin v. Wisconsin*, 483 U.S. 868 (1987).

[137] *Samson v. California*, 547 U.S. 843 (2006).

show that someone's constitutional rights have been violated; he must show that *his* constitutional rights have been violated."[138] Even though the person whose rights have been violated may complain and in fact may bring a civil action against the officers, the party who has no substantial possessory interest in the property or legitimate presence on the premises cannot complain. It is also important to note that when a defendant challenges the admissibility of physical evidence or makes a motion to suppress, he or she bears the burden of establishing his or her standing to challenge the admissibility of such evidence.[139]

In *Jones v. United States*,[140] the U.S. Supreme Court ruled that the person aggrieved by an unlawful search and seizure must have been a victim of the search and seizure, but liberalized the "standing" requirements. The decision in *Jones* was that a person on the premises could challenge the search of the apartment because he or she was "legitimately on the premises."

In *Rakas v. Illinois*, the U.S. Supreme Court overturned *Jones* and rejected the "legitimately on the premises" standard, stating:

> We think that *Jones* on its facts merely stands for the unremarkable proposition that a person can have a legally sufficient interest in a place other than his own home so that the Fourth Amendment protects him from unreasonable government intrusions into that place.[141]

The Court determined that the fact that the defendants were charged with "possession" would not give them any standing to challenge the constitutionality of this search. The Court then included this comment:

> Today we hold that defendants charged with crimes of possession may only claim the benefits of the exclusionary rule if their own Fourth Amendment rights have been violated. The automatic standing rule of *Jones v. United States* . . . is therefore overruled.

The U.S. Supreme Court was again called upon to determine the extent of the "standing to challenge" rule in the 1990 case of *Minnesota v. Olson*.[142] In *Olson*, the suspect was located in the home of two women, where he was an overnight guest. Without seeking permission and with weapons drawn, police officers

---

[138] *Lopata v. State*, 307 A.2d 721 (Md. 1973).
[139] *People v. Berrios*, 270 N.E.2d 709 (N.Y. 1971).
[140] *Jones v. United States*, 362 U.S. 257 (1960).
[141] *Rakas v. Illinois*, 439 U.S. 128 (1978).
[142] *Minnesota v. Olson*, 495 U.S. 91 (1990).

entered the home, found Olson hiding in a closet, and arrested him. Shortly after the arrest, he made an inculpatory statement that the trial court refused to suppress. The Minnesota Supreme Court reversed the murder conviction, ruling that Olson had a sufficient interest in the women's home to challenge the legality of his warrantless arrest, that the arrest was illegal because there were no exigent circumstances to justify the warrantless entry, and that his statement was tainted and should have been suppressed. The Supreme Court agreed that Olson had a subjective expectation of privacy and that the search of the home violated the Fourth Amendment. The Court noted that:

> We need go no further than to conclude, as we do, that Olson's status as an overnight guest is alone enough to show that he had an expectation of privacy in the home that society is prepared to recognize as reasonable.

Among the factors relevant in deciding whether a defendant has standing to challenge an alleged unconstitutional search or seizure are: the defendant's ownership, possession, and/or control over the areas searched or items seized; the historical use of the property or item; the defendant's ability to regulate access; the totality of the circumstances surrounding the search; the existence or nonexistence of subjective anticipation of privacy; and the objective reasonableness of the defendant's expectations of privacy in light of the specific facts of the case.[143] In *United States v. Gumez*, the court held that defendants who fail to prove a sufficiently close connection to relevant places or objects searched have no standing to claim that they were searched or seized illegally. To make the "standing to challenge" exception more clear, some examples of other situations in which the defendant did not have standing to challenge are discussed in this section.

A property owner did not have a reasonable expectation of privacy in a house in one state while she lived in another state and allowed another individual to live in the house.[144] An individual who was merely present in the home did not have standing to challenge the search, and did not possess a legitimate expectation of privacy in a package addressed to someone else.[145] A state court also held that the defendants did not have standing to complain of a search made of a third party's car when the search took place immediately after the third party had left the defendants' home, as the

---

[143] *United States v. Gumez*, 16 F.3d 254 (8th Cir. 1994).

[144] *Bonds v. Cox*, 20 F.3d 697 (6th Cir. 1994).

[145] *United States v. Daniel*, 982 F.2d 146 (5th Cir. 1993). See, however, *State v. Brown*, 612 N.W.2d 104 (Iowa 2000), in which the court held that a legitimate expectation of privacy in an invited place is not so narrowly construed as to mean only a person's home; rather, even an overnight guest has a legitimate expectation of privacy in the host's home.

search was not directed toward the defendants.[146] Similar reasoning was followed in a case in which evidence of a crime was obtained from the home of the mother of one of the defendants, when the defendant was not living in the house and had no possessory rights in it.[147]

In *Palmer v. State*,[148] the court held that a thief has no standing to challenge the search of an automobile he stole. The court explained that no valuable social purpose could conceivably be served by extending the protection of the Fourth Amendment to a thief in a stolen automobile. Likewise, this doctrine is legitimately applied when the automobile is misappropriated, even if not actually stolen. For example, where a defendant obtained an automobile from a car rental corporation by misrepresentation, he committed "larceny by trick" and therefore did not have standing to object to the search of the automobile.[149] The U.S. Supreme Court has supported the "no standing" reasoning in holding that a passenger in an automobile cannot complain if an illegal search is made when he or she has neither a property nor a possessory interest in the automobile searched, nor an interest in the property seized.[150]

§ 7.11 Stop-and-Frisk

In previous chapters, the authority to detain where there is probable cause to arrest was discussed. The question that presents itself in relation to search and seizure is the extent to which an officer may seize weapons or evidence from a suspect when there is no probable cause to make an arrest, and therefore no justifiable search incident to the arrest. This relates to what has become known as "stop-and-frisk."

Until *Terry v. Ohio*[151] in 1968, there was considerable doubt as to whether a police officer could stop suspicious persons on the street, ask them questions, and then frisk them for weapons. At least some of the doubt was removed in the *Terry* case. In *Terry*, a police officer stopped a suspect on a downtown street after he observed the suspect and two other men "casing" a jewelry store. Without putting the suspects under arrest, the police officer patted down their outside clothing for weapons and later removed a pistol from Terry's overcoat pocket.

Admitting that there was no probable cause to make an arrest, the Supreme Court was faced with two questions. First: did the officer have the authority to detain; and second, did the officer have the authority to frisk the detained suspects for weapons?

---

[146] *State v. Valdez*, 562 N.W.2d 64 (Neb. Ct. App. 1997).
[147] *United States v. Salvucci*, 448 U.S. 83 (1980).
[148] *Palmer v. State*, 286 A.2d 572 (Md. 1972). See cases cited therein.
[149] *Shope v. State*, 307 A.2d 730 (Md. 1973).
[150] *Rakas v. Illinois*, 439 U.S. 128 (1978).
[151] *Terry v. Ohio*, 392 U.S. 1 (1968).

The Court was careful to distinguish this "stop-and-frisk" from a search incident to a lawful arrest, explaining:

> The sole justification for the search in the present situation is the protection of the police officer and others nearby, and must therefore be confined in scope to an intrusion reasonably designed to discover guns, knives, clubs, or other hidden instruments for the assault of the police officer.

Two findings are important in this case. First, officers do not need probable cause to make a *Terry* stop-and-frisk. All that is needed is reasonable suspicion.[152] Second, the frisk authorized in this detention situation is only for the protection of the officer and is limited to patting down, rather than a full-scale search. For example, this "frisk" authorization did not extend to an officer who, while patting down a suspect, found a small package of narcotics.[153] The Court explained that, while there is a self-protective search for weapons, the officer must be able to point to particular facts from which he or she reasonably inferred that the individual was armed and dangerous.

Terry was based on an officer's direct observation and experience to justify the stop-and-frisk. There are times, however, when the officer may not have personal knowledge, and may be informed of weapons, and such by another person. In *Adams v. Williams*,[154] an officer was told by an informant with whom the officer was familiar that Adams, who was in a nearby vehicle, was in possession of illegal drugs and had a pistol in the waistband of his pants. The officer went to the car and asked Adams to open the car door. When Adams rolled down the window instead, the officer reached inside the car and removed the pistol from the location where the informant said it would be. Adams was arrested for unlawful possession of a weapon; and a search incident to the arrest revealed more weapons and illegal drugs. The Supreme Court ruled that an officer does not have to have direct observation to initiate a stop-and-frisk. Because reasonable suspicion is all that is required, officers may combine information from another person along with their own observation to make a stop-and-frisk for weapons.

This line of reasoning was extended further in *United States v. Hensley*,[155] when officers stopped Hensley because he was the subject of a wanted poster for armed robbery. The Supreme Court held that the wanted poster was sufficient for a brief, *Terry*-type stop to further investigate the officers' suspicions. The Court stopped short, however, of ruling that reasonable suspicion could be based on an anonymous tip.

---

[152] See *Alabama v. White*, 496 U.S. 325 (1990).
[153] *Sibron v. New York*, 392 U.S. 40 (1968).
[154] *Adams v. Williams*, 407 U.S. 143 (1972).
[155] *United States v. Hensley*, 469 U.S. 221 (1985).

In *Florida v. J.L.*,[156] officers responded to a tip that a young, black male was standing at a particular bus stop wearing a plaid shirt and carrying a gun. When officers observed the person matching the description at that bus stop, they frisked J.L. and found a pistol. The Supreme Court held here that an anonymous tip, without more from the officers to test the validity of the information, is not sufficient to constitute reasonable suspicion.

Like many other lines of Fourth Amendment cases, the ultimate legal determination of what constitutes reasonable suspicion in stop-and-frisk situations is "totality of the circumstances."[157] What represents "totality of the circumstances" in stop-and-frisk situations is not always apparent, however, and has to be decided (by both officers and the courts) on a case-by-case basis.

Officers must be aware of the difference between a full search incident to a lawful arrest and a "frisk for weapons" predicated on a frisk after a detention. As was pointed out in *Chimel*, when a search is made incident to a lawful arrest, the person of the arrestee and the immediate area may be searched for weapons and evidence that may be destroyed or concealed; however, when the officer does not have an arrest warrant or sufficient reasonable grounds for an arrest, but does have sufficient evidence to detain as provided in the *Terry* rule, he or she may pat down the outer clothing only for *weapons* or *means of escape*. If the officer discovers evidence or obtains information that will give him or her probable cause or reasonable grounds to arrest, the officer may place the suspect under arrest and make a full-scale search.

The stop-and-frisk rule has resulted in many seizures of evidence and hundreds of cases challenging the seizures. A review of the cases makes it clear that some seizures are justified if within the scope of the *Terry* frisk; however, a lawful detention for questioning does not necessarily give the officers the authority to conduct a pat-down search for weapons.[158] The courts have increasingly demanded that the requirement be strictly interpreted. For example, in *State v. Patterson*, the court held that the officer's belief that his safety or that of others was in danger, justifying a frisk after a stop for questioning was not reasonable unless the officer was able to point to particular facts from which he reasonably inferred that the individual was armed and dangerous. An unsupported statement by the officer that he feared for another officer's safety, on its own, was insufficient to justify a search for weapons on Patterson, who was stopped on suspicion of resisting an officer. The issue here was that the officer did not testify as to any facts from which he could have based a reasonable suspicion that Patterson, while being interviewed with at least two federal agents present, either presented a danger or possessed a weapon.

---

[156] *Florida v. J.L.*, 529 U.S. 266 (1999).
[157] *United States v. Arvizu*, 534 U.S. 266 (2001).
[158] *State v. Patterson*, 758 So. 2d 955 (La. 2000).

In a Nebraska case, the court affirmed that during a lawful *Terry* stop, officers are entitled, for the protection of themselves and others in the area, to conduct a carefully limited search of the outer clothing of the person to discover weapons that might be used to assault the officer, but a "second pass" by police officers to palpate the subject's clothing for drugs is improper in the context of a *Terry* stop.[159]

In 1993, the U.S. Supreme Court clarified and expanded the *Terry* rule. In *Minnesota v. Dickerson*,[160] the Court held:

> In this case, we consider whether the Fourth Amendment permits the seizure of contraband detected through a police officer's sense of *touch* during a protective pat down search. (Emphasis added.)

The facts of this case indicate that the officer, upon observing Dickerson's seemingly evasive actions when approached by the police officer and the fact that he had just left a building known to be a location for cocaine trafficking, decided to investigate further and ordered the suspect to submit to a pat-down search. The search revealed no weapons, but the officer who conducted the search testified that he felt a small lump in the suspect's jacket and, upon examining it with his fingers, believed it to be a lump of crack cocaine. The officer then reached into the pocket and retrieved a small bag of cocaine.

The Supreme Court decided that the seizure of the cocaine was an unconstitutional seizure; explaining that under the Minnesota court's interpretation of the record, the officer never thought the lump was a weapon, and did not immediately recognize it as cocaine. Rather, he determined that it was contraband only after he squeezed, slid, and otherwise manipulated the pocket's contents. Even though *Terry* entitled him to place his hand on the respondent's jacket and to feel the lump in the pocket, his continued exploration of the pocket after he concluded that it contained no weapon was unrelated to the justification for the search under *Terry*. Because the additional search was unconstitutional, the Court decided that the seizure of the cocaine that followed was, likewise, unconstitutional.

Although the decision in *Dickerson* permitted a seizure of contraband detected through a police officer's sense of touch (plain touch), the detection must be made possible as a result of a protective pat-down search within the lawful bounds marked by *Terry*. The Court, in its decision, added another caveat, stating that:

> Regardless of whether the officer detects the contraband by sight or by touch, however, the Fourth Amendment requirement that the officer have probable cause to believe that the item was contraband before seizing it ensures against excessively speculative seizure.

---

[159] *State v. Gutierrez*, 611 N.W.2d 853 (Neb. Ct. App. 2000).
[160] *Minnesota v. Dickerson*, 508 U.S. 366 (1993).

As was inevitable, the lower courts have been called upon to further interpret the extent of seizures like these under the *Terry* rule. One question left unanswered by *Terry* was whether an article that did not feel like a knife or club could be a dangerous weapon and therefore subject to seizure. A second question was whether the officer, while in the process of seizing the weapon, could legally seize other articles that were not considered dangerous to the officer.

According to the California Supreme Court, an officer may pat down a suspect for atypical weapons if the officer can articulate facts that reasonably support a suspicion that the particular suspect is armed with a weapon such as a "sap."[161] This would indicate that if the officer can articulate facts that reasonably lead him or her to believe the person is carrying razor blades, brass knuckles, or other atypical weapons peculiar to the area, he or she can reasonably pat down the suspect and seize such weapons.

As to the authority of the officer to seize evidence other than weapons obtained while checking the suspect in a stop-and-frisk situation, it is apparent that the seizure without a warrant rule applies. If the officer, to protect him- or herself, reaches into a suspect's pocket to obtain a weapon, but in addition to, or instead of, a weapon, finds other contraband, the use of such contraband as evidence is legitimate.[162] For example, the Fourth Circuit Court of Appeals approved the seizure of cocaine that came into the view of an officer after he had detained a suspect and checked a zipper bag for weapons.[163] The Fourth Circuit Court of Appeals held that the seizure of narcotics did not depend for its validity upon probable cause for arrest, but was justified by the guidelines for protective searches established by *Terry v. Ohio*.

In *Terry*, the Court approved the frisk of a pedestrian. Following that case, courts were asked to consider whether a *Terry*-type frisk could be made of the occupants of a car following the issuance of a traffic citation. In *Pennsylvania v. Mimms*,[164] police officers stopped a vehicle with an expired license plate for the purpose of issuing a traffic summons. When the driver stepped out of the car, the officer noticed a large bulge under the motorist's jacket and, fearing that the bulge might be a weapon, frisked the motorist and discovered a loaded .38 caliber revolver. The Supreme Court explained that such a frisk is not unreasonable, commenting:

> We think it too plain for argument that the state's proffered justification—the safety of the officer—is both legitimate and weighty. Certainly it would be unreasonable to require that police officers take unnecessary risks in the performance of their duties.

---

[161] *People v. Collins*, 463 P.2d 403 (Cal. 1970).
[162] *People v. Woods*, 86 Cal. Rptr. 264 (1970).
[163] *United States v. Poms*, 484 F.2d 919 (4th Cir. 1974).
[164] *Pennsylvania v. Mimms*, 434 U.S. 106 (1977).

Noting that roadside encounters between police and suspects are especially hazardous, in determining whether an officer's pat-down search of a defendant was objectively reasonable, a Texas court held that an officer had an objectively reasonable concern for his safety, and thus was constitutionally justified in patting down a defendant for weapons where the officer stopped the defendant pursuant to an articulable suspicion that he was trafficking in cocaine, and weapons and violence were frequently associated with drug transactions.[165]

Mimms and other cases dealt with the authority of officers to make a *Terry* stop-and-frisk of the driver of a vehicle. The Supreme Court has also addressed whether this applies to passengers. In several cases, the Court has ruled that all passengers are subject to a *Terry* pat-down within the guidelines of *Terry* stops. In *Maryland v. Wilson*,[166] the Supreme Court ruled that an officer may order the passengers out of a vehicle subjected to a traffic stop. In *Brendlin v. California*,[167] the Court ruled that passengers are seized during a traffic stop. This allowed the Supreme Court to determine whether passengers could be subjected to a *Terry* pat-down during a traffic stop.[168] In this case, the Court ruled "that a lawful roadside stop begins when a vehicle is pulled over for investigation of a traffic violation." They further argued that all occupants are seized for the duration of the stop (typically, when police inform the driver and passengers they are free to leave). As such, officers may order the driver and passengers out of the vehicle and subject them to a *Terry* pat-down if justified by the circumstances. The Court also ruled in this case that "[a]n officer's inquiries into matters unrelated to the justification for the traffic stop do not convert the encounter into something other than a lawful seizure, so long as the inquiries do not measurably extend the stop's duration." This issue is further addressed in the next paragraph.

Another issue related to *Terry* is how long an officer may hold the occupants of a vehicle and what authorizes an officer to change the investigation from the purpose of the initial stop. In *United States v. Brigham*,[169] an officer stopped a car Brigham was driving for following too closely. The officer asked for Brigham's driver's license and vehicle registration. The vehicle was rented to a 50-year-old woman from Memphis, but Brigham's driver's license was from Arkansas. The officer questioned Brigham about his purpose, who owned the car, and other questions in an attempt to determine if he was in legal possession of the vehicle. When Brigham's story did not make sense to the officer, he also questioned other passengers in the vehicle. After making checks of the identification of the occupants, the officer issued a warning and told Brigham

---

[165] *Carmouche v. State*, 10 S.W.3d 323 (Tex. 2000).
[166] *Maryland v. Wilson*, 519 U.S. 408 (1997).
[167] *Brendlin v. California*, 551 U.S. 1 (2007).
[168] *Arizona v. Johnson*, 555 U.S. 323 (2009).
[169] *United States v. Brigham*, 382 F.3d 500 (2004).

he was free to go. The officer then commented about his duty to control drugs and weapons on the highway and asked if Brigham possessed anything illegal. Brigham denied any illegal items and consented to a search. During the search, the officer found illegal narcotics. Brigham challenged the stop, saying the officer exceeded his authority under *Terry*. The court in this case held that there were two issues important to *Terry* that were related to traffic stops: the extent to which the officer may make inquiry as to the occupants, and how much the officer may deviate from the purpose of the initial stop. The court held that the officer did not exceed his authority in continuing to ask questions of Brigham and others because their stories continued to raise questions in the officer's mind. Further, the officer was within the guidelines of *Terry* to ask for consent to search the vehicle for drugs. The court in this case stated "we reject any notion that a police officer's questioning, even on a subject unrelated to the purpose of a routine traffic stop, is itself a Fourth Amendment violation."

The next issue considered by the Supreme Court was whether the passenger compartment of a car may be frisked under the *Terry* doctrine when there is no probable cause to make a search incident to the lawful arrest. The Court approved the seizure of weapons from the passenger compartment of an automobile when the driver of the car walked toward the car after a police officer arrived at the scene.[170] Shining his flashlight into the car, the officer saw something under the armrest and, upon lifting the armrest, saw an open pouch that contained what appeared to be marijuana. The Court agreed that the protective search of the passenger compartment was reasonable under the principle articulated in *Terry*.

From this and other cases, it can be concluded that, if an officer stops a car to issue a traffic citation, he or she may, for his or her own protection, order the driver and any passengers to step out of the car, and if the facts available justify a person of reasonable caution to conclude that the person is armed or poses a serious and present danger to the safety of the officer, a pat-down or frisk for weapons is justified. Also, if the officer can articulate reasons for believing a present danger exists, he or she may search the passenger compartment of the car for weapons. If, during the protective search of the passenger compartment for weapons, the officer comes upon contraband or illegally possessed evidence, he or she may seize that evidence under the plain view principle.

The final issue related to *Terry*, which has still not been completely resolved, is whether a person is compelled to provide identification to officers and whether he or she can be arrested and prosecuted for failing to provide that identification. This issue is typically referred to as "stop and identify." One of the first cases to address this issue was *Brown v. Texas*.[171] In this case, the Court ruled that a stop and identify must

---

170 *Michigan v. Long*, 463 U.S. 1032 (1983).
171 *Brown v. Texas*, 443 U.S. 47 (1979).

be ". . . based on specific, objective facts establishing reasonable suspicion to believe the suspect was involved in criminal activity" (using the wording from *Terry*). Later, the Court also overturned a statute as too vague that required a suspect to provide "credible and reliable" identification when asked by an officer for identity.[172] The Court held that the statute provided no standard for what a person must do to provide "credible and reliable" identification.

At least for the purposes of a *Terry* stop, the Court resolved the issue of stop and identify in *Hiibel v. Sixth Judicial District Court of Nevada*.[173] In this case, officers responded to a domestic disturbance call. When the officer arrived at the scene, he asked Hiibel for identification. Hiibel refused. Over the course of several minutes, the officer asked Hiibel a total of 11 times for his name. Finally, the officer arrested Hiibel pursuant to a Nevada law requiring individuals to disclose their name when asked by an officer who has reasonable suspicion of criminal activity. The U.S. Supreme Court took this case, stating "[a]lthough it is well established that an officer may ask a suspect to identify himself during a *Terry* stop, it has been an open question whether the suspect can be arrested and prosecuted for failure to answer" (internal citations omitted). The Court ruled that, if the requirements of *Terry* are met to make an initial stop, state law may require the person to disclose his or her name or face arrest and prosecution. The Court based this ruling solely on *Terry* (Fourth Amendment) rather than Fifth Amendment testimonial grounds, because there was no danger in this case of Hiibel incriminating himself by providing his name. The Court left open, however, the possibility of a Fifth Amendment claim should "a case arise where there is a substantial allegation that furnishing identity at the time of a stop would have given the police a link in the chain of events needed to convict the individual . . ."

The Supreme Court's approval of the *Terry* stop-and-frisk has been very helpful to police officers in carrying out their responsibilities. However, the officer must be cautious not to overstep the line and use the procedure as a subterfuge for making an illegal search.

§ 7.12 Seizure of Verbal Evidence via Recorders or Microphones: Electronic Searches

In *On Lee v. United States*,[174] an undercover federal narcotics agent, wearing a small microphone and an antenna concealed in his overcoat, entered the laundry of an old acquaintance. Unknown to the suspect, a second narcotics agent was stationed

---

[172] *Kolender v. Lawson*, 461 U.S. 352 (1983).
[173] *Hiibel v. Sixth Judicial District Court of Nevada*, 542 U.S. 177 (2004).
[174] *On Lee v. United States*, 343 U.S. 747 (1952).

outside with a radio receiver tuned in on that conversation. At the trial, the second agent was permitted to testify as to matters he heard. This procedure was challenged on the ground that it was an illegal search and seizure in violation of the Fourth Amendment. Two questions were presented in this situation: (1) whether the seizure of verbal evidence by way of a microphone or a recorder comes within the purview of the Fourth Amendment; and (2) if words as well as tangible evidence are protected by the Fourth Amendment, whether the conduct of the officer violated established search and seizure standards. The Court held in this case that there is no violation of the Fourth Amendment if one party to a conversation consents to police listening to the conversation.[175] The Court has also allowed such conversations to be recorded by officers for later use at trial, explaining:

> For constitutional purposes, no different result is required if the agent, instead of immediately reporting and transcribing his conversations with the defendant, either (1) simultaneously records them with electronic equipment which he is carrying on his person or (2) carries radio equipment which simultaneously transmits the conversations either to recording equipment located elsewhere or to the other agents monitoring the transmitting frequency.[176]

Although federal and state laws generally have an exception that allows interception of communications if one party consents, the consent must be voluntary. It is involuntary when it is coerced by either explicit or implicit means or by an implied threat or covert force.[177] Even if there is no constitutional objection to the use of electronic surveillance equipment when one party consents, and there is no objection to this under federal law, a state statute or constitutional provision may prohibit this use.[178] It is therefore essential that state wiretapping and eavesdropping laws be consulted and interpreted before such devices or techniques are used.

It is clear that officers may electronically eavesdrop when one of the parties agrees to the search. This is not the case, however, when police listen to conversations where none of the parties consents to monitoring. A series of cases decided by the Supreme Court leaves no doubt that the Court considers eavesdropping by electronic devices, or "bugging," as a search regulated by the Fourth Amendment.[179] Therefore, all of the Amendment's safeguards that apply to the seizure of tangible goods also apply to the

---

[175] See also *Lopez v. United States*, 373 U.S. 427 (1963); *Osborn v. United States*, 385 U.S. 323, (1966); and *United States v. Caceres*, 440 U.S. 741 (1979).

[176] *United States v. White*, 401 U.S. 745 (1971).

[177] *United States v. Antoon*, 933 F.2d 200 (3d Cir. 1991).

[178] *People v. Beavers*, 227 N.W.2d 511 (Mich. 1975). Electronic surveillance where the officer is not present, or where neither party has consented to the surveillance, is regulated by federal law at 18 U.S.C. §§ 2510-2520.

[179] *Katz v. United States*, 389 U.S. 347 (1967); *Berger v. New York*, 388 U.S. 41 (1967).

"seizure" of verbal evidence.[180] The Court noted that, in the case of electronic seizures, the need to particularly describe the evidence sought is especially necessary due to the expectation of privacy. Specifically, the Court held in *Berger* that the following requirements must be met for electronic eavesdropping:

1. There must be a showing of probable cause to believe that a specific crime has been or is being committed;
2. A warrant must be obtained, which must describe with particularity the conversations to be overheard;
3. The wiretap must be for a limited period, although extensions may be obtained by an adequate showing of necessity;
4. The suspects whose conversations are to be overheard must be named in the judicial order;
5. A return must be made to the court, showing what conversations were intercepted; and
6. The wiretapping must terminate when the desired information has been obtained.

These six requirements were, in effect, enacted into law by Title III of the Omnibus Crime Control and Safe Streets Act of 1968, along with many other provisions. Some of these requirements have been relaxed somewhat by legislation following the terrorist attacks of September 11, 2001, but the general requirements have not lessened.

In *Katz v. United States*, the Court dealt with the issue of using electronic devices to overhear telephone conversations. In this case, police placed a listening device on the outside of a public telephone booth known to be used by Katz. The police argued that because they did not intrude on a private place (a public telephone booth where anyone who was standing nearby could hear the conversation), there was no expectation of privacy. The Court disagreed, and held that any form of electronic surveillance constitutes a search, and therefore must meet the requirements of the Fourth Amendment. This provision was lessened somewhat in *United States v. Willoughby*.[181] In this case, officers recorded telephone conversations between a person inside a correctional institution and a party on the outside. The Court held that one of the parties to the communication gave prior consent because the institution advised inmates that their telephone calls would be monitored and such notice was prominently posted. Therefore, the inmate's use of the telephone constituted implied consent.[182]

---

[180] See *United States v. Jackson*, 213 F.3d 1269 (10th Cir. 2000), which held that the use of a silent video surveillance must comply with the Fourth Amendment, but the use of a silent video surveillance camera installed without a warrant on telephone poles outside the defendant's residence did not violate the Fourth Amendment because the cameras were incapable of viewing inside the residence.

[181] *United States v. Willoughby*, 860 F.2d 15 (2d Cir. 1988).

[182] See *United States v. Amen*, 831 F.2d 373 (2d Cir. 1987).

Excluded from the statutory coverage are instances in which the listening is accomplished without the aid of any sound-amplifying or "bugging" apparatus. Therefore, if a government agent is standing a few feet from the defendant while the defendant is placing a call at a public telephone, and, without the aid of any listening device, overhears sports wagering information, there is no Fourth Amendment violation.[183]

§ 7.13 Airport Searches

Procedures have been established to examine the bags of airline passengers. The practice has been challenged as violating the Fourth Amendment. In *United States v. Edwards*,[184] a Deputy United States Marshal examined a beach bag as Edwards was preparing to board a flight. During the investigation, he found a total of 1,664 glassine envelopes, each containing a white powder that was later determined to be heroin. The court indicated that to brand such a search as unreasonable would go far beyond any fair interpretation of the Fourth Amendment. After reviewing other cases, the *Edwards* court summarized:

> Although no one could reconcile all of the views expressed in the opinion of the various circuits or, indeed, of this circuit alone, a consensus does seem to be emerging that an airport search is not to be condemned as violating the Fourth Amendment simply because it does not precisely fit into one of the previously recognized categories for dispensing with a search warrant, but only if the search is "unreasonable" on the facts.

At present, the search of passengers and luggage at airports has been held to be reasonable under the Constitution. However, if government agents are found to be abusing their authority and using an airport search, not for the purpose intended, but as a general means for enforcing the criminal laws, then evidence seized may be inadmissible unless the procedure complies with the general rules concerning searches.

§ 7.14 Search of Pervasively Regulated Businesses

A somewhat different issue is whether regulated businesses such as those licensed to sell alcoholic beverages or those licensed under the Gun Control Act to sell firearms have the same constitutional protections as others. Depending upon the statutes

---

[183] *United States v. McLeod*, 493 F.2d 1186 (7th Cir. 1974).
[184] *United States v. Edwards*, 498 F.2d 496 (2d Cir. 1974).

and ordinances, these businesses may not have the same protections. For example, in *United States v. Biswell*,[185] a Treasury agent, acting under the authority of the Gun Control Act of 1968, requested entry into a locked gun storeroom and was admitted after showing the owner the provisions of the statute. There he found and seized illegally possessed weapons. The Gun Control Act authorizes entry into the premises during business hours for purposes of inspecting or examining records and documents required for firearms or ammunition stored by the dealer at such premises. The Supreme Court approved the seizure of illegally possessed firearms, explaining that close scrutiny of trafficking in firearms is justified and that this limited threat to the dealer's expectation of privacy is reasonable. The Court explained:

> When a dealer chooses to engage in this type of pervasively regulated business and to accept a federal license, he does so with the knowledge that his business records, firearms, and ammunition will be subject to effective inspection.

Explaining the difference between the search of a home and the warrantless inspection of business premises, a federal court established some guidelines for the inspection of a pervasively regulated industry. The court commented that a warrantless inspection of a business in a pervasively regulated industry will be considered reasonable if: (1) the regulatory presence is so comprehensive and defined that the business owner cannot help but be aware that his or her commercial property will be subject to periodic inspections undertaken for specific purposes, such that the governmental regulation of the industry is pervasive; (2) there is a substantial governmental interest that informs a regulatory scheme pursuant to which inspection is made; (3) warrantless inspections are necessary to further the regulatory scheme; and (4) the statute's inspection program performs the two basic functions of a warrant in that it advises the owner of the premises that the search is being conducted pursuant to the law and within properly defined scope, and it limits discretion of inspecting officers.[186]

§ 7.15   Summary

Although there are no provisions in the Fourth Amendment that authorize a search without a warrant, courts have held that it was not the intent of the framers of the Constitution to condemn all warrantless searches. However, if a search cannot be made under a warrant or one of the recognized exceptions, it is very likely that the evidence seized will be inadmissible.

---

[185] *United States v. Biswell*, 406 U.S. 311 (1972).
[186] *Lesser v. Espy*, 34 F.3d 1301 (7th Cir. 1994). See comments in *Whren v. United States*, 517 U.S. 806 (1996).

The courts authorize a search without a warrant when it is made incident to a lawful arrest. For such a search to be legal and the evidence admissible, the arrest must be lawful and the search must be made contemporaneously with the arrest. If someone is lawfully arrested, his or her person may be searched and articles on his or her person seized, even though the articles are unconnected with the crime. Also, the search may extend to the area within his or her reach for weapons or evidence that might be destroyed or concealed.

A person may waive the rights that are guaranteed by the Fourth Amendment if done so voluntarily and freely. There are some dangers, however, in relying on a consent search. First, the search is limited to the exact words or meaning of the consent. Second, the consent may be withdrawn at any time. Third, the person giving consent must have the legal capacity to do so.

The third warrantless search authorized by the courts is the search of movable vehicles and objects. In approving this exception, the courts have recognized that it is often impossible to obtain timely warrants for objects that may be moved from the jurisdiction. In such a case, the search may nevertheless be made if there is probable cause that would have justified the issuance of a search warrant and if the vehicle or article is moving or about to be moved.

Because the Constitution only protects against *unreasonable* searches and seizures, a seizure of articles does not violate the Constitution where there is no search. For the plain view exception to apply, the officer must be lawfully present on the premises when he or she views the object and must have probable cause to believe that the article is contraband, illegally possessed, or otherwise subject to seizure.

The general rule is that an officer who is legitimately conducting an inventory search of a lawfully impounded car may seize evidence coming within his or her possession as a result of such inventory. However, recent Supreme Court decisions have indicated that standardized criteria or an established routine must regulate the opening of containers found during inventory searches. Also, if the inventory is turned into a purposeful and general means of discovering evidence of crime rather than making an inventory, the evidence will be inadmissible. As some states have limited the scope of the inventory search, state law must be studied to determine whether the inventory search is permitted in a particular state.

Because the constitutional prohibitions operate only against official action, evidence seized by a private person without the knowledge or acquiescence of an official may be used in evidence even if the search would have been illegal otherwise. Also, the Fourth Amendment relates only to persons, houses, papers, and effects. Other property is not protected by the Constitution. Thus, the search of unprotected property, such as open fields, does not violate the Fourth Amendment, and the evidence will probably be admissible.

Only a person whose rights are violated may challenge the illegal search. The defendant who has no proprietary or possessory interest in the premises and is not on the premises may not challenge the search.

Even though the officer sometimes has no probable cause to make an arrest, he or she may have the authority to stop and frisk a suspect. Where the sole justification for the frisk is to protect the officer and others nearby, the officer may pat down the outer clothing and seize guns, knives, clubs, or other hidden instruments that might be used to assault the police officer. This evidence may be used in court. There is some legal justification for seizing evidence other than weapons when this other evidence comes within the view or possession of the officer while he or she is legitimately searching for or seizing weapons.

Although words as well as tangible evidence are protected by the Fourth Amendment, there is no federal constitutional objection to the electronic recording or transmitting of conversations with others if one party to the conversation is aware of and agrees to the recording procedure. The rationale is that a person who voluntarily converses with another assumes the risk that the other will report or later transcribe the conversation (this is, of course, unless the person has requested an attorney—see *Edwards*, above). For constitutional purposes, there is no different result if the law enforcement officer, instead of immediately reporting and transcribing the conversation with the defendant, records or transmits the conversation by means of electronic equipment.

In balancing the need to search passengers boarding an airplane and their luggage against the need to protect individual rights, airport searches have been upheld. The courts have generally agreed that the government has a compelling interest in dispensing with the search warrant requirement in making airport searches when the risk is to thousands of human lives and millions of dollars in property damage.

The laws related to search and seizure are complicated, and sometimes difficult to interpret. That is why this area of police work is one of the most litigated of all legal issues. There are many issues not addressed in this chapter simply because the material would fill a book much larger than this one to give adequate coverage of all cases. It is also important to remember that there is often a close link between searching and the questioning of suspects (one often leads to the other). Questioning suspects is the topic of the next chapter.

Chapter 8
Questioning Suspects

In dealing with statements obtained through interrogation, we do not purport to find all confessions inadmissible. Confessions remain a proper element in law enforcement. Any statement given freely and voluntarily without any compelling influence is, of course, admissible in evidence.

Miranda v. Arizona, 384 U.S. 436 (1966)

§ 8.1   General Considerations

Every police officer must be familiar with the rules relating to questioning suspects. Improper questioning may not only contaminate the statements obtained, but also the evidence obtained as a result of the improper questioning. This does not mean, however, that all questioning is improper. The U.S. Supreme Court, in

Miranda v. Arizona,[1] pointed out that its decision was not intended to hamper the traditional function of police officers in investigating crime. The Court specifically approved the questioning of persons not under restraint, general on-the-scene questioning as to facts surrounding a crime, and other general questioning of citizens in the fact-finding process. They argued that the use of questions in ferreting out the guilty is a proper and necessary tool in protecting society.[2]

What the Court has condemned and continues to condemn is the improper use of questioning, or using questioning as a substitute for a thorough investigation. An officer who is familiar with the rules relating to questioning can determine when it is preferable to question a suspect and when it is advisable to remain silent. Questioning is only one technique that can be used to solve a crime, and should be used only when that technique has been determined to be preferable after considering other investigative techniques.

Before a confession may be admissible as evidence for most purposes, it must pass at least five tests. First, a confession must be given freely and voluntarily. Second, with some exceptions, a confession will not be admitted into court if the *Miranda* warnings are not given. Third, a confession is not admissible if it is tainted by an illegal arrest or an illegal search. Fourth, a confession may be inadmissible if there is a failure to provide the suspect with counsel. Finally, a confession must meet the requirements established by the U.S. Supreme Court in the *McNabb* and *Mallory*[3] cases, or the *delay in arraignment* requirements. Additionally, independent corroborative evidence must be introduced. These tests and hurdles are discussed in the following sections.

A sign of the current criminal justice situation in the United States is the number of people from foreign countries who come into contact with the police. These people must be subjected to searches and seizures, and generally enjoy the same constitutional protections as U.S. citizens. There are also some additional protections offered to foreign nationals. One of these is a treaty signed by the United States stating that foreign nationals have a right to have their country's consulate notified of their detention.[4] These rights come into play in relation to police interrogation in the case of *Sanchez-Llamas v. Oregon*.[5] In this case (actually two cases combined at the U.S. Supreme Court), two defendants were arrested and interrogated. Both were read their

---

1   *Miranda v. Arizona*, 384 U.S. 436 (1966).

2   Out-of-court confessions and admissions are admitted, as an exception to the hearsay rule, for the limited purpose of impeaching the credibility of a testifying defendant. *People v. Crisset*, 681 N.E.2d 1010 (Ill. 1997).

3   *McNabb v. United States*, 318 U.S. 332 (1943); *Mallory v. United States*, 354 U.S. 449 (1957).

4   Article 36 of the Vienna Convention on Consular Relations, Apr 24, 1963.

5   *Sanchez-Llamas v. Oregon*, 548 U.S. 331 (2006).

At the Phoenix Police Museum in Phoenix, Arizona, retired police captain Carroll Cooley demonstrates how Ernesto Miranda was fingerprinted in the 1960s. Cooley was the arresting officer featured in *Miranda v. Arizona*, the landmark self-incrimination case that resulted in the mandatory reading of *Miranda* warnings by law enforcement when arresting a suspect. (*AP Photo/Matt York*)

Miranda warnings, but were not informed of their Article 36 rights. Both sought suppression of the statements made following waiver of their *Miranda* rights. The Supreme Court in these cases held that there is nothing in Article 36 that invokes the exclusionary rule for violation of its provisions. Based on this, the Court ruled that as long as the accused had his or her *Miranda* warnings read and there was nothing else unlawful about their arrest, the confessions would be admissible.

§ 8.2   The Free and Voluntary Rule

The traditional test used to determine the admissibility of a confession is known as the *free and voluntary* rule. Although the free and voluntary rule has been in effect throughout the history of the United States, the scope of the rule has been broadened in recent years. This rule was developed in England, and was applied in the courts of the United States at the time of the adoption of the Constitution. The rule states that the confession of a person accused of crime is admissible in evidence against the accused only if it was freely and voluntarily made; that is, made without duress, fear, or compulsion in its inducement and with the suspect's full knowledge of the nature and consequences of the confession.[6]

Although the free and voluntary rule has been followed by state and federal courts since the adoption of the U.S. Constitution, efforts to explain the rationale for the rule and to frame a consistent definition continue today. The historic justification for the rule was that only voluntary confessions could be relied upon as trustworthy.

Traditionally, some of the factors courts considered relevant in determining whether a confession was voluntary included the use of force, making threats or promises, and psychological coercion. If force is used to obtain a confession, the confession will, obviously, be inadmissible.[7] Not only will physical force make a confession inadmissible, but threats of bodily harm or other threats that cause a suspect to make statements against his or her will may also make a confession inadmissible.[8] One court noted that, in assessing the circumstances surrounding the taking of a confession, the court must consider any promises or misrepresentations made by the interrogating officers.[9] In discussing psychological coercion, another court cautioned that both physical and psychological pressure can lead to an involuntary confession.[10]

The investigator who makes false promises while interviewing a suspect treads on dangerous ground. If a police officer makes a false promise that misleads the suspect, and the suspect gives a confession because of that false promise, that confession has not been voluntarily, knowingly, and intelligently made.[11] In *Pyles v. State*, the court held that a police officer's statement to a murder suspect, who was a prior acquaintance of the officer, that the officer would "do everything in the world that he could for this suspect," was a false promise that resulted in the involuntary confession, and made the confession inadmissible. The court explained that this false promise was made when the suspect was emotional and tired from a long interrogation and while the suspect, who had a prior relationship with the officer, held the officer's hand and wept. Even though law enforcement agents may employ some degree of trickery in obtaining a confession, a deceptive practice that distorts the suspect's rational

---

6   *Arizona v. Fulminante*, 499 U.S. 279 (1991).
7   *United States v. Jenkins*, 938 F.2d 934 (9th Cir. 1991).
8   *Payne v. Arkansas*, 356 U.S. 560 (1958).
9   *United States v. Springs*, 17 F.3d 192 (7th Cir. 1994).
10   *United States v. Miller*, 984 F.2d 1028 (7th Cir. 1993).
11   *Pyles v. State*, 947 S.W.2d 754 (Ark. 1997).

choice may render the confession involuntary.[12] For example, a federal court held that a government agent coerced the defendant's confession by stating that the defendant would be killed unless he told the informant what "really happened."[13] In this case, the defendant was drug dependent and frightened that the government agent was about to kill him.

Similarly, using a trick or ruse to obtain a confession may result in a violation of the Fifth Amendment. For example, in *Rogers v. Richmond*,[14] the Supreme Court held that threats to take family members into custody, even though the officers had no intention of doing so, were considered coercive and therefore rendered the confession involuntary.

Tricks alone, however, do not automatically render a confession involuntary. For example, an officer telling a suspect his accomplice had already confessed did not make his confession coerced.[15] Nor was the confession suppressed when police sent an intentional message to an officer's pager stating they were on the way to question and detain his girlfriend.[16]

Many courts apply the "totality of circumstances" test in determining whether a confession is admissible. In one case, the court held that a confession is "voluntary" if, taking into consideration the totality of circumstances, it is a product of the accused's free and rational choice, and is made with the awareness of a right being abandoned and the consequences of that decision.[17] According to a federal court in Illinois, the proper inquiry for determining whether a confession was improperly coerced looks to the totality of circumstances, rather than a single factor of deceitful tactics by police.[18] According to that court, in determining whether a confession was improperly coerced, factors or considerations other than deceitful tactics by the police are age, duration of questioning, occurrence of physical punishment, receiving advice of constitutional rights, and level of education of the accused.

In discussing the totality of circumstances rationale, a federal appeals court indicated that to determine whether a confession is voluntary, the court must assess the totality of all the surrounding circumstances, both the characteristics of the accused and

---

[12] *United States v. Drake*, 934 F. Supp. 953 (N. D. Ill. 1996). See also *State v. Burdette*, 611 N.W.2d 615 (2000), which held that it is fundamental that a statement be suppressed if it is obtained by offensive police practices; however, mere deception will not render a statement involuntary or unreliable. The test for determining the admissibility of a statement obtained by police deception is whether that deception produced a false or untrustworthy confession or statement.

[13] *United States v. McCullah*, 87 F.3d 1136 (10th Cir. 1996).

[14] *Rogers v. Richmond*, 365 U.S. 534 (1961).

[15] *Frazier v. Cupp*, 394 U.S. 731 (1969).

[16] *United States v. Blue*, 122 Fed. Appx. 427 (10th Cir. 2005).

[17] *United States v. Ornelas-Rodriguez*, 12 F.3d 1339 (5th Cir. 1994).

[18] *Williams v. Peters*, 843 F. Supp. 427 (N.D. Ill. 1994).

the details of the interrogation.[19] The court continued by stating that the inquiry focuses on whether there was any police overreaching, and the factors to be considered included the accused's level of education, intelligence, the lack of any advice to the accused of his constitutional rights, the length of the detention, the repeated and prolonged nature of the questioning, and use of physical punishment, such as deprivation of food or sleep. Although it is not necessary that all of these factors be considered, the court must inquire into the totality of the circumstances in assessing the conduct of law enforcement officials and the defendant's capacity to resist pressure.[20]

In a case that reached the United States Supreme Court in 1999, the primary issue was whether the legislature could modify the rule laid down in *Miranda v. Arizona*. Included in the decision is a comprehensive review of the history of the law governing the admissibility of confessions. The court made it clear that the voluntary test still applies, stating:

> We have never abandoned this due process jurisprudence, and thus continue to exclude confessions that were obtained involuntarily, and;

> The requirement that *Miranda* warnings be given does not, of course, dispense with the voluntariness inquiry.[21]

Even if there is sufficient evidence to support a conviction without a coerced confession, the conviction may be reversed if the coerced confession was improperly introduced at the trial. In *Payne v. Arkansas,* the U.S. Supreme Court stressed that, regardless of the amount of other evidence, "the admission in evidence, over objection, of the coerced confession vitiates the judgment." In explaining the reason for this rule, the Supreme Court included this statement:

> Where, as here, a coerced confession constitutes a part of the evidence before the jury and a general verdict is returned, no one can say what credit and weight the jury gave to the confession.[22]

In 1991, a sharply divided Supreme Court veered from this and other rulings and held that defendants whose coerced confessions were improperly used as evidence are not *always* entitled to a new trial.[23] In this case, a paid informant for the FBI,

---

[19] *Waldrop v. Jones*, 77 F.3d 1308 (11th Cir. 1996).
[20] *United States v. Jacobs*, 97 F.3d 275 (8th Cir. 1996). *See also Klueg v. Groose*, 106 F.3d 239 (10th Cir. 1997), which stated that the legal test for evaluating whether a confession was coerced is whether, in light of the totality of circumstances, the pressures exerted upon the suspect overbore his or her will.
[21] *Dickerson v. United States*, 530 U.S. 428 (2000). This case is considered more comprehensively in § 8.3.
[22] *Payne v. Arkansas*, 356 U.S. 560 (1958).
[23] *Arizona v. Fulminante*, 499 U.S. 279 (1991).

masquerading as an organized crime figure, told the defendant, who was a cellmate of the informer, that he would protect the defendant in exchange for the truth about the killing of an 11-year-old child. This statement to the informant was used at the trial and the defendant was convicted of murder and sentenced to death.

The Supreme Court ruled that the use of this confession, which the Court held to be involuntary, may be considered "harmless error" if other trial evidence was sufficient to convict the defendant. The nine-member Court yielded three distinct votes, but on the question of the "harmless error" application to confessions, five justices held that the harmless error analysis applies to coerced confessions. Applying the harmless error test, the Court ruled that the state had not carried its burden of demonstrating that their error was harmless and accordingly affirmed the judgment of the state court in reversing the defendant's conviction. This case stands for the proposition that if a defendant's coerced confession was improperly used as evidence, the conviction will be reversed even though there was other ample evidence, aside from the confession, to support the conviction, unless the state meets the burden of demonstrating beyond a reasonable doubt that the admission of the confession did not contribute to the defendant's conviction.[24]

An issue in admitting confessions is what degree of proof is necessary in determining the voluntariness of a confession. After years of doubt, the Supreme Court in 1972 determined that the Constitution required only a preponderance of the evidence.[25] This means that the weight of the evidence must show that the confession is voluntary, but it is not necessary to show that the confession is voluntary beyond a reasonable doubt.

It should be noted that while federal courts apply the "preponderance of the evidence" test, some states require a higher standard. For example, an Indiana court held that the state must prove the voluntariness of the defendant's statement to the police beyond a reasonable doubt.[26]

§ 8.3   Warning and Waiver Requirements (*Miranda* Rule)

Because of difficulties in establishing whether a confession was free and voluntary, the Supreme Court decided in *Miranda v. Arizona* that when an individual is taken into custody or otherwise deprived of his or her freedom by the authorities and is subject to questioning, he or she must be given the following warnings:

1. The right to remain silent.
2. Any statement made could be used in a court of law.

---

[24] According to *Chapman v. California*, 386 U.S. 18 (1967), "[b]efore a federal constitutional error can be held harmless, a court must be able to declare a belief that it was harmless beyond a reasonable doubt."

[25] *Lego v. Twomey*, 404 U.S. 477 (1972). See also Nelson v. Walker, 121 F.3d 828 (2d Cir. 1997).

[26] *Turner v. State*, 682 N.E.2d 491 (Ind. 1997). See also *State v. Cole*, 695 A.2d 1180 (Me. 1997).

3. The right to have an attorney present during questioning.
4. If a person cannot afford an attorney, one will be appointed prior to any questioning if desired.[27]

Not only must these warnings be given initially, but the opportunity to exercise these rights must be given throughout questioning. If the accused indicates at any stage of the questioning that he or she does not wish to be interrogated or that he or she wishes to consult with an attorney, questioning must stop.

The decision in *Miranda* was unacceptable to many, including some police personnel, prosecutors, and members of Congress. In the wake of that decision, Congress enacted legislation that, in essence, made the admissibility of such statements turn solely on whether they were made voluntarily.[28] The statute, 18 U.S.C. § 3501, provided that the trial judge, in determining the issue of voluntariness, should take into consideration all the circumstances surrounding the giving of the confession, including: (1) the time elapsing between the arrest and the arraignment of the defendant making the confession, if it was made after arrest and before arraignment; (2) whether the defendant knew the nature of the offense with which he or she was suspected at the time of making the confession; (3) whether the defendant was advised or knew that he or she was not required to make any statement and that any such statement would be used against him or her; (4) whether the defendant had been advised prior to questioning of his or her right to the assistance of counsel; and (5) whether the defendant was without the assistance of counsel when questioned and when giving the confession. The presence or absence of any of these factors to be taken into consideration by the judge need not be conclusive on the issue of voluntariness.

In *Dickerson v. United States*,[29] the U.S. Supreme Court agreed that there was an obvious conflict between the *Miranda* decision and § 3501. Dickerson was indicted for bank robbery, conspiracy to commit bank robbery, and using a firearm in the course of committing a crime of violence. Before trial, Dickerson moved to suppress a statement made to the FBI on the grounds that he had not received the *Miranda* warnings before being interrogated. The prosecutor argued that *Miranda* warnings were not necessary as long as the confession met the requirements of § 3501. As a result, the Supreme Court had to address whether Congress had the constitutional authority to supersede *Miranda*. After providing a brief historical account of the law governing the admission of confessions, the Court held:

---

[27] *Miranda v. Arizona*, 384 U.S. 436 (1966).
[28] 18 U.S.C. § 3501.
[29] *Dickerson v. United States*, 530 U.S. 428 (2000).

In sum, we conclude that *Miranda* announced a constitutional rule that Congress may not supersede legislatively. Following the rule of *stare decisis*, we decline to overrule *Miranda* ourselves.

The effect of this decision is that all of the rules established in the *Miranda* decision (as modified by decisions following *Miranda*) will continue to be binding.

As is the case with other constitutional rights, this right may be waived; however, the waiver must be given voluntarily, knowingly, and intelligently. A waiver will not be presumed simply from the silence of the accused after the warnings are given. Also, the waiver will not be considered voluntary if there is evidence that the accused was threatened, tricked, or cajoled.

One of the issues surrounding *Miranda* warnings is whether the person was in custody at the time of the interrogation. The warnings are not required unless the individual is taken into custody and subjected to questioning. This is addressed in the next section.

A. *Judicial Interpretation of "Custody"*

In *Miranda*, the Supreme Court indicated that the warnings must be administered if the accused is "in custody or otherwise deprived of his freedom of action in any significant way." Both the Supreme Court and lower courts have been called upon to determine the meaning of these words.

The facts to be considered when the court is asked to determine whether the person interviewed is in custody are: (1) the number of officers present; (2) the attitude toward the person being questioned; (3) the stage of the investigation; (4) the environment in which the interview takes place; and (5) whether the interviewee is free to leave. It should be noted, however, that the determining factor is not whether the suspect is in his or her home or in the police station, but whether, in fact, he or she is free to leave.

The Fifth Circuit Court of Appeals has held that a suspect who was surrounded at his place of business by 20 armed agents was "in custody" because he was not free to leave, and evidence obtained after he had been asked if he had any concealed weapons nearby was not admissible.[30] Another circuit court, however, found that a suspect was not in custody even when questioned at a police station because she never attempted to leave and appeared at police headquarters of her own free will.[31]

---

[30] *United States v. Castellana*, 488 F.2d 65 (5th Cir. 1974).

[31] *Freije v. United States*, 408 F.2d 100 (1st Cir. 1969). For a discussion of the *Miranda* warning requirement when a prisoner is questioned by a jail official, see *Garcia v. Singletary*, 13 F.3d 1487 (11th Cir. 1994).

The Supreme Court in *Orozco v. Texas*[32] reasoned that the suspect was in custody when officers entered his bedroom and questioned him in the early hours of the morning. The officers in this case admitted that the suspect was not free to leave. The Supreme Court ruled in *Oregon v. Mathiason*,[33] however, that a burglary suspect who was invited to the police station and appeared of his own free will was not in custody. Some of the news media indicated that *Mathiason* in effect reversed *Miranda*. This, of course, is not the case because the decision merely defined "custody" more specifically. This paragraph from the case more fully explains the Court's thinking:

> In the present case, however, there is no indication that the questioning took place in the context where respondent's freedom to depart was restricted in any way. He came voluntarily to the police station, where he was immediately informed that he was not under arrest. At the close of one-half hour's interview, respondent did in fact leave the police station without hindrance. It is clear from these facts that Mathiason was not in custody "or otherwise deprived of his freedom of action in any significant way."

One court, in discussing the custody issue, commented that the ultimate inquiry in determining whether a suspect is in custody for *Miranda* purposes is simply whether there is a formal arrest or restraint on the freedom of movement of the degree associated with a formal arrest.[34] But the court also stated that in determining whether the suspect was in custody for *Miranda* purposes, the courts should inquire how a reasonable person in the suspect's position would have understood his situation.

In *Stansbury v. California*,[35] the question presented to the U.S. Supreme Court was whether the interrogating officers had focused their suspicion on the individual being questioned, or on another suspect, relevant for the purpose of determining "custody." In this first-degree murder, rape, and kidnapping case, the officers asked the defendant to go with them to the station to answer some questions. Because the focus of the investigation at the time was on another suspect, the California court held that the defendant was not in custody and the *Miranda* warnings were unnecessary. The U.S. Supreme Court, however, reversed the conviction, commenting:

> Our decisions make clear that the initial determination of custody depends on the objective circumstances of the interrogation, not on the subjective views harbored by either the interrogating officers or the person being questioned.

---

[32] *Orozco v. Texas*, 394 U.S. 324 (1969).
[33] *Oregon v. Mathiason*, 429 U.S. 711 (1977).
[34] *United States v. Hicks*, 967 F. Supp. 242 (E.D. Mich. 1997). See also *Manchester v. State*, 487 S.E.2d 449 (1997).
[35] *Stansbury v. California*, 511 U.S. 318 (1994).

In this case, the suspect was in custody and the *Miranda* warnings should have been administered prior to questioning.

The custody question has reached numerous reviewing courts in both federal and state cases. For example, in a federal case, the defendant was in custody during interrogation in his apartment and was entitled to the *Miranda* warnings, even though the police officer's conduct was not coercive and the officers did not use bodily restraint even though the defendant was prevented from contacting anyone other than the officers, including his roommate. Officers required the defendant to stay in the kitchen while they searched the apartment for weapons and did not tell the defendant that he was free to leave after the search was completed or that he could refuse to answer questions. Between three and six officers were in the apartment, and the interrogation lasted more than an hour.[36]

In Pennsylvania, a defendant was "in custody," for purposes of determining whether he should have been provided the *Miranda* warnings, where the police asked the defendant to accompany them to the police station and he waited in an interview room for almost two hours before interrogating officers arrived. The defendant was interviewed for two hours, received one bathroom break, and had no chance to smoke, eat, or drink.[37]

In *Yarborough v. Alvarado*,[38] the U.S. Supreme Court was asked to address whether age and experience with the criminal justice system were pertinent in an individual's ability to determine whether he or she is in custody or is free to leave. In this case, officers left a message on Alvarado's answering machine that they wished to speak to him. His parents brought him to the station, where they waited while he was interviewed without being read his *Miranda* warnings. Following the interview, Alvarado was returned to his parents to be taken home. The Court ruled that he was not in custody because of the nature of the interview. The Court then addressed the issue of whether Alvarado had the capacity, based on his age and inexperience with the criminal justice system, to understand that he was free to terminate the interview and leave. The Court stated that it had never considered age or experience as factors in deciding whether a person should be given *Miranda* warnings because it would require officers to make subjective assumptions about the person. The Court held that age and experience with the criminal justice system are not required in addressing the ability of a person to formulate a proper decision of whether he or she could terminate an interview.

As a practical matter, the suspect may not be in custody during the initial stages of the interview, but at some point during the interview facts may be developed that

---

[36] *United States v. Bunnell*, 106 F. Supp. 2d 60 (D. Me. 2000).

[37] *Commonwealth v. Hayes*, 755 A.2d 27 (Pa. 2000).

[38] *Yarborough v. Alvarado*, 541 U.S. 933 (2004).

indicate knowledge of the crime, in which case the suspect would not be free to leave. If the officer has made such a determination or if the court finds that such a determination should logically have been made under the circumstances, the suspect is then "in custody" and the *Miranda* warnings must be administered if questioning continues.

An issue that is of considerable concern to police officers, especially those involved in traffic duty, is whether a person who is stopped for a traffic offense is considered "in custody," so as to require *Miranda* warnings. The Supreme Court was asked to make this determination in *Berkemer v. McCarty*.[39] In *Berkemer*, the Supreme Court decided that roadside questioning during a routine traffic stop does not constitute custodial interrogation unless the officer subjects the motorist to treatment that renders him or her "in custody" for practical purposes. The Court reasoned that the concerns underpinning *Miranda* are absent in a routine, minor traffic stop situation. The Court continued by explaining that the traffic stops are usually temporary, brief, and public, and that the relatively noncoercive nature of routine traffic stops makes them more analogous to investigative stops than arrests. If, however, the treatment of the motorist is such that it in fact renders him or her "in custody" for practical purposes, he or she will be entitled to the full protection prescribed by *Miranda*. An example here might be with driving under the influence of alcohol. When the officer stops the vehicle and asks some preliminary questions, there is no requirement to administer the *Miranda* warnings. However, once the officer decides that an arrest will be made, *Miranda* warnings must be given before questioning.

B. Judicial Determination of "Questioning"

The Court in *Miranda* indicated that when an individual is taken into custody and is subjected to questioning, the privilege against self-incrimination is jeopardized. If no questions are asked, however, even though the suspect is in custody, the *Miranda* warnings are not required. If, for example, the suspect is taken into custody and, without questioning, voluntarily admits his or her guilt on the way to the station, the statements will be admissible. Also, a general inquiry at the scene of the crime will not be considered questioning so as to make the volunteered statements inadmissible. Following this reasoning, the Illinois Court of Appeals refused to exclude statements given to the officers when they arrived at the scene of a crime and asked, "What happened?" Such statements are admissible as responses to general on-the-scene questioning by the police as to facts surrounding the crime.[40]

---

[39] *Berkemer v. McCarty*, 468 U.S. 420 (1984).
[40] *People v. Routt*, 241 N.E.2d 206 (Ill. 1968).

The issue of what is "questioning," however, is not always easily resolved. Although it would seem that questioning is asking questions, this is not necessarily the definition given by the courts. Questioning not only includes asking direct questions of the suspect, but also words or actions on the part of the officer that would be reasonably likely to elicit incriminating responses from the suspect.

The seminal case related to what constitutes questioning is *Brewer v. Williams*.[41] In this case, a young girl disappeared from a YMCA building. Williams was seen leaving the building with a large bundle wrapped in a blanket and "two legs in it and they were skinny and white." When Williams' car was found with clothing belonging to the missing child, a search was begun between that spot and the YMCA. Williams was also arrested and arraigned in a nearby town. Williams was then transported to Des Moines. Officers told Williams' counsel that he would not be interrogated. During the trip, however, the officer began a conversation with Williams in which he said that the girl ought to be given a Christian burial before a snowstorm (which later became known as the "Christian burial speech"), which might prevent the body from being found. As Williams and the officer neared the town where the body was hidden, Williams agreed to take the officer to the child's body. At trial, a motion to suppress the evidence was denied and Williams was convicted of first-degree murder. The Supreme Court held that the officer's actions in this case amounted to an interrogation, in violation of the Fifth Amendment.

In *Rhode Island v. Innis*,[42] the Court reached a different conclusion based on different facts. In this case, Innis and two officers were in a car when the officers, without bringing Innis into the conversation, engaged in a conversation between themselves concerning a missing shotgun. One of the officers stated that there were "a lot of handicapped children running around in this area and God forbid one of them might find a weapon with shells and they might hurt themselves." The statement was not directed to Innis nor did the officers indicate that they expected an answer. However, Innis interrupted the conversation, suggesting that the officers turn the car around so he could show them where the gun was located. After the Rhode Island Supreme Court set aside the conviction, the U.S. Supreme Court stated the rule as to what is "questioning" or "interrogation":

> We conclude that *Miranda* safeguards come into play whenever a person in custody is subjected to either express questioning or its functional equivalent. That is to say, the term "interrogation" under *Miranda* refers not only to express questioning, but

---

[41] *Brewer v. Williams*, 430 U.S. 387 (1977).
[42] *Rhode Island v. Innis*, 446 U.S. 289 (1980).

also to any words or actions on the part of the police . . . that the police should know are reasonably likely to elicit incriminating responses from the suspect.

In *Innis*, the Court found that the dialogue between the two officers did not amount to "interrogation." Nevertheless, the rule has been clearly defined and must be applied in future cases.

In a 2000 federal case, the court reiterated the rule expressed in *Innis* that "interrogation" for *Miranda* purposes refers not only to express questioning, but also to any words or actions on the part of the police that they should know are reasonably likely to elicit an incriminating response from the suspect.[43] Applying this rule, the court held that a police officer who found concealed weapons on the defendant's person and stated his opinion that the defendant was "stupid for not getting rid of the gun," should have known that the statement to the defendant was reasonably likely to elicit an incriminating response, and therefore the defendant's response was obtained in violation of his *Miranda* rights.

In *Arizona v. Mauro*,[44] the Supreme Court again was confronted with the question of whether the activities of the officers involved amounted to questioning after the suspect indicated his intention not to answer any questions. At the insistence of Mauro's wife, she was allowed to meet with him in the office where he was interviewed. The police agreed to the meeting on the condition that an officer be present and that the conversation be recorded. During the meeting in which the wife expressed despair, Mauro told her not to answer any questions until a lawyer was present. The prosecution used the information on the tape to rebut Mauro's insanity defense, and he was convicted and sentenced to death. The Supreme Court ruled that this activity was not "questioning," because the police officers did not directly question Mauro, nor did they use subterfuge or a "psychological ploy" to try to get the suspect to say something incriminating. In rejecting the claim that this was questioning, the Court explained: "Officers do not interrogate a suspect simply by hoping he will incriminate himself."

The rule gleaned from these cases is that "questioning" includes express questioning or its functional equivalent—that is, any words or actions on the part of the police that the police should know are reasonably likely to elicit an incriminating response from the suspect. However, merely allowing the suspect to make statements is not questioning.

Even though the rule seems straightforward, a case decided in 1990 emphasizes the difficulty of applying the rule. In *Pennsylvania v. Muniz*,[45] the defendant was

---

[43]   *United States v. Braxton*, 99 F. Supp. 2d 567 (E.D. Pa. 2000).

[44]   *Arizona v. Mauro*, 481 U.S. 520 (1987).

[45]   *Pennsylvania v. Muniz*, 496 U.S. 582 (1990).

arrested for driving under the influence on a Pennsylvania highway. Without being advised of his rights under *Miranda*, he was taken to a booking center where, as was the routine practice, he was told that his actions and voice would be videotaped. Still without having been advised of his *Miranda* rights, he answered seven questions regarding his name, address, height, weight, eye color, date of birth, and current age, stumbling over two responses. He was then asked, and was unable to give, the date of his sixth birthday. In addition, he made several incriminating statements while he performed physical sobriety tests and when he was asked to submit to a Breathalyzer test. Both the video and audio portions of the tape were admitted at trial and he was convicted.

The Supreme Court held first that Muniz was in custody for the purposes of *Miranda*. Concerning the questions relating to his name, address, height, weight, eye color, date of birth, and current age, the Court held these were of a routine booking nature and were not intended to elicit information for investigatory purposes; therefore, the *Miranda* warnings were not required. Also, Muniz's incriminating utterances during the sobriety and Breathalyzer tests were not prompted by interrogation within the meaning of *Miranda* and should not have been suppressed. The Court explained that the privilege against self-incrimination protects an accused from being compelled to testify against him- or herself or otherwise provide the state with evidence of a testimonial or communicative nature, but not from being compelled by the state to produce "real or physical evidence." However, the Court found that Muniz's response to the sixth birthday question was incriminating because the *content* of the answer supported an inference that his mental state was confused. His response was testimonial because he was required to communicate an express or implied assertion of fact or belief, and thus, was confronted with the "trilemma" of truth, falsity, or silence.

The "booking" issue was comprehensively discussed in a case in which an officer asked the defendant how he received an injury to his arm.[46] The Court first made it clear that there is no *per se* exception to *Miranda* for questions asked during booking. Although the police may ask questions during booking concerning basic biographical data essential to the booking process, police questions as to how the suspect received an injury to his arm are not routine booking questions. The Court admonished that the availability of the privilege against self-incrimination does not turn upon the type of proceeding in which the protections are invoked but upon the nature of the statement or admission invited by the questioning of the suspect. The Court concluded the booking exception to the *Miranda* rule did not apply, and thus, the defendant was subjected to "interrogation" in violation of his Fifth Amendment privilege against self-incrimination.

---

[46] *Franks v. State*, 486 S.E.2d 594 (Ga. 1997).

C. Interpretation of "Warning" and "Waiver"

If a suspect has been taken into custody and questions are asked, *Miranda* warnings are required. The suspect may waive his or her rights, but must do so knowingly and voluntarily. The prosecution must demonstrate that the warnings were given and the protected rights were waived by the suspect. A waiver will not be presumed simply from the silence of the accused after the warnings are given, nor will a waiver be considered voluntary if there is evidence that the accused was threatened into giving the waiver. Not only must the warnings be given initially, but the opportunity to exercise these rights must be given throughout questioning.

Miranda provided that a suspect must be warned when he or she is in custody and before he or she is questioned. The question that arose in *California v. Prysock*[47] was whether the warnings must be given in the exact terms as stated in the *Miranda* case. In *Prysock*, a murder suspect was given the warnings, but not in the exact terms as stated in *Miranda*. The court of appeals reversed the conviction and ordered a new trial. The Supreme Court disagreed, holding that "nothing in these observations suggests any desirable rigidity in the form of the required warnings."

The *Miranda* warnings need not be given in the exact terms as they are printed in the *Miranda* case, however any substitute must meet the "fully effective equivalent test."[48] It is preferable to give the *Miranda* warnings in the form in which they appear in the case; however, if the warnings effectively advise the suspect of his or her rights, the confession will most likely be admitted.

Allowing some flexibility, the Supreme Court has also indicated that there is no legal requirement that the suspect make an express statement that he or she waives his or her rights after the *Miranda* warnings have been given. In *North Carolina v. Butler*,[49] a lower court reversed a conviction because the suspect had said during the interview that "I will talk with you but I am not signing any form." The lower court indicated this was not a specific waiver as required by *Miranda*. The Supreme Court disagreed, advising that *Miranda* did not hold that an express statement is indispensable to the finding of a waiver. The question of waiver is not one of form, but of substance. The prosecution must demonstrate that the defendant knowingly and voluntarily waived his or her rights, but the waiver may be in the form of actions of indirect affirmation.

Although the question of waiver is not one of form but of substance, there is no doubt that the prosecution bears the burden of establishing beyond a reasonable doubt that the statement made to the investigators is voluntary.[50] A Massachusetts court held

---

[47] *California v. Prysock*, 453 U.S. 355 (1981).
[48] See also *Duckworth v. Egan*, 492 U.S. 195 (1989).
[49] *North Carolina v. Butler*, 441 U.S. 369 (1979).
[50] *State v. Cole*, 695 A.2d 1180 (Me. 1997).

that the government bears the burden of proving beyond a reasonable doubt that the defendant's waiver of his *Miranda* rights was valid.[51]

If a suspect indicates during questioning or prior to questioning that he or she does not want to answer questions, or he or she has invoked his or her right to counsel, questioning must cease. In 1981, the U.S. Supreme Court formulated what has become known as the *Edwards* rule. In *Edwards v. Arizona*,[52] after the police advised Edwards of his rights, he answered, "I want an attorney before making a deal." Questioning ceased at that time, but later, two detectives, colleagues of the officers who had previously interrogated Edwards, came to the jail to see Edwards. After being told by a guard that he had to talk to the two officers, the officers again informed him of his *Miranda* rights, and Edwards indicated that he was willing to talk, but that he first wanted to hear the taped statements of an alleged accomplice. He thereafter implicated himself in the crime and was convicted. The Arizona Supreme Court held that he waived his right to remain silent and his right to counsel when he voluntarily gave the statement after being informed of his rights the second time. The Supreme Court disagreed, however, commenting:

> We further hold that an accused, such as Edwards, having expressed his desire to deal with police only through counsel, is not subject to further investigation by the authorities until counsel has been made available to him, *unless the accused himself initiates further communications, exchanges, or conversations* with the police. (Emphasis added.)

As noted in *Edwards*, police-initiated questioning must cease if the suspect expresses a desire to speak with police only through counsel, and the suspect cannot be subjected to further questioning until counsel has been made available to him or her or the suspect initiates further questioning. But what if there is a break in custody? For example, what if a person is in custody and invokes the *Miranda* privileges, but is then released from custody? If the person is brought back into custody, does the previous invocation of *Miranda* still apply, or can officers readminister *Miranda* warnings and get a confession?

This issue was addressed in *Maryland v. Shatzer*.[53] In this case, a police detective tried to question Shatzer in 2003 concerning a child sexual abuse case. Shatzer was incarcerated at a Maryland prison at that time. Shatzer invoked his *Miranda* right to have counsel present during interrogation, so the detective terminated the interview. Shatzer was released back into the general prison population, and the investigation

---

[51] *Commonwealth v. Rodriguez*, 682 N.E.2d 591 (Mass. 1997).
[52] *Edwards v. Arizona*, 451 U.S. 477 (1981). This rule was reaffirmed in 1984 in the case of *Solem v. Stumes*, 465 U.S. 638 (1984).
[53] *Maryland v. Shatzer*, 559 U.S. 98 (2010).

was closed. In 2006, another detective reopened the investigation and again attempted to interrogate Shatzer, who was still incarcerated. Shatzer waived his *Miranda* rights and made inculpatory statements. The trial court ruled that *Edwards* did not apply in this case because there was a "break in custody" between the first and second interrogations. The Supreme Court affirmed the decision, ruling that "where a suspect has been released from custody and returned to his normal life for some time before the later attempted interrogation, there is little reason to think that his change of heart has been coerced." In *Edwards* and subsequent cases, the courts ruled that a person held in custody would feel coerced by subsequent attempts to question him or her, and believe his or her future release is controlled by police and a willingness to talk. Even though Shatzer stayed in prison the whole time between interrogations, the Court ruled that when he was released from the first interrogation, he returned to his normal life in prison and there was nothing to indicate a second interrogation had any relation to continued confinement.

This protection also applies if a suspect requests counsel at arraignment. But what if counsel has been made available to the suspect, an appointed attorney has met with the suspect on two or three occasions, and then the suspect is told again that he would "have to talk" to an officer and "could not refuse"? The Mississippi Supreme Court reasoned that if counsel has been made *available*, then the police could initiate further questioning; however, the Supreme Court again disagreed.[54] The Court explained that if there were any ambiguities in their earlier cases on this point, "we now hold that when counsel is requested, interrogation must cease, and officials may not reinstate interrogation without counsel present, whether or not the accused has consulted with his attorney." The mere fact that the suspect has talked with counsel does not authorize the police to initiate additional questioning without counsel being present.

The *Edwards* decision does not foreclose finding a waiver of the Fifth Amendment protection after counsel has been requested, however, provided that the accused initiated the conversation or discussions with the authorities.[55] If an accused "knowingly and intelligently," without any attempts by officials to persuade the accused to waive his or her rights, elects to proceed without counsel and in fact initiates questioning, the uncounseled statements he or she then makes need not be excluded at the trial.[56]

How a suspect initiates the conversation has been an issue for the *Edwards* rule. In one case, the Supreme Court determined that a suspect who had claimed his right to counsel "initiated further questioning" when he asked the officers, "Well, what is

---

[54]   *Minnick v. Mississippi*, 498 U.S. 146 (1990).

[55]   *Edwards v. Arizona*, 451 U.S. 477 (1981).

[56]   *Patterson v. Illinois*, 487 U.S. 285 (1988).

going to happen to me now?"[57] In a New Jersey court, the question was whether the prosecution was required to show that the defendant waived his Fifth Amendment rights after he waived his Sixth Amendment rights by initiating further discussion.[58] In that case, the court held that once the state has demonstrated that the defendant has initiated discussion even after invoking his or her right to counsel, the state must establish beyond a reasonable doubt that the defendant made a knowing, intelligent, and voluntary waiver of his or her privilege against self-incrimination.

The Supreme Court was again asked to determine whether the *Edwards* rule applies when a defendant has requested counsel, questioning has ceased, but the interrogation concerning an unrelated crime is initiated by enforcement agents. In *Arizona v. Roberson*,[59] the suspect, after being arrested at the scene of a burglary and advised of his *Miranda* rights, replied that he wanted a lawyer before answering any questions. Questioning ceased at this point, but three days later, while the suspect was still in custody, a different officer, unaware that the suspect had requested counsel, advised him of his rights and interrogated him about a different burglary, obtaining an incriminating statement about that crime. At the trial, this statement was suppressed in reliance upon the decision in *Edwards*. The U.S. Supreme Court held that the *Edwards* rule applied even though Roberson was reinterrogated by a different officer about an unrelated offense. In concluding their opinion, the Court commented:

> Whether a contemplated reinterrogation concerns the same or a different offense, or whether the same or different law enforcement authorities are involved in the second investigation, the same need to determine whether the suspect has requested counsel exists. The police department's failure to honor that request cannot be justified by the lack of diligence of a particular officer.

In still another case, the Supreme Court agreed that a suspect waived his right to counsel when he told the officers he was willing to *talk* about the incident but that he would not make a *written* statement.[60] Barrett was advised three times by the police of his right to counsel and each time agreed to make an oral statement. Stating the reason for allowing the statement to be admitted, the Court made this comment:

> The fact that officials took the opportunity provided by Barrett to obtain an oral confession is quite consistent with the Fifth Amendment. *Miranda* gives the defendant the right to choose between speech and silence, and Barrett chose to speak.

---

[57] *Oregon v. Bradshaw*, 462 U.S. 1039 (1983).
[58] *State v. Chew*, 695 A.2d 1301 (N.J. 1997); see also *Patterson v. Illinois*, 487 U.S. 285 (1988).
[59] *Arizona v. Roberson*, 486 U.S. 675 (1988).
[60] *Connecticut v. Barrett*, 479 U.S. 523 (1987).

In *Oregon v. Elstad*,[61] a suspect, without having been given *Miranda* warnings, was asked some preliminary questions at his home concerning a burglary and replied, "Yes, I was there," thereby implicating himself. After he had been transported to the sheriff's headquarters approximately one hour later, he was advised for the first time of his *Miranda* rights. At this point, the defendant waived his right to counsel as well as his rights under the Fifth Amendment and agreed to make a statement.

The Oregon Court of Appeals reversed the conviction, noting that the "cat was sufficiently out of the bag" when the first questions were asked, and this had a coercive influence on the later admission. The U.S. Supreme Court, however, distinguished this from the *Edwards* situation, because in this case no *Miranda* warnings had been given and counsel was not requested. The Court made this comment:

> It is an unwarranted extension of *Miranda* to hold that a simple failure to administer the warnings unaccompanied by any actual coercion or circumstances calculated to undermine the suspect's ability to exercise his free will, so taints the investigatory process that a subsequent, voluntary and informed waiver is ineffective.

If coercion or improper tactics are used in obtaining an unwarned statement, then the *Elstad* ruling would not apply; that is, such improper tactics in obtaining the first statement would so contaminate the second statement that it would be inadmissible even if the warnings were administered before the second statement. Also, if the suspect has requested counsel, with or without warnings, the questioning must cease unless the suspect him- or herself initiates further questioning.

The decision in *Elstad* is not easily interpreted, however. For example, one court ruled that, although the response to an officer's question at the scene of an arrest concerning who owned a gun had to be suppressed because the suspect was in custody and had not been read his *Miranda* warnings, subsequent statements by the suspect where he continued to shout at the officer that the gun was not his, even after waiving his *Miranda* warnings and without any prompting from officers, did not have to be suppressed.[62]

Because of the decision in *Elstad,* some police agencies and police training groups began a practice known as "question-first." Officers would question a suspect without reading him or her the *Miranda* warnings. Once a confession was obtained, the officer would then read the *Miranda* warnings, hoping to obtain a waiver of rights, then obtain a restatement of the confession.[63] Although the U.S. Supreme Court acknowledged continued support for *Elstad*, it found several contrasts between *Seibert* and *Elstad*. These included "the completeness and detail of the question and

---

[61]   *Oregon v. Elstad*, 470 U.S. 298 (1985).
[62]   *United States v. Cole*, 315 F.3d 633 (6th Cir. 2003).
[63]   *Missouri v. Seibert*, 542 U.S. 600 (2004).

answers in the first round of interrogation, the overlapping content of the two statements, the timing and setting of the first and the second, the continuity of police personnel, and the degree to which the interrogator's questions treated the second round as continuous with the first." The overriding principle here is whether the two events could be seen as separate and distinct interrogations where the reasonable person would believe he or she is free to disregard the first and assert his or her rights on the second. The Court ruled that, when officers deliberately create a situation in which it would not be clear in a suspect's mind that he or she truly had a right to refuse to speak the second time, the warnings of *Miranda* were ineffective. The Court, therefore, held this practice to violate the Fifth Amendment.

In a case that reached a Louisiana appeals court, the question presented was whether *Miranda* warnings are required when a defendant makes a statement to a parole officer over the phone.[64] In this case, the reviewing court decided that Maise's statement to a probation officer during a telephone conversation, in which Maise admitted to sexually penetrating a child victim, were not invalidated by a probation officer's failure to advise him of his *Miranda* rights. The court explained that the defendant was not under arrest, was not in the physical presence of the probation officer, was not in custody at the time he made the statement, so was not subject to inherently coercive custodial interrogation, and his privilege against self-incrimination was not violated because he was not compelled to make the statement.

A final issue that may present itself in police questioning is what crimes may be covered as a part of a single waiver of the *Miranda* rights. In *Colorado v. Spring*,[65] police obtained a signed waiver from Spring and began asking him questions about firearms transactions. The officers then asked him about a murder in which they suspected him of being involved. Ultimately, Spring confessed to the murder. At trial, Spring sought to suppress the confession because the officers did not tell him as a part of his *Miranda* waiver that they would ask him about the murder. The Supreme Court stated that a suspect's waiver of *Miranda* rights is valid even if he or she believes the interrogation will focus on minor crimes but the police shift the questioning to cover a different and more serious crime.

§ 8.4   Exclusion Related to the Fourth Amendment

In addition to the challenges discussed in the preceding sections, statements introduced in court may be challenged on a fourth ground. This challenge relies on the *fruit of the poisonous tree* doctrine, sometimes referred to as the *Wong Sun* doctrine.

---

[64]   *State v. Maise*, 759 So. 2d 884 (La. 2000).
[65]   *Colorado v. Spring*, 479 U.S. 564 (1987).

This rule provides that if a confession is derived immediately from an unlawful arrest or unlawful search, the confession is "tainted" and neither it nor its fruits may be used against the defendant, whose Fourth Amendment rights are violated.

In *Wong Sun v. United States,*[66] an oral statement implicating an accused was held inadmissible because it was made immediately following an unlawful entry and an unlawful arrest. After finding that the arrest was illegal, the judge reasoned that such statements were fruits of the agent's unlawful action and that the exclusionary prohibition relating to evidence obtained by an illegal search extends to the indirect as well as to the direct products of such invasions.

Even if the suspect who is arrested illegally is given the *Miranda* warnings, there is a good possibility that a confession obtained after these warnings will remain contaminated. In a case that was before the Supreme Court in 1975, a confession was obtained after an arrest. Prior to questioning, the officers properly advised the arrestee of his rights, and Brown voluntarily agreed to make statements to the police.[67] The prosecution argued that because Brown had waived his Fifth Amendment rights voluntarily, the fact that an illegal arrest preceded the advice should not taint his confession. The Supreme Court held that there was a causal connection between the illegality of the arrest and the confession, and that giving the *Miranda* warnings alone does not attenuate the taint of the illegal arrest. The Court agreed that Fifth Amendment rights are protected by giving the *Miranda* warnings, but that this, in itself, does not protect the Fourth Amendment rights; despite *Miranda* warnings, the Fourth and Fourteenth Amendments require the exclusion of statements obtained as the fruit of an illegal arrest.

Three cases have reaffirmed the rule that a confession is contaminated if there is a causal connection between the confession and an illegal search or arrest. In *Dunaway v. New York*, the Supreme Court reversed the conviction of a suspect where incriminating statements and sketches were obtained during the petitioner's illegal detention. In that case, the Court pointed out that:

> Where there is a close causal connection between the illegal search and the confession, not only is the exclusion of the evidence more likely to deter similar conduct in the future, but the use of the evidence is more likely to compromise the integrity of the courts.[68]

In a second case, the Supreme Court ruled that a robbery suspect's confession, six hours after his illegal arrest, was not sufficiently purged of the taint of that illegality

---

[66]   *Wong Sun v. United States*, 371 U.S. 471 (1963).
[67]   *Brown v. Illinois*, 422 U.S. 590 (1975).
[68]   *Dunaway v. New York*, 442 U.S. 200 (1979).

to render it admissible in evidence.[69] In a third case, the Court reiterated the rule that a confession immediately following an illegal arrest or search will be inadmissible if there is a causal connection between the illegality of the arrest and the statement, even though the *Miranda* warnings have been given. Emphasizing this point, the Supreme Court stated:

> Under well-established precedent, the fact that a confession may be voluntary for purposes of the Fifth Amendment, in the sense that the *Miranda* warnings were given and understood, is not by itself sufficient to purge the taint of the illegal arrest.[70]

In each of these three cases, evidence obtained from a defendant following arrest was suppressed because the police lacked probable cause to make an arrest. They stand for the familiar proposition that the indirect fruits of an illegal search or arrest should be suppressed when they bear a significantly close relationship to the underlying illegality.

Following these Supreme Court cases, lower federal courts and state courts have applied the rules in diverse situations. In a federal case, the court held that a confession made by the defendant following an unlawful arrest, although voluntary, was impermissibly tainted by the arrest and was inadmissible.[71] The court explained that there was no significant lapse in time between the arrest and confession because the confession occurred approximately two hours after the illegal arrest and no intervening circumstances existed that would dissipate the effect of the unlawful arrest. A second federal court pointed out that even if the *Miranda* waiver and subsequent confession are valid under the Fifth Amendment, the confession may not be sufficiently purged of the taint of the Fourth Amendment violation to be admissible.[72] The court held in that case that the taint of the illegal arrest was not purged and the confession was inadmissible where the defendant was forcibly restrained in handcuffs without probable cause for the arrest and remained in handcuffs with a uniformed officer for at least 45 minutes prior to the confession. However, a third federal court, citing previous cases, recognized that even if the arrest were illegal, the custodial statement is admissible if it was voluntary and lacked any causal connection to the illegal detention.[73]

Despite the fact that the courts have reiterated that a confession is tainted if it is derived immediately from an unlawful arrest or unlawful search, many cases still reach both federal and state courts on this issue. In a 2000 federal case, the court held

---

69 *Taylor v. Alabama*, 457 U.S. 687 (1982).
70 *Lanier v. South Carolina*, 474 U.S. 25 (1985).
71 *Craig v. Singletary*, 80 F.3d 1509 (11th Cir. 1996).
72 *United States v. Robinson*, 932 F. Supp. 1271 (D.N.M. 1997).
73 *United States v. Johnson*, 121 F.3d 1141 (8th Cir. 1997).

that the defendant's post-arrest statements to law enforcement officers should have been suppressed as the fruit of the illegal search and subsequent arrest, when police conducted an unlawful search of a vehicle trunk.[74] A state court advised that in determining the threshold question of whether there has been a seizure, in connection with a determination of whether a defendant's statements should be suppressed as fruit of the poisonous tree, the court examines the effects of the police conduct at the time of the alleged seizure, applying an objective standard.[75]

A different instance of the relationship between confessions and the Fourth Amendment is where an illegal confession leads to physical evidence. In *United States v. Patane*,[76] the Court addressed the issue of whether the failure to give a suspect *Miranda* warnings requires suppression of the physical fruits of the unwarned but voluntary statements. The Court held that because *Miranda* protects against violations of the self-incrimination clause, it is not violated by the introduction at trial of physical evidence resulting from voluntary statements (in this case, telling police where a pistol is located). The Court based its ruling on three foundations. First, the Court held that "the core protection afforded by the Self-Incrimination Clause is a prohibition on compelling a criminal defendant to testify against himself at trial." Because there was no testimony in this instance, the self-incrimination clause did not apply. Second, the Court stated that "[o]ur cases make clear the related point that a mere failure to give *Miranda* warnings does not, by itself, violate a suspect's constitutional rights . . ." Potential violations occur, if at all, only upon the admission of unwarned statements into evidence at trial. Finally, the Court reiterated that the exclusionary rule was created to control police conduct. The Court noted that the *Miranda* rule is not aimed at police conduct, and police do not violate the Constitution by failure to warn: "Thus, unlike unreasonable searches under the Fourth Amendment or actual violation of the due process clause or the self-incrimination clause, there is, with respect to mere failures to warn, nothing to deter. There is therefore no reason to apply the 'fruit of the poisonous tree' doctrine of *Wong Sun*."

§ 8.5   Right to Counsel

As with many protections of the Bill of Rights, the guarantee of counsel to assist in the criminal justice process has not always been in force. Prior to *Powell v.*

---

[74]   *United States v. Wald*, 216 F.3d 1222 (10th Cir. 2000).
[75]   *State v. Banks*, 755 A.2d 279 (Conn. 2000).
[76]   *United States v. Patane*, 542 U.S. 630 (2004).

Alabama,[77] a defendant was not always guaranteed counsel if he or she could not afford a private attorney. In *Powell*, the Court held:

> In a capital case, where the defendant is unable to employ counsel, and is incapable adequately of making his own defense because of ignorance, feeblemindedness, illiteracy, or the like, it is the duty of the court, whether requested or not, to assign counsel for him as a necessary requisite of due process of law; and that duty is not discharged by an assignment at such a time or under such circumstances as to preclude the giving of effective aid in the preparation and trial of the case.

This case granted the right to counsel to defendants involved in trials where the death penalty was a possible punishment. After several smaller extensions of *Powell*, this right was extended to all persons standing trial for a felony offense (in both state and federal courts) in *Gideon v. Wainwright*.[78] Neither of these cases involved the police because the right to counsel considered here was only at trial. There was no right to counsel for suspects during interrogation or other pretrial procedures. That would change in 1964 with *Escobedo v. Illinois*.[79]

In *Escobedo*, the defendant was arrested and released on the same day on a writ of habeas corpus. He told the police nothing at the time. He was rearrested about 11 days later and, before making any statement, requested an opportunity to consult with his attorney. His attorney likewise made repeated efforts to gain access to his client. Each was told that he could not see the other until the police had finished with the interrogation. In the course of questioning, Escobedo stated that another person had committed the shooting, thereby admitting knowledge of the crime and implicating himself. At the trial, he moved to suppress the incriminating statements, but his motion was denied.

The U.S. Supreme Court, in reversing the conviction and declaring the confession inadmissible, designated the point in the criminal process at which the right to counsel attaches. The Court's decision concluded with this admonition:

> When the process shifts from the investigatory to the accusatory—when its focus is on the accused and its purpose is to elicit a confession—our adversary system begins to operate, and, under the circumstances here, the accused must be permitted to consult with his lawyer.

There were two problems with this statement, and with the decision in *Escobedo* in general. The first was how to ensure that the person knew his or her rights to

---

[77] *Powell v. Alabama*, 287 U.S. 45 (1932).
[78] *Gideon v. Wainwright*, 372 U.S. 335 (1963).
[79] *Escobedo v. Illinois*, 378 U.S. 478 (1964).

counsel. In *Escobedo*, the accused asked to consult with his lawyer. But what if the defendant was ignorant of his rights and had not made a demand on the police? Must he be advised in every case of his right to counsel? Another issue was that "when the process shifts from the investigatory to the accusatory" is different in almost every case, depending on the circumstances. This is the reason *Miranda* was decided two years later. Even with the decisions in *Escobedo* and *Miranda*, there were additional issues that had to be addressed concerning the right to counsel. Many of these related to issues later in the criminal justice process, but others related to the police and are discussed below.

An issue central to the protection of the right to counsel is what amounts to a request for counsel in determining whether the defendant has invoked the right to counsel. The answer is that a suspect is not required to express his or her desire to obtain counsel with lawyer-like precision; all that is required is that he or she make the desire to consult with an attorney clear. In *Robinson v. Borg*,[80] the Ninth Circuit Court of Appeals held that the suspect's statement "I have to get me a good lawyer, man. Can I make a phone call?" constituted an unambiguous and unequivocal invocation of his right to counsel, and thus it was incumbent upon the police to cease interrogation. Their failure to do so rendered inadmissible any statement made by the suspect in response to their continued questioning.

In a later case, the Supreme Court provided more guidance concerning what constitutes a valid request for an attorney. In *Davis v. United States*,[81] a suspect in a murder was given his *Miranda* warnings, which he waived. Approximately one and one-half hours into the interview, Davis stated, "Maybe I should get a lawyer." When agents asked if he was asking for an attorney, he replied he was not. Following a break, agents reminded Davis of his rights and continued the interview. After another hour, Davis stated, "I think I want a lawyer before I say anything else." At that time, the interview ceased. The Supreme Court ruled that statements made after Davis's first statement could be admitted into court because he had not unequivocally requested an attorney; and agents properly ended the interview when Davis did request an attorney.

Davis did not necessarily end issues with when a person truly asks for an attorney, however. In *James v. Marshall*,[82] James called the police and told them he thought he killed someone. Police read James his *Miranda* rights prior to talking to him, and he agreed to make a statement. James then agreed to have the questioning videotaped. The officer then reread James his rights on camera. When the officer asked, "Do you wish to make a statement at this time?" James replied, "Nope." The

---

[80]   *Robinson v. Borg*, 918 F.2d 1387 (9th Cir. 1990).
[81]   *Davis v. United States*, 512 U.S. 452 (1994).
[82]   *James v. Marshall*, 322 F.3d 103 (1st Cir. 2003).

office then said, "Okay. Can I talk to you about what happened earlier tonight?" To which James replied, "Yup." At trial, James sought to have the confession suppressed because he had invoked his right to remain silent based on his response "Nope." The court disagreed, holding that James had been very cooperative prior to that point and had agreed on multiple occasions to make a statement. Further, when the officer rephrased his question, James agreed to speak. The court reasoned that James was simply stating that he had no formal statement to make at that time but was willing to be questioned, rather than making an unequivocal request for an attorney or to remain silent.

Further extending the decision in *Davis*, the Court ruled in *Berghuis v. Thompkins*[83] that that silence after being read the *Miranda* warning combined with the statement made to the police represent a valid waiver to remain silent. In this case, Thompkins remained silent when asked to read a statement of his *Miranda* warnings and during the first part of an interrogation. Later in the interrogation, he did make brief statements that were used to convict him of murder. The Supreme Court ruled these statements were admissible, holding "Thompkins did not say that he wanted to remain silent or that he did not want to talk to the police. Had he made either of these simple, unambiguous statements, he would have invoked his 'right to cut off questioning.' [Internal citations omitted.] Here he did neither, so he did not invoke his right to remain silent."

In *Miranda*, the Court decided that a suspect who is in custody must be advised of his or her right to counsel prior to questioning. Also, a suspect who is in custody must be allowed to consult with an attorney, if he or she so requests, prior to any questioning. But is it necessary for the police to advise the suspect in custody that an attorney has been retained by someone else to represent him or her? The Supreme Court, in *Moran v. Burbine*, answered this question in the negative.

In *Moran v. Burbine*,[84] Burbine was arrested on a breaking and entering charge. Unknown to Burbine, his sister, who was unaware that he was under suspicion of another charge, sought help from the public defender's office. The assistant public defender agreed to represent Burbine and telephoned the detective division, stating that she would act as his counsel. She was informed that Burbine would not be questioned until the next day. Burbine was not advised that counsel had been retained to represent him, nor that counsel had contacted the detective. He did, however, validly waive his self-incrimination and counsel rights after being warned and made a confession. In a habeas corpus proceeding, Burbine argued that the police conduct, in failing to inform him about the attorney's call and in conducting interviews after telling the attorney there would be no interviews, tainted his waivers. The Supreme

---

[83] *Berghuis v. Thompkins*, 560 U.S. 370 (2010).
[84] *Moran v. Burbine*, 475 U.S. 412 (1986).

Court determined that the confession should be admitted, expressing this reasoning:

> The police failure to inform the respondent of the attorney's telephone call did not deprive him of information essential to his ability to knowingly waive his right to remain silent and to the presence of counsel.

This is because the suspect himself was aware of his right to counsel as well as his Fifth Amendment rights. The fact that he was not advised that counsel had been retained and the fact that counsel had not been advised concerning the questioning did not influence his ability to make the decision. Had Burbine requested counsel or had he been denied permission to contact counsel before making the statements, the decision in this case would have been different.

In a Kansas case, the court considered the issue of waiver of counsel after the accused has asserted his or her constitutional right to be silent or have counsel present during the custodial interrogation.[85] The court first reiterated that an accused may waive *Miranda* rights by his or her own acts and words in initiating a conversation with police. The court continued by stating that an accused's waiver of a previously asserted right to be silent or have counsel present during custodial interrogation must be knowing, voluntary, and intelligent under the totality of circumstances. The court then warned that when the accused has invoked his or her right to have counsel present during the custodial interrogation, a valid waiver of that right cannot be established by showing only that he or she responded to further police-initiated custodial interrogation, even if he or she was advised of the *Miranda* rights. Finally, the court established some rules to be followed. The court advised that in determining whether events subsequent to the accused's exercise of the constitutional right to be silent or have counsel present during the custodial interrogation constitute a waiver of the previously asserted right, the court must first determine whether the accused actually invoked the right, and, if so, the court must then determine whether the accused initiated further discussions with the police and knowingly and intelligently waived the previously asserted rights.

The right to counsel protection also comes into play when an informant cellmate obtains information from an indicted defendant at the request of law enforcement officials. Because the rule in the cellmate cases is very technical, it is necessary to discuss four cases because each had a different result.

In the first of these cases, *United States v. Henry*,[86] an informant who was the cellmate of Henry was advised by an FBI agent to be alert to any statements made, but not to initiate any communications with or question Henry. After the informant

---

[85]   *State v. Lane*, 940 P.2d 422 (Kan. 1997).
[86]   *United States v. Henry*, 447 U.S. 264 (1930).

initiated a discussion, Henry did, in fact, tell the informant some details of the crime, and the informant testified at the trial. The U.S. Supreme Court reversed the conviction, including this statement in its decision:

> By intentionally creating a situation likely to induce Henry to make incriminating statements without the assistance of counsel, the government violated Henry's Sixth Amendment right to counsel.

In *Henry*, the informant cellmate had not asked questions directly, but had stimulated the conversation.

In a second "cellmate confession" case, *Kullman v. Wilson*,[87] the informant obeyed police instructions only to listen to the defendant for the purposes of identifying his confederates in the robbery and murder, but not to question him about any crimes. The Supreme Court distinguished this case from *Henry*, noting that the Sixth Amendment does not forbid admission of an accused's statement made to a jailhouse informant who is placed in close proximity to the defendant in the jail, but who makes no effort to stimulate the conversation about the crime with which the defendant is charged. If the informant cellmate merely listens and does not elicit any incriminating remarks, the right to counsel is not violated even if the suspect has been indicted and counsel appointed. In *Kullman*, the Supreme Court indicated that the burden is on the defendant to demonstrate that the police and their informant took some action beyond merely listening that was deliberately designed to elicit incriminating remarks. If the defendant does not prove improper action on the part of the police or informant, the statements made to the informant are admissible.

In *Illinois v. Perkins*,[88] police placed an undercover agent in a cell block with Perkins, who was incarcerated on charges unrelated to the murder that the police were investigating. When the undercover agent asked Perkins if he had killed anybody, Perkins made statements implicating himself in the murder. He was then charged with murder. The trial court granted Perkins' motion to suppress the statements on the ground that he had not been given the warnings as required by *Miranda*. The U.S. Supreme Court distinguished this case from *Henry*, because, in this case, the defendant had not been indicted. In explaining the difference, the Court made this comment:

> We held in those cases that the government may not use an undercover agent to circumvent the Sixth Amendment right to counsel once the suspect has been charged

---

[87] *Kullman v. Wilson*, 477 U.S. 436 (1986). See also *United States v. Stubbs*, 944 F.2d 828 (11th Cir. 1991), which held that inculpatory statements made by a defendant to a jailmate were admissible when the jailmate did not interrogate the suspect by eliciting incriminating information or by initiating any discussion about crimes with which the defendant was charged.

[88] *Illinois v. Perkins*, 496 U.S. 292 (1990).

with a crime. After charges have been filed, the Sixth Amendment prevents the government from interfering with the accused's right to counsel. . . . In the instant case
no charges had been filed on the subject of the interrogation, and our Sixth Amendment precedents are not applicable.

In a more recent case, the Supreme Court ruled that testimony from a cellmate
confession could be used to impeach a defendant's testimony even if it violated the
defendant's Sixth Amendment rights and could not have been admitted into court
itself. In this case, Ventris and another person were charged with murder and other
crimes. Prior to trial, an informant placed in Ventris' cell heard him admit to shooting
and robbing the victim. At trial, Ventris testified that the other person committed the
crimes. The informant was then called to testify over Ventris' objection.

As in the case of the waiver of Fifth Amendment rights, an accused may waive
his or her Sixth Amendment right to counsel if he or she does so voluntarily, knowingly, and intelligently. According to the Eighth Circuit Court of Appeals, there is "no
compelling reason to hold that he (the accused) may not voluntarily, knowingly, and
intelligently waive his right to have counsel present at an interrogation after counsel
has been appointed."[89] The burden, however, is always on the government to show
that the waiver was knowingly and intelligently made.

In discussing "a knowing and intelligent waiver," a federal court agreed that
mental retardation does not, by itself, render a defendant incapable of waiving his or
her *Miranda* rights; however, the court held that the defendant's waiver of his
Miranda rights in this case was not knowing or intelligent, given the defendant's
extreme lack of education; his unfamiliarity with key words contained in the *Miranda*
warning; his mental retardation; his inability to understand, without repetition and
clarification, concepts implicit in *Miranda* warnings; the haste with which the rights
were read and his waiver was made; and his total lack of familiarity with the criminal
justice process.[90]

The right to counsel is sometimes inextricably linked with the protection from
self-incrimination. The Supreme Court first addressed this issue in *Massiah v. United
States*,[91] in which the Court ruled that obtaining incriminating statements after the
filing of formal charges without the presence of counsel violated Massiah's Sixth
Amendment rights. This came to be known as the "deliberate elicitation standard," in
which officers are not to elicit incriminating statements without counsel after formal
charges have been filed. The Court further clarified this rule in *Fellers v. United
States*.[92] In this case, officers went to Fellers' home after he was indicted to "discuss

---

[89]   *Moore v. Wolff*, 495 F.2d 35 (8th Cir. 1974).
[90]   *United States v. Robles-Ramirez*, 93 F. Supp. 2d 762 (W.D. Tex. 2000).
[91]   *Massiah v. United States*, 377 U.S. 201 (1964).
[92]   *Fellers v. United States*, 540 U.S. 519 (2004).

his involvement in methamphetamine distribution." They also told him they had a federal warrant for his arrest, and ultimately placed him under arrest. While at Fellers' home, they questioned him related to others involved in the crime. When they arrived at jail, the officers first read Fellers his *Miranda* warnings. He signed a waiver of his rights and reiterated the statements. The U.S. District Court suppressed the statements made at Fellers' home, but admitted statements made after he waived his *Miranda* warnings based on the decision in *Elstad*. The Supreme Court acknowledged their continued support for the deliberate elicitation standard, but "expressly distinguished this standard from the Fifth Amendment custodial-interrogation standard." The Court ruled that both statements had to be suppressed because in both cases, Fellers was questioned without proper representation of counsel after being indicted. Had Fellers not been indicted, it is likely that the second set of statements would have been admitted pursuant to *Elstad* (which was the controversy in the lower courts).

§ 8.6   The Delay in Arraignment Rule

Some statements are challenged because they were obtained "prior to arraignment," even though they were admittedly freely and voluntarily made. If the officer "unnecessarily" delays taking the apprehended person before a judicial officer as required by state or federal law, a confession or statement made during the delay probably will not be admitted. This rule was first announced in 1943 in *McNabb v. United States*.[93] In this case, federal officers obtained a confession from suspects who were held for several days without being taken before a magistrate. The Supreme Court, in reversing the conviction, based its holding solely on the ground that evidence was secured in disregard of the federal statutory procedures established by Congress.

The *delay in arraignment* rule was revived and reemphasized in a case that received national recognition. In *Mallory v. United States*,[94] the defendant was apprehended between 2:00 P.M. and 2:30 P.M. the day following a rape in Washington, D.C. Rather than taking the arrestee before a commissioner as required by federal law, the suspect was questioned until about 8:00 P.M., when he first admitted involvement in some part of the crime. The commissioner could not be located that evening and the suspect was not taken before the commissioner until the following morning. In reversing the conviction, the Supreme Court stated, "[w]e cannot sanction this extended delay, resulting in confession, without subordinating the general rule of prompt arraignment to the discretion of arresting officers in finding exceptional

---

93   *McNabb v. United States*, 318 U.S. 332 (1943).
94   *Mallory v. United States*, 354 U.S. 449 (1957).

circumstances for its disregard." In this case, the Court did not consider the free and voluntary test, but reversed the decision because there had been a delay in bringing the accused before the United States Commissioner.

The delay in arraignment (*McNabb-Mallory*) rule first applied only in federal cases. Initially, state courts refused to adopt the rule; but in 1961 the rule was made applicable in state courts as well.[95]

Because *Mallory* did not state or define what was "unnecessary delay," hundreds of cases have been decided in an attempt to reach a definition. It is only "unnecessary" delays that make the statement inadmissible. If there is a necessary delay, such as a magistrate not being available, the confession will be admissible if otherwise qualified.[96]

Congress, recognizing that the *Mallory* rule was not only ambiguous but placed an unnecessary burden on officers, enacted legislation in 1968 that modified the *McNabb-Mallory* requirements.[97] This act, in effect, states that a confession shall not be inadmissible in a federal court if the confession was obtained during a delay in arraignment. The act establishes the time as six hours between an arrest and the making of the confession, but gives judges discretion to admit the confession even if more than six hours have elapsed if the judge finds the delay reasonable. This left unanswered whether a confession obtained within the six-hour period is *per se* reasonable, or whether a confession obtained after the six-hour period is *per se* unreasonable.

Federal courts have taken the position that if a confession is obtained during the six-hour period between arrest and arraignment, it is *per se* reasonable.[98] Courts have also held that statutes providing that a confession shall not be inadmissible solely because of delay in bringing the person before the magistrate, if a confession was given within six hours immediately following the arrest, do not render inadmissible all confessions obtained more than six hours after the arrest.[99] In determining whether a confession obtained more than six hours after arrest is admissible, the court will consider the circumstances. If the delay in bringing the person before a magistrate is found by the trial judge to be reasonable, considering the means of transportation and the distance to be traveled to the nearest available judicial officer, the limitations do not apply.[100] However, when a pre-arraignment delay of more than six hours occurs so the investigator would have additional time to interrogate the defendant, the delay is

[95] *Culombe v. Connecticut*, 367 U.S. 568 (1961).

[96] *United States v. Mitchell*, 322 U.S. 65 (1944).

[97] 18 U.S.C. § 3501(c) (1970).

[98] *United States v. Tham*, 815 F. Supp. 1325 (N.D. Cal. 1993); *United States v. Rojas-Martinez*, 968 F.2d 415 (5th Cir. 1992).

[99] *United States v. Perez-Bustamante*, 963 F.2d 48 (5th Cir. 1992).

[100] 18 U.S.C. § 3501(c).

unreasonable and any confession during that time must be suppressed.[101] A Pennsyl-vania court ruled in 1999 that there was no violation of the rule requiring that the arrestee be arraigned within six hours of the arrest where the defendant made no statements to the police during an interview prior to the arraignment, but gave his oral confession and taped confession *after* he was arraigned.[102]

To avoid problems, it is preferable to take the person arrested before a magistrate within a reasonable time. If the usual practice is followed and the person arrested is not discriminated against, the confession will probably be admissible. On the other hand, if the usual practice is to take an arrestee before a magistrate on the morning following the evening when the arrest was made, and the suspect is not taken before the magistrate as is the customary procedure, a confession obtained during the delay will probably be inadmissible.

§ 8.7   Corroboration

A defendant cannot be convicted on his or her own uncorroborated confession without proof that a crime has been committed by someone—that is, without proof of the *corpus delicti*.[103] Although a person may not be convicted of an offense solely upon a confession or admission made by him or her, additional proof may consist of circumstantial evidence that the crime occurred and such evidence need not directly connect the defendant to the crime.[104]

The term *corpus delicti* refers to the body of the crime or evidence that a crime was committed at the place alleged in the indictment, and the state needs only slight evidence of the *corpus delicti* to corroborate a confession and sustain a conviction.[105] The courts are apparently inconsistent in determining whether an accomplice's testimony may be corroborated by the testimony of another accomplice. In a Georgia case, the court held that evidence was sufficient to corroborate an accomplice's testimony in a prosecution for armed robbery and aggravated assault.[106] However, a

---

[101] *United States v. Tham*, 815 F. Supp. 1325 (N.D. Cal. 1993). See also *United States v. Alvarez-Sanchez*, 511 U.S. 230, (1994), in which the Supreme Court decided that in the absence of a "collusive arrangement between state and federal agents," an arrest by state authorities on state criminal charges is not "an arrest or other detention" within the meaning of the statute, when the defendant is tried on a federal charge. See also *United States v. Headdress*, 953 F. Supp. 1272 (D. Utah 1996).

[102] *Commonwealth v. Marielli*, 690 A.2d 203 (Pa. 1997).

[103] *State v. Fountain*, 647 So. 2d 1254 (La. 1994). See also *United States v. Banks*, 78 F.3d 1190 (7th Cir. 1996).

[104] *People v. Curro*, 556 N.Y.2d 364 (1990). See also *United States v. Clark*, 57 F.3d 973 (10th Cir. 1994) and *Ward v. State*, 529 S.E.2d 378 (2000).

[105] *State v. Smith*, 24 S.W.3d 274 (Tenn. 2000).

[106] *Arnold v. State*, 532 S.E.2d 458 (Ga. 2000).

Minnesota case held that an accomplice's testimony may not be corroborated solely by the testimony of another accomplice.[107]

§ 8.8   Exceptions to Right to Counsel and Self-Incrimination

Too often, a police investigator, after reading Supreme Court decisions, is convinced that no questioning is authorized and no statements will be admissible. This is not the case. The Supreme Court in *Miranda* emphasized that the Court did not purport to find all confessions inadmissible. The Court remarked, "[c]onfessions remain a proper element in law enforcement." The Court went on to explain that statements given freely and voluntarily are admissible. The Court also stated that the police are not required to stop a person who enters the station and states that he or she wishes to confess to a crime, calls the police to make a confession, or to make any other statement. In addition, the courts in recent years have established specific instances in which confessions may be admissible even though some of the technical rules have not been followed. Some of these are discussed in the following paragraphs.

A.   Use of Statements for Impeachment Purposes

Even if a confession is inadmissible to establish guilt because the *Miranda* warnings were not administered, that confession may nevertheless be admissible to impeach the credibility of the defendant if he or she takes the stand in his or her own behalf.[108] The Supreme Court explained the reasoning in approving the use of a confession for limited impeachment purposes:

> Every criminal defendant is privileged to testify in his own defense or to refuse to do so. But that privilege cannot be construed to include the right to commit perjury . . . having voluntarily taken the stand, petitioner was under an obligation to speak truthfully and accurately, and the prosecution here did no more than utilize the traditional truth-testing devices in the adversary process.

The U.S. Supreme Court has been consistent in approving the limited use of custodial statements for impeachment purposes. In *Oregon v. Hass*[109] the Court

---

[107] *State v. Pederson*, 614 N.W.2d 724 (Minn. 2000).
[108] *Harris v. New York*, 401 U.S. 222 (1971).
[109] *Oregon v. Hass*, 420 U.S. 714 (1975).

reiterated its approval of the use of the statements given without having administered the *Miranda* warnings for impeachment purposes. Carrying the "impeachment admission" rule one step further, the Supreme Court approved the use of a statement taken in violation of the *Michigan v. Jackson* rule when the statement was used only for impeachment purposes. The *Jackson* rule provides that once a criminal defendant invokes his or her Sixth Amendment right to counsel, a subsequent waiver of that right, even if voluntary, knowing, and intelligent under traditional standards, is presumed invalid if secured pursuant to a police-initiated conversation.[110] In overturning this rule, the Court allowed statements taken in violation of *Jackson* to be used only for impeachment purposes. As stated above, the Supreme Court has also allowed statements to be admitted to impeach a defendant's testimony even if they violate the *Henry* rule against cellmate informant confessions.

While custodial statements that are inadmissible under *Miranda* may nonetheless be admissible for limited impeachment purposes, silence of the accused after warnings may not be used for impeachment purposes.[111] As an accused has the right to remain silent during police interrogation, any reference to his or her silence under such circumstances carries with it an intolerable prejudicial influence. The police therefore are not justified in relying on a suspect's silence in intimating the guilt of the suspect or even for impeachment purposes.

The rules expressed in *Harris v. New York* and *Oregon v. Hass* that a confession taken without the proper *Miranda* warnings may be used for impeachment purposes do not apply if the confession is obtained involuntarily.[112] Although a confession obtained without reading the *Miranda* warnings is admissible for impeachment purposes if trustworthy by established legal standards, an involuntary statement cannot be used in any way against a defendant at his or her trial.

B. Use of Statements Made at Grand Jury Hearings

The Supreme Court has also held that *Miranda* warnings need not be given to a grand jury witness who is called upon to testify about criminal activities in which he or she may be personally involved.[113] The Court indicated that the warnings enumerated in *Miranda* were aimed at police interrogation of a person in custody, and not necessarily required in other situations.

---

[110] *Michigan v. Jackson*, 475 U.S. 625 (1986); see also *Michigan v. Harvey*, 494 U.S. 344 (1990) and *DiJoseph v. Vuotto*, 968 F. Supp. 244 (E.D. Pa. 1997).

[111] *United States v. Hale*, 422 U.S. 171 (1975).

[112] *Mincey v. Arizona*, 437 U.S. 385 (1978).

[113] *United States v. Mandujano*, 425 U.S. 564 (1976).

C. Nonofficial Questioning

In the absence of state involvement, voluntary statements made to private citizens are admissible even if no *Miranda* warnings are given. As in the case of the Fourth Amendment, the Fifth Amendment prohibitions operate only against official action; therefore, if a private individual obtains information without the encouragement or knowledge of a police officer, that evidence is admissible even if no warnings are given. For example, incriminating statements that the defendant made to a journalist did not violate his Sixth Amendment right to counsel absent a showing that the journalist acted on behalf of the state in obtaining an interview.[114] Further, a defendant's statements to a friend while they were seated in a patrol car were not required to be suppressed even though the *Miranda* warnings had not been given.[115] Nonetheless, because the free and voluntary rule is based in part on the rule that evidence must be trustworthy, a defendant would have grounds for challenge if force were used, even if this force were exerted by a private citizen. On the other hand, if the challenge is predicated only on the *Miranda* rule or the delay in arraignment rule, statements made to a private person would be admissible.[116]

D. Public Safety Exception

After 20 years of adherence to the literal language of the *Miranda* decision, which provided that evidence would be inadmissible unless the warnings were given, the Supreme Court acknowledged in 1984 that it was time to pull back. The Court announced a narrow *public safety* exception to the requirement that a suspect be advised of his or her rights prior to custodial interrogation.

In *New York v. Quarles*,[117] a police officer entered a grocery store after being told by a rape victim that her assailant, who was carrying a gun, had entered the supermarket. After the suspect was apprehended in the grocery store, the officer noticed that the suspect was wearing an empty shoulder holster. At this point, the officer asked the suspect, "Where is the gun?" The suspect indicated that the gun was in some empty cartons and said, "The gun is over there." The suspect was in custody, questions were asked, but the *Miranda* warnings were not administered. The U.S. Supreme Court, in this ruling, coined what has become known as the *public safety*

---

[114] *Wilcher v. State*, 697 So. 2d 1123 (Miss. 1997).

[115] *State v. Dreps*, 558 N.W.2d 339 (S.D. 1996).

[116] *United States v. Casteel*, 476 F.2d 152 (10th Cir. 1973); *Commonwealth v. Mahnke*, 335 N.E.2d 660 (Mass. 1975).

[117] *New York v. Quarles*, 467 U.S. 649 (1984).

exception to the *Miranda* requirement. The Court indicated that the need for answers in this situation outweighed the need for a strict rule. The rule in *Quarles* is that, when police officers ask questions reasonably prompted by a concern for public safety, the suspect's incriminating statements may be admitted into evidence even if the *Miranda* warnings were not administered.

The public safety exception to *Miranda* also applied when the investigation and the search were for vials of freeze-dried bubonic plague bacteria.[118] In this case, Harris was asked only questions needed to locate a dangerous instrumentality and the officer read Harris his rights after the questions were asked. The court allowed the admission of the statements even though the immediate risk to the public was not as significant as the officers thought at the time. The police captain testified that no one in the city had previously participated in a search for a deadly bacteria and that the officers were motivated by concerns for public safety when they questioned the defendant prior to reading him his rights.

A consideration of the public safety exception is that the person giving the statements will repeat them at trial and have the opportunity for cross-examination (the *confrontation clause* of the Constitution). But what if the person cannot be made available for confrontation at trial (typically because the person is dead)? The Supreme Court has ruled that statements made to police *may* be admitted at court in exigent circumstances even though the person is not read the *Miranda* warnings or has the right to counsel.[119] In this case, a victim told police before he died that he was shot by Bryant through Bryant's back door. The police went to Bryant's house and found a bullet hole in the back door and found the victim's wallet outside the house. The Court stated "Statements are nontestimonial when made in the course of police interrogations under circumstances objectively indicating the primary purpose of the interrogation is to enable police assistance to meet an ongoing investigation." In essence, this case extended *Quarles* to include cases where there is not the ability to cross-examine the witness.

In dealing with hostage situations, a New York court held that even assuming that the defendant was subjected to custodial interrogation while holding hostages inside a building and talking with negotiators over the telephone, the public safety exception to the *Miranda* rule applied to his statements to negotiators, given the direct threat he posed to public safety, where the defendant advised investigators that he was armed and indicated a willingness to harm the hostages, the police, and himself.[120]

---

[118] *United States v. Harris*, 961 F. Supp. 1127 (S.D. Ohio 1997).

[119] *Michigan v. Bryant*, 562 U.S. ___, No. 09-150 (2011).

[120] *People v. Scott*, 710 N.Y.S.2d 228 (2000).

§ 8.9   Admissibility of a Second Confession After an Inadmissible First Confession

If a confession is obtained in violation of the Constitution, that confession and derivative evidence will not be admitted, with some exceptions. The question that arises is whether an inadmissible first confession will taint a second confession. As a general rule, once a confession has been made under improper influences, the presumption arises that a subsequent confession of the same crime flows from the same influences, even though made to a different person from the one to whom the first confession was made.[121] If, however, the police ask preliminary questions without giving the *Miranda* warnings and later continue the questioning after the full *Miranda* warnings have been administered, statements made at the first session do not necessarily contaminate those made at the second session.[122]

Elaborating on the rule established in *Elstad*, a federal court observed that the voluntariness of a Mirandized confession that follows a prior non-Mirandized confession is a totality of circumstances inquiry, and depends upon such factors as surrounding circumstances, the combined effect of the course of the officer's conduct upon the defendant, including the effect of previously having made the confession, and the manner in which officers utilize the prior confession in obtaining a second confession.[123] If coercion tactics are used in obtaining the first confession or first statement, then the second statement would be inadmissible even if the *Miranda* warnings were given in full at the time the second statement was taken.[124] As stated above in the case of *Missouri v. Seibert*, officers cannot purposely gain a confession without *Miranda* warnings and then Mirandize the person to get an admissible confession. This tactic will result in the confession being inadmissible in court.

§ 8.10 Summary

Although the courts have condemned improper questioning and have criticized the police for interrogating suspects rather than conducting thorough investigations, those courts have specifically approved the use of questioning as a means of investigation when it is done within the established rules. To protect those who

---

[121] *Westover v. United States*, 384 U.S. 436 (1966). Note: *Westover* was part of the *Miranda v. Arizona* decision.

[122] *Oregon v. Elstad*, 470 U.S. 298 (1985).

[123] *United States v. Polanco*, 93 F.3d 555 (9th Cir. 1996).

[124] *Desire v. Attorney General of California*, 969 F.2d 802 (9th Cir. 1992). See also *People v. Thomas*, 839 P.2d 1174 (Colo. 1992).

are accused of crime, many admissibility tests have been covered and explained in this chapter.

The first test is the *free and voluntary* test. This provides that, for a statement to be admissible in court, the prosecution has the burden of proving that the statement was made freely and voluntarily; that is, without force or duress. Even if the confession is free and voluntary, it may not be admissible if the officer unnecessarily delays in taking the apprehended person before a judicial officer, as required by law.

Perhaps the best-known requirements are those that were established in *Miranda v. Arizona*. In that case, the Supreme Court established the rule that a confession will be inadmissible unless the provisions established in that case were followed. The *Miranda* rule provides that if a person is in custody and subject to questioning, he or she must be warned prior to any questioning that: (1) he or she has a right to remain silent; (2) anything he or she says can and will be used in a court of law; (3) he or she has the right to the presence of an attorney; and (4) if he or she cannot afford an attorney, one will be appointed prior to any questioning, if he or she so desires. In addition to these warnings, the suspect must be given an opportunity to exercise these rights throughout questioning. If, however, the suspect is not in custody or is in custody and is not questioned, the warnings are unnecessary. Additionally, these rights may be waived, provided the waiver is made voluntarily, knowingly, and intelligently.

One method of enforcing the Sixth Amendment's right to counsel is to exclude a statement made by the defendant if this safeguard is not met. The accused, if in custody, must be warned of his or her right to counsel prior to questioning and must be given the opportunity to have counsel present. Even if not in custody, the accused must be *permitted* to have counsel present if incriminating questions are asked.

A confession that is free and voluntary, that is not obtained during an unnecessary delay in arraignment, and that is obtained after the suspect is given the *Miranda* warnings and waives his or her rights, may nevertheless be inadmissible if it is derived from an unlawful arrest or search. The reasoning is that a confession that derives from an unlawful entry or an unlawful search is considered to be the fruit of an official illegality and therefore constitutionally tainted.

Finally, an extrajudicial confession, standing alone, will not support a conviction. Independent evidence must be introduced to corroborate the statements made in the confession.

Notwithstanding the requirements that must be met prior to the introduction of a confession into evidence, some statements are admissible even though these requirements are not met. In *Miranda*, the Court specifically stated that confessions are admissible if they are made freely and voluntarily. The Supreme Court also approved general on-the-scene questioning as to facts surrounding a crime. Later cases have indicated that an officer does not have to give the warnings as required in *Miranda* unless the suspect is in custody and is being questioned. A suspect will not be considered in custody if he or she is free to leave.

The Supreme Court has approved the use of extrajudicial confessions to impeach the in-court testimony of defendants who take the stand in their own behalf, even though the *Miranda* warnings were not given. The Supreme Court has also adopted a rule that warnings need not be given to a grand jury witness who is called upon to testify about criminal activities, and statements made to private citizens without official involvement are admitted into evidence, because only official conduct is prohibited by the Fifth Amendment.

The Supreme Court has also relaxed the rules relating to the admission of a confession given without *Miranda* warnings and have reasoned that the *Miranda* warnings need not be administered prior to questioning if the safety of the officer or others reasonably requires that the questions be asked immediately.

In many instances, it is not necessary to question the suspect to make a case. Despite court restrictions, interrogation is still a useful and legitimate means of investigating crime. The knowledgeable officer will not only be aware of the questioning requirements, but will be able to select the best investigative tool.

Chapter 9
Pretrial Identification Procedures

. . . [T]he confrontation compelled by the State between the accused and the victim or witnesses to a crime to elicit identification evidence is peculiarly riddled with innumerable dangers and variable factors which might seriously, even crucially, derogate from a fair trial . . . [I]n practice the issue of identity may (in the absence of other relevant evidence) for all practical purposes be determined there and then, before the trial.

United States v. Wade, 388 U.S. 218 (1967)

§ 9.1   General Considerations

As part of the investigative process, it is often appropriate, and even essential, to identify the suspect. As a general procedure, the first step after arrest is to fingerprint and photograph the suspect. Often, it is good investigative practice to have the suspect appear before a victim or a witness to determine whether the investigation is proceeding along the proper lines. Sometimes the confrontation immediately follows the apprehension to eliminate suspects, and sometimes the confrontation is by means of a lineup that might take place some days later. The taking of fingerprints and photographs and the confrontation for identification have been challenged on at least three constitutional grounds—self-incrimination, right to counsel, and due process.

The law relating to fingerprinting and photographing has developed over a period of years and is fairly well established. The case decisions regarding lineups and other confrontations for identification are not quite as well established. It is not the lineup or confrontation itself that is challenged; it is the in-court identification that might be contaminated by improper confrontation (lineup) procedures that is objectionable. The danger is that a witness who is called upon to identify the suspect in court may make that identification not from what occurred at the scene of the crime but from what occurred at the later confrontation for identification.

Especially since the turn of the twenty-first century, more and more scientific methods have been used in efforts to solve crimes. This is particularly the case in terms of using DNA to match a person to (or eliminate the person from) the crime. Even before then, however, voice exemplars, blood samples, and other means of identification were utilized in the criminal processing system. All of these issues are presented and discussed in the sections that follow.

§ 9.2   Fingerprinting and Photographing Suspects

Although fingerprinting and photographing suspects are now common practices, these procedures have not always gone unchallenged. The primary challenge is that subjecting a person to fingerprinting and photographing for identification purposes requires the suspect to incriminate him- or herself in violation of the Fifth Amendment. One of the early Supreme Court decisions on this matter was *Holt v. United States*.[1] In that case, the Court distinguished between compelling a person to give verbal evidence and requiring him or her to submit to fingerprinting.

The line of demarcation was clearly established in the case of *Schmerber v. California*, in which the Court stated:

> We hold that the privilege (self-incrimination) protects an accused only from being compelled to testify against himself or otherwise provide the state with evidence of a testimonial or communicative nature.[2]

---

[1]   *Holt v. United States*, 218 U.S. 245 (1910).
[2]   *Schmerber v. California*, 384 U.S. 757 (1966).

This set the standard that the Fifth Amendment applies only to spoken evidence, not "real evidence," such as a photograph or fingerprint. Regarding the taking of fingerprints, the Supreme Court held:

> It [the self-incrimination privilege] offers no protection against compulsion to submit to fingerprinting, photographing, or measurements, to write or speak for identification, to appear in court, to stand, to assume a stance, to walk, or to make a particular gesture.

In an even more comprehensive statement, a federal court advised that evidence of one's fingerprints, handwriting, vocal characteristics, stance, stride, gestures, or blood characteristics, as well as evidence of an intoxicated person's slurring of speech and other evidence of lack of muscular coordination, does not violate the Fifth Amendment privilege against self-incrimination.[3] The manner of speech (not what is said) does not require administration of *Miranda* warnings. In *Mimms*, the Supreme Court ruled that checking a person for slurred speech or even asking questions that require logic but the answer is irrelevant (like saying the ABCs backward) are not testimonial, and therefore are admissible. If the answer to the question is relevant (in this case the date of the suspect's sixth birthday), then the material becomes testimonial and is protected by the Fifth Amendment; therefore, the *Miranda* warnings are required for it to be admissible.

Taking palmprints or fingerprints does not violate the self-incrimination protection of the Constitution if the person in lawful custody is required to submit to photographing and fingerprinting as part of a routine identification process.[4] Nor is there any violation of the Fourth Amendment if the person whose fingerprints are taken has been properly arrested. If, however, the sole purpose of the detention is to obtain fingerprints and the arrest is not justified, the Fourth Amendment search and seizure provisions are violated and this becomes an illegal search.[5] However, authorization by a judicial officer to schedule a time for the fingerprinting of a suspect may be proper even though the suspect has not been formally arrested.[6]

Asking a suspect to sign a fingerprint identification card also does not violate the Fifth Amendment privilege against self-incrimination, and a suspect is not required to be Mirandized before signing the card because there is no constitutional right not to be fingerprinted.[7] Alternatively, a defendant does not have the right to draw adverse

---

3   *United States v. Veiarde-Gomez*, 224 F.3d 1062 (9th Cir. 2000). See also *Pennsylvania v. Muniz*, 496 U.S. 582 (1990).

4   *Smith v. United States*, 324 F.2d 879 (D.C. Cir. 1963). See also *Barnes v. State*, 763 So. 2d 216 (Miss. 2000).

5   *Davis v. Mississippi*, 394 U.S. 721 (1969).

6   For a discussion of this point, see *Davis v. Mississippi*, 394 U.S. at 728-729.

7   *United States v. Snow*, 82 F.3d 935 (10th Cir. 1996).

inferences against the government based on the government's failure to introduce fingerprint evidence or to take fingerprints.

In *United States v. Hoffman*,[8] Hoffman claimed that the district court committed reversible error by preventing defense counsel from arguing to the jury that it could draw various adverse inferences against the government because the government agent failed to take fingerprints. The reviewing court acknowledged that it would not have been improper for the defense counsel to point out to the jury that the government had not presented any evidence concerning fingerprinting. It would have been improper, however, to allow Hoffman to go beyond merely pointing out the lack of fingerprint evidence and arguing that its absence weakened the government's case. The lower court properly prohibited the defense from arguing that: (1) the police did not attempt to obtain fingerprints from the plastic bag containing narcotics; (2) this failure violated standard police procedure; and (3) the fingerprint evidence, if obtained, would have been favorable to the defendant.

§ 9.3   Lineup—Self-Incrimination Challenge

At trial in a criminal case, witnesses are often instructed to identify the perpetrator of a crime as part of their in-court testimony. There is a real danger that the identification could be made not because of what the witness observed at the time of the incident, but as a result of a lineup or showup prior to trial. Recognizing this possibility, courts in many cases have established procedures that must be followed at pretrial lineups or showups. The procedure followed in pretrial confrontation for identification has been challenged on three constitutional grounds: self-incrimination, right to counsel, and due process provisions. Although the lineup, or confrontation, has been challenged on other constitutional grounds, defendants have had little success in challenging this procedure as a violation of the self-incrimination protections.

In *United States v. Wade*,[9] the Court expressly stated that compelling the accused to exhibit his or her person for observation by a prosecutor's witness prior to trial "involves no compulsion of the accused to give evidence having 'testimonial significance.'" The courts, including the Supreme Court in the *Schmerber* case cited earlier, have been consistent in holding that the viewing of a suspect under arrest by an eyewitness does not violate this constitutional privilege because the prisoner is not required to be an unwilling witness against himself or herself. There is clearly a

---

8   *United States v. Hoffman*, 964 F.2d 21 (D.C. Cir. 1992).
9   *United States v. Wade*, 388 U.S. 218 (1967). See also *United States v. Montgomery*, 100 F.3d 1404 (8th Cir. 1996), in which the court held that the Fifth Amendment does not protect people from having to try on clothing.

distinction between a bodily view and requiring an accused to give oral testimony against him- or herself or to communicate ideas.

§ 9.4   Lineup—Right to Counsel Challenge

The right to counsel challenge is not so easily addressed. In a decision in which the members of the Supreme Court had little consensus, the post-indictment lineup was determined to be a critical stage of the proceedings if the in-court identification of the accused could be jeopardized.[10] The reasoning of the Court was that if the lineup, or other confrontation procedure followed by the police, suggests that a suspect is the one who committed the crime, there is a serious danger of misidentification at trial.

Contrary to some opinions expressed following the *Wade* decision, the Supreme Court did not require counsel at all lineups and did not hold that the in-court identification would be disallowed. The Supreme Court held that counsel must be present if requested by the suspect or if one has been appointed. Even in this situation, however, failure to have counsel at the post-indictment lineup does not necessarily contaminate the in-court identification. Even if the lineup is not admitted, the in-court identification can be admitted if it can be proven that the person identifying the suspect did so based on his or her own recollection, independent of the police misconduct.[11]

The holding in *Wade* left many questions unanswered. In *Wade*, the lineup was conducted after an indictment. Soon after that case was decided, the question arose as to whether the same rule would apply to a police showup that took place before the defendant was indicted, or otherwise formally charged with any criminal offense. This question was considered by the Supreme Court in *Kirby v. Illinois*.[12]

The Court in *Kirby* refused to extend the right to counsel protection of the Sixth Amendment to a pre-indictment identification. In that decision, the Court ruled:

> The initiation of judicial criminal proceedings is far from a mere formalism. It is the starting point of our whole system of adversary criminal justice. For it is only then that the government has committed itself to prosecute, and only then that the adverse positions of government and defendant have solidified . . . It is this point, therefore, that marks the commencement of the "criminal prosecutions" to which alone the explicit guarantees of the Sixth Amendment are applicable.

---

[10]   *United States v. Wade*, 388 U.S. 218 (1967).
[11]   *United States v. Crews*, 445 U.S. 463 (1980).
[12]   *Kirby v. Illinois*, 406 U.S. 682 (1972).

Based on the reasoning of this case, counsel generally is not required at the scene of arrest, when an officer is merely trying to determine whether he or she has the correct suspect.[13] But the arresting officer must recognize that even though counsel may not be required in the case of a pre-indictment confrontation or street confrontation, the in-court identification may still be contaminated if the procedure is so suggestive as to violate the due process provisions of the Constitution.

Although Supreme Court decisions have made a distinction between the right to counsel at the identification process before the formal proceedings have been initiated, some states established more rigorous standards. For example, in California, Alaska, and Michigan, the courts have declared that a criminal suspect has the right to counsel at a lineup or showup occurring before formal proceedings have been initiated, as well as after formal proceedings have been initiated.[14]

§ 9.5   Lineup—Due Process Challenge

One reason the Supreme Court and other courts have taken a close look at lineups and other confrontations is because, in many instances, the rights of individuals have been abused. If the lineup, showup, or other confrontation is so unnecessarily suggestive as to be conducive to irreparable mistaken identification, the procedure violates due process. For example, if a suspect is in a six-person lineup with five other people of a different race, this would make the procedure unfair, and the in-court identification unconstitutional.

This unlawful behavior was exemplified by the procedures followed in *Foster v. California*.[15] In this case, a witness to an armed robbery was called to the police station to view a lineup. In the lineup were three men, including Foster. Foster was six feet tall while the other two men in the lineup were about five feet, six inches tall. Additionally, only Foster wore a leather jacket that was similar to one the witness said he saw on the robber. At the first lineup, the witness could not positively identify the robber and was called to view a second lineup. At the second lineup, there were five men in the lineup, but Foster was the only person in the second lineup who was in the first lineup. This time, the witness was convinced that Foster was the man he had seen at the scene of the robbery. The Supreme Court, in reversing the conviction, condemned this procedure as a violation of the due process clause of the Fourteenth Amendment.

---

13   See also *Smith v. State*, 534 So. 2d 903 (2000).
14   *People v. Bustamante*, 634 P.2d 727 (Cal. 1981); *Blue v. State*, 558 P.2d 636 (Alaska 1977); *People v. Jackson*, 217 N.W.2d 22 (Mich. 1974).
15   *Foster v. California*, 394 U.S. 440 (1969).

To be constitutional, a lineup or other confrontation for identification must not be suggestive. If the makeup of the lineup, or the action of the officer at the lineup, is such that the witness would be influenced in determining the identity of the suspect, the in-court identification will be contaminated and disallowed. On the other hand, if it is clear that a witness positively identified the defendant as a result of observations made at the scene rather than at the showup, the in-court identification will be allowed.[16] The Supreme Court, in this case, explained that the primary evil to be avoided is the likelihood of irreparable misidentification. Five factors that should be considered in evaluating the likelihood of misidentification are:

1. The witness's opportunity to view the criminal during the crime;
2. The witness's degree of attention;
3. The accuracy of the witness's prior description of the criminal;
4. The level of certainty demonstrated by the witness at the confrontation; and
5. The length of time between the crime and the confrontation.

Although the wording used by the lower courts may be somewhat different from that of the Supreme Court, lower courts have applied the guidelines established by the Supreme Court. A Louisiana court applied these guidelines and held that the victim's identification of an attempted carjacking defendant was reliable because the victim had ample opportunity to clearly see Jones' face and stature, the victim's recitation of details of the incident showed that he was attentive, the victim's description of Jones was corroborated by the victim's wife, and the victim expressed no doubt that the person who entered his car was Jones.[17]

In establishing some guidelines for determining whether the in-court identification is contaminated by the pretrial procedures, one court outlined a two-step process. The court pointed out that, in examining the constitutionality of pretrial identification procedures under the due process clause, the court must first determine whether the procedure was unnecessarily suggestive and must then weigh the corrupting influence of the suggestive procedure against the reliability of the identification itself.[18]

A pretrial identification procedure is impermissibly suggestive when it leads the witness to an all but inevitable identification of the defendant as the perpetrator or when it is the equivalent to the authorities telling the witness "this is our suspect."[19] Interpreting the test to be applied, one court commented that reliability is the linchpin in determining admissibility of identification testimony at the trial. If the

---

[16] *Neil v. Biggers*, 409 U.S. 188 (1972).

[17] *State v. Jones*, 765 So. 2d 1191 (La. 2000). See also *State v. Brannon*, 341 S.C. 272 (2000).

[18] *Grubbs v. Hannigan*, 982 F.2d 1483 (10th Cir. 1993). See also *United States v. Jackman*, 837 F. Supp. 468 (D. Mass. 1993).

[19] *Cowan v. State*, 531 S.E.2d 785 (Ga. 2000).

identification procedure itself is unduly suggestive, the central question then becomes whether, under the totality of circumstances, the identification was reliable.[20]

If the pretrial identification takes place at a showup rather than a lineup, improper procedures will also contaminate the in-court identification. Generally, one-on-one identifications are not favored; however, this type of confrontation between the suspect and the victim is permissible when justified by the overall circumstances, particularly when the accused is apprehended within a relatively short period after the occurrence of the crime and has been returned to the crime scene.[21] If, considering the totality of circumstances, the identification was impermissibly suggestive, in-court identification of the suspect will be disallowed. For example, the use of a showup identification procedure at the scene of a second robbery to permit an eyewitness to the first robbery to identify the suspect was improper—the witness should have been transported to the precinct for a lineup, absent any unbroken chain of events or exigent circumstances justifying the showup; the showup occurred after the defendant was apprehended at the scene of the second robbery, and witnesses who had already been interviewed at the precinct and returned to their place of business were transported to the scene of the second robbery and identified the defendant as he sat on the floor, bleeding from the head.[22]

§ 9.6   Pretrial Photographic Identification

One method of identifying or eliminating suspects is the use of mug shots, photographs, or videotapes. This procedure is closely related to the lineup identification procedure, and is usually challenged on the same grounds.

Because the accused is required to do nothing whatsoever, certainly not to give information of a testimonial or communicative nature, the self-incrimination challenge has no merit. Also, because the suspect is not expected to appear in person, he or she has little claim of being denied the right to counsel as required by the Sixth Amendment. On the other hand, the defendant may claim in court that the identification made at the time of the trial was contaminated by a suggestive photographic identification.

In *Simmons v. United States*,[23] snapshots of a suspect were shown to five bank employees who witnessed a bank robbery, and each witness identified Simmons as one of the robbers. The Supreme Court refused to prohibit the use of this technique

---

[20]   *United States v. Hicks*, 967 F. Supp. 242 (E.D. Mich. 1997).
[21]   *State v. Day*, 762 So. 2d 264 (La. 2000).
[22]   *People v. Johnson*, 711 N.Y.S.2d 440 (2000).
[23]   *Simmons v. United States*, 390 U.S. 377 (1968).

but indicated that each case must be decided on its own merits. The Court cautioned that the witness identification at trial, following a pretrial identification by photographs, would be set aside if the photographic identification procedure was so suggestive that it would create a substantial likelihood of irreparable misidentification.

It is preferable to make use of multiple photographs of persons who are reasonably alike in appearance. The use of a single photograph was held by the Sixth Circuit Court of Appeals case to be suggestive and a denial of due process.[24] This is not to say that in all instances the use of a single photograph will make an in-court identification impermissible, because each case is decided on its own facts. Care should be taken, however, to establish identification procedures to avoid successful challenge of the process used.

Applying the "totality of circumstances" test, a Texas court held that showing a wounded police officer a single photograph did not make the identification unreliable, in view of the fact that the officer was alert at the time he identified the suspect from the photograph, and the fact that the officer had a clear view of the assailant at the time of the shooting, even though the officer died before trial.[25] A New York court determined that a photo array shown to two witnesses was not unduly suggestive where all the pictures were of people similar to the defendant in skin color and facial features.[26] The court noted that there is no requirement for all photographs to have virtually identical characteristics. Pointing out that the totality of circumstances test must be applied, a Connecticut court determined that a photographic array containing photographs of men, including the defendant, with facial hair, which was a characteristic that did not conform to the description of a clean-shaven robber that was given by the witnesses, was not unnecessarily suggestive.[27]

To avoid a challenge of the in-court identification, a record of the photographic array used in a pretrial photographic identification procedure should be maintained. In a federal case, the court held that when the government fails to preserve a photographic array used in a pretrial lineup, there will exist a presumption that an array is impermissibly suggestive, even if the record discloses no evidence of bad faith on the part of the government.[28] However, a New York court decided that the procedure by which the robbery victim selected defendants' photographs from binders containing more than 100 photographs of black females, which was compiled specifically for the defendant's case, militated against a presence of suggestiveness.[29]

---

24   *Workman v. Cardwell*, 471 F.2d 909 (6th Cir. 1972). See also *United States v. Crews*, 445 U.S. 463 (1980).

25   *Herrera v. Collins*, 904 F.2d 944 (5th Cir. 1990).

26   *People v. Adams*, 660 N.Y.S.2d 950 (N.Y. Supp. 1997).

27   *State v. Banks*, 755 A.2d 951 (Conn. 2000).

28   *United States v. Honer*, 255 F.3d 549 (5th Cir. 2000).

29   *People v. Hunter*, 714 N.Y.S.2d 331 (2000).

§ 9.7   Dental Examination

Another means of identification, although certainly more rare than fingerprinting, is dental examination. In a Pennsylvania case, the prosecution sought to admit evidence of a dental examination to prove the defendant had a missing tooth in the area of his mouth pinpointed by one of the witnesses.[30] Applying the *Schmerber* reasoning, the U.S. District Court for the Eastern District of Pennsylvania concluded that the suspect's self-incrimination protection was not violated when he was required to have a dental examination, nor was this a violation of the Fourth Amendment or due process protection under the facts of the case. The court explained that the compelled display of identifiable physical characteristics infringes on no interest protected by the privilege against compulsory self-incrimination.

§ 9.8   Voice Exemplars

Another method of identifying a suspect is through the sound of his or her voice, or patterns of that sound. Not all courts accept spectrograph evidence to prove identity in criminal cases. Further, use of such evidence has been challenged on the grounds that it violates the Constitution or is unreliable. The U.S. Supreme Court decided in 1973 that compelling a suspect to produce voice exemplars did not violate the Fifth Amendment.[31] The Court explained that, because the comparisons were to be used for identification purposes and not for their testimonial or communicative content, this procedure did not involve self-incrimination.

Federal courts are divided on the question of the reliability of spectrographic voice identification to prove the identity of a person. In *United States v. Maivia*,[32] the U.S. District Court for the District of Hawaii reviewed the decisions of federal courts and concluded that the use of spectrographic evidence to identify voices is no longer considered unreliable, and expert testimony is admissible for voice comparison purposes. In *Maivia*, the court proposed the following safeguards be applied when the spectrographic analysis is offered: (1) two or more minutes of each speech sample; (2) a signal-to-noise ratio where the signal is higher by 20 decibels; (3) a frequency of 3,000 hertz or better; (4) an example in the same words, the same rate, and the same way, spoken naturally and fluently; and (5) a responsible examiner.

---

[30]   *United States v. Holland*, 378 F. Supp. 144 (E.D. Pa. 1974).

[31]   *United States v. Dionisio*, 410 U.S. 1 (1973).

[32]   *United States v. Maivia*, 928 F. Supp. 1471 (D. Haw. 1990). For a more detailed explanation of the scientific principles of speech mechanics, the spectrograph, and the spectrogram, see *United States v. Williams*, 583 F.2d 1194 (2d Cir. 1978).

A 1989 article discussed the Computer Assisted Voice Identification System (CAVIS). The article compared the spectrograph technique with the CAVIS procedure. According to the article, the conventional method of comparing voices in criminal cases can take several hours, days, or even weeks, depending upon the nature of the recording. With the spectrograph, examiners need at least 20 words or approximately 30 seconds of speech to make an accurate comparison. With the use of the computer, however, a voice examiner can compare the tone of the voice and the way the energy vibrates from the vocal cords and make the identification in a shorter period.[33]

§ 9.9   Footprint Comparisons and Other Body Examinations

At one time, some courts prohibited the use of footprint comparison evidence if the suspect was forced to place his or her foot in the print. This, according to these courts, required the suspect to take an active part, thereby incriminating him- or herself. Since the *Schmerber* holding, this is no longer considered a violation of the Fifth Amendment because there is no testimony or communication. In *United States v. Cortez*,[34] footprints were one of the items of evidence used to establish the "totality of circumstances" in a case.

It is also not a violation of the self-incrimination provisions to examine a suspect's body for traces of blood,[35] or to take epidermal scrapings or saliva samples from a suspect.[36] Applying the *Schmerber* rationale, it is doubtful if taking hair samples, fingernail scrapings, or other evidence from the body would be considered violations of the self-incrimination provisions. There is a possibility that a Fourth Amendment challenge might stand if the person from whom this evidence is taken is not legally arrested or if there is no court order justifying the seizure.

Neither due process nor the statutory privilege against self-incrimination is implicated by the choice in cases of driving while intoxicated granted by the implied consent statute of whether to submit to a chemical test of bodily substances such as blood, breath, or urine.[37] The court explained in *State v. Coe* that, under proper circumstances, the state can force the defendant to produce evidence from his or her body.

---

[33]   *International Association of Chiefs of Police News*, Vol. 3, No. 10 (Oct. 1989).
[34]   *United States v. Cortez*, 449 U.S. 411 (1981).
[35]   *McFarland v. United States*, 150 F.2d 593 (D.C. Cir. 1945).
[36]   *Brent v. White*, 276 F. Supp. 386 (E.D. La. 1967).
[37]   *State v. Coe*, 533 S.E.2d 104 (Ga. 2000).

§ 9.10 Deoxyribonucleic Acid (DNA) Tests

Researchers have made a significant breakthrough in using the deoxyribonucleic acid code present in blood and other body fluids to link evidence such as bloodstains or semen specimens to a specific individual. The issue for the courts is whether this technique violates constitutional rights. This is an important area for criminal justice, but often has little to do with the police. Many cases reach the appellate or Supreme Court level, but most involve courtroom issues or those at the crime lab or expert witness level rather than involving the actions of the police. A few of the main cases related to DNA are addressed in this section. A better understanding of the legal issues surrounding DNA are best left to other legal documents.

Since the courts cautiously accepted DNA tests in the 1980s, there has been widespread acceptance of the technique. During this period, techniques for determining DNA profile and identification have been improved and new methods have received acceptance.[38] In *United States v. Martinez*, the U.S. Court of Appeals for the Eighth Circuit stated, "we conclude that the Second Circuit's conclusion as to the reliability of the general theory and techniques of DNA profiling are valid under the Supreme Court holding in *Daubert v. Merrell Dow Pharmaceuticals*,[39] and hold that in the future, courts can take judicial notice of their reliability." Although there is still some criticism about the underlying principles and methodology surrounding the use of DNA matches, the technique generally has been accepted by the scientific community, as required in the case of *Daubert v. Merrell Dow Pharmaceuticals*.

Most of the criticism and challenges to the use of DNA evidence for identification purposes are not that the scientific principles have not been officially established, but that the procedures and methodology for conducting DNA testing have not met acceptable standards.[40] A New York court pointed out that once the *Frye v. United States*[41] standard for reliability of scientific procedure is satisfied, the question is whether the accepted techniques were employed by the experts in the case at hand. The focus moves from the general reliability of the procedures followed to generate the evidence proffered and whether they establish a foundation for the reception of the evidence at trial.[42]

To avoid the necessity of proving the reliability of the procedure in each case, some states have enacted statutes providing that DNA testing is a reliable scientific

---

[38] *United States v. Bonds*, 12 F.3d 540 (6th Cir. 1993). See also *United States v. Martinez*, 3 F.3d 1191 (8th Cir. 1993).

[39] *Daubert v. Merrell Dow Pharmaceuticals*, 509 U.S. 579 (1993).

[40] *United States v. Bonds*, 12 F.3d 540 (6th Cir. 1993).

[41] 293 F. 1013 (D.C. Cir. 1923).

[42] *People v. Klinger*, 713 N.Y.S.2d 823 (2000).

technique.[43] In a Virginia case, the court held that the purpose of the statute was to recognize the reliability of scientific techniques that underlie DNA testing and profile comparisons, thereby eliminating the need for exhaustive proof in each case of how and why profiling is scientifically reliable before the DNA evidence can be admitted.

Now that DNA testing is becoming more commonplace, challenges are beginning to take the form of more traditional challenges. A 2013 Supreme Court case addressed one of these challenges.[44] In this case, a man broke into a woman's home in 2003 and raped her. Police were not able to identify him but did obtain a DNA sample of the assailant from the victim. In 2009, King was arrested for assault. As a part of the booking, he had a DNA sample taken from him, which was found to match the rape case. King moved to have the DNA excluded because it violated his Fourth Amendment rights. The Supreme Court ruled the taking of the sample as a part of

California Attorney General Jerry Brown, right, is shown defending a state law enforcement policy that allows police to collect DNA samples from people who have been arrested but not convicted of any crime. Also pictured are Mark Sconce, member of Surviving Parents Coalition, left, and Michael Chamberlain of the Attorney General's office. (*AP Photo/Jeff Chiu*)

---

43   *Crawford v. Commonwealth*, 534 S.E.2d 332 (Va. 2000).
44   *Maryland v. King*, 569 U.S. ___, 133 S. Ct 1958 (2013).

routine booking procedures was valid. It is somewhat unclear from the Supreme Court decision, however, the circumstances that may lead to the collection. The Maryland statute in this case was somewhat restrictive—only allowing DNA collection if the person was arrested for violent crimes or burglary, requiring the test to not be conducted until the person was arraigned, and mandating destruction of the DNA sample if the person was not convicted. Law enforcement should be aware that taking of DNA samples is most likely to be supported when it follows the provisions set out by Maryland in this case. Collecting DNA samples for other reasons (say for less than "serious" crimes) should be undertaken with caution and may be subject to exclusion in court.

§ 9.11 Summary

Fingerprinting, photographing, lineups, dental examinations, and the use of evidence from the body of an accused all have been challenged under one or more of four constitutional provisions. These types of investigative procedures have been challenged as violating Fourth Amendment unreasonable search provisions, Fifth Amendment self-incrimination provisions, Sixth Amendment right to counsel provisions, or the Fifth and Fourteenth Amendment due process clauses.

Fingerprinting and photographing suspects for identification purposes do not violate self-incrimination provisions, or the Fourth Amendment, if there is a legal arrest. The courts have held that admission of physical evidence such as fingerprints, voice exemplars, or photographs cannot be self-incriminating because they are not testimonial in nature. A court can rule these inadmissible if there was an improper arrest or search in violation of the Fourth Amendment, but not the Fifth Amendment.

Although lineups and showups are challenged under self-incrimination, right to counsel, and due process provisions, only the latter two challenges have had any success. The accused should be permitted to have counsel at post-indictment lineup proceedings. If counsel is not present or this right is not properly waived, the burden is on the prosecution to show the procedure at the lineup did not influence the in-court identification. Counsel is generally not required at a pre-indictment confrontation for identification. If, however, a lineup or other confrontation is so suggestive as to cause a likelihood of irreparable misidentification at trial, the in-court identification will probably be successfully challenged as violating the due process clause. Pretrial photographic identification procedures may also be condemned if they are so suggestive as to cause the witness to misidentify the accused at the trial.

The courts have been almost unanimous in holding that a dental examination and reasonable examination of a suspect's body for evidence do not violate the Fifth or Fourth Amendments. This is based on the same rationale as above, where dental exams are physical evidence and therefore do not violate the Fifth Amendment. As discussed above, however, they can violate the Fourth Amendment if there is an illegal search or arrest.

Techniques designed to identify individuals by the use of spectrographic voice identification have not been universally recognized, but the technique has been approved by some federal and state courts. Although the technique does not violate the Fifth Amendment self-incrimination provisions, some courts have found that the technique is not sufficiently reliable to be recognized by the courts.

Most state and federal courts have concluded that DNA profiling for identification purposes is sufficiently reliable to prove identity. If the constitutional standards are followed in obtaining the samples of tests and if the tests are performed in accordance with appropriate laboratory standards and controls to ensure reliability, the results are generally admissible.

Chapter 10
Taking the Law to the Streets

The "reasonableness" of a particular [legal issue] must be judged from the perspective of a reasonable officer on the scene, rather than with the 20/20 vision of hindsight.

Graham v. Connor, 490 U.S. 386 (1989)

§ 10.1 General Considerations

The actions of police officers are, by necessity, one of the most regulated parts of the criminal justice system—or any governmental system. The law related to the actions of police officers covers everything from simple traffic stops to the authority of police to take the life of another person. There are thousands of laws and court decisions that cover almost everything police officers do in their jobs. There are even hundreds of cases at the U.S. Supreme Court level that cover the actions of all officers. This is an indication of how important it is for police officers to "get it right" when dealing with the public.

In this book, we have worked to give you a strong overview of the critical legal issues in law enforcement. There is no way we could cover all of the legal issues that govern the actions of the police; so we chose those we felt were most important. They are important to students who never plan to be police officers because, if a person has any contact with the criminal justice system, it is most likely going to be with the police. So, a better understanding of what the police do and the issues that surround policing are important to understand how the front end of the criminal justice system works. It is also important for students who are not police officers but who plan to go into law enforcement. You should learn as much as you can now; it will only get more complicated when you are on the job. It is also important for current police officers. As good as training academies are, it is hard to teach the law in training because there is little context to understand the realities of legal decisions. Once a person has been working in law enforcement for a while, the laws can make more sense (or less sense). For those officers and agencies that use this book for promotions and for training, we hope it provides you with the most up-to-date and useful material to allow officers to do their job to the best of their ability.

The rest of this chapter provides some conclusions and thoughts about the topics covered in the book. Through this discussion, we look to provide some context of the law as it applies on the streets. There is not as much reference material and we rely more on our thoughts and experiences from our time in law enforcement and in the legal system. To make it organizationally easy, the sections are arranged by the chapters in the book.

§ 10.2 The Consequences of Not Complying with the Law

It might seem somewhat strange that we begin the book by discussing liability of police officers, having evidence excluded in court, and generally the bad things that can happen when the legal mandates on police officers are not followed. We felt it was important to impress on the reader right away that this is not "legal fiction" or the courts coddling offenders. The subject of this book is critical to almost everything police officers do in their jobs. And there are consequences for not doing it within the boundaries of the law.

As a general rule, the Supreme Court seeks to understand the intricacies of law enforcement in practice. The Court reasoned in *Graham v. Connor*[1] that their decisions should be drawn "from the perspective of a reasonable officer on the scene, rather than with the 20/20 vision of hindsight." That means the Court tries to see things as officers would see them rather than as they might be argued in a courtroom

---

[1] *Graham v. Connor*, 490 U.S. 396 (1989).

when there are months to prepare for the argument. That does not mean, however, that the Courts will always rule in favor of the police. Even independent of the makeup of the court (which can change to be more pro-rights or more pro-law enforcement), the courts routinely draw lines where they rule police officers exceeded their authority. In those cases, the evidence is often excluded from being used in court. While this may seem like the courts are "letting the criminals walk free," it is a reality that is a central element of our criminal justice system. We must understand the law and know how to work within it.

At the extreme is where officers are held personally liable for their actions. It is tragic for everyone when an officer is tried for manslaughter when he or she shot a person and it turned out the actions were outside the boundaries of police authority and law. These cases where an officer may be criminally tried for his or her actions are beyond the purview of this book; but there are cases where officers (and their agencies) are held civilly liable. The Supreme Court has held that officers generally have *qualified immunity*[2] in their actions, and sometimes have *absolute immunity*[3] for their actions. So, at the present time, officers can expect the following immunity in performance of their duties:

1. Absolute immunity when testifying;
2. Qualified immunity under federal law, but only if it does not rise to the level of "deliberate indifference"; and,
3. Officers at the state level cannot be sued under federal law in a state court except for civil rights violations.

Beyond this, officers may not enjoy qualified or absolute immunity for their actions; so staying within the boundaries of the law (and therefore knowing the boundaries of the law) is the best course of action.

More often, the actions of police officers may have negative consequences in terms of the evidence being excluded from trial. The exclusionary rule is a legal concept that the courts have wrestled with since the founding of the U.S. It gained acceptance and broadened over the years beginning in 1886[4] through the decision in *Mapp v. Ohio*[5] that applied the exclusionary rule to the states. The exclusionary rule now applies to almost all of the actions of law enforcement (particularly those related to searches, arrests, and interrogations).

There are many exceptions to the exclusionary rule that allow evidence to be admitted in court even though it was obtained through means not authorized by law.

---

[2]   See *Saucier v. Katz*, 533 U.S. 194 (2001).
[3]   See, for example, *Briscoe v. LaHue*, 460 U.S. 325 (1983).
[4]   *Boyd v. United States*, 116 U.S. 616 (1886).
[5]   *Mapp v. Ohio*, 367 U.S. 643 (1961).

These include a *good faith exception,*[6] where police believe their actions are valid even though they are later determined to be illegal; an *independent source exception,*[7] where the court determines the evidence would have been found by legal means anyway; and a *public safety exception,*[8] where an emergency exists that overrides Fourth Amendment protections.

Although there are calls for the exclusionary rule to be done away with,[9] at the current time, it is still very much a part of police work. This means the chapters in the book are important to understand.

§ 10.3 Detention and Arrest

In many instances, initial contact with the police is minimal and unobtrusive (you either get a traffic ticket or not). As such, there are not a lot of legal considerations for these kinds of encounters. It is when the encounters become more intrusive that legal issues arise.

Possibly, the least intrusive encounter with the police that has resulted in a Supreme Court case is stopping to check driver's license and registration. This brings up two issues—the circumstances under which the stop can take place, and the time it takes to complete the stop. The Supreme Court has ruled that there must be some legal justification to stop a vehicle[10] or a person,[11] and that a random stop is not justified.[12] While the Supreme Court has set no time limits on how long a stop may take, it did rule that 20 minutes was reasonable. The Court indicated that the length of a detention would rest on several factors, including:

1. The purpose of the stop;
2. The means of investigation used; and
3. The reasonableness of the time used for that type of investigation.

For example, it takes longer to call for a drug detection dog to examine a vehicle than it would to simply issue a traffic citation.

---

[6] *United States v. Leon,* 468 U.S. 897 (1984).

[7] *Murray v. United States,* 487 U.S. 533 (1988).

[8] *New York v. Quarles,* 467 U.S. 649 (1984).

[9] See Jeffery T. Walker, and Rick Dierenfeldt (2015), "The Restriction and Likely Elimination of the Exclusionary Rule." In Craig Hemmens (ed.), *Current Legal Issues in Criminal Justice*. New York, NY: Oxford University Press.

[10] *Delaware v. Prouse,* 440 U.S. 648 (1979).

[11] *Terry v. Ohio,* 392 U.S. 1 (1968).

[12] *United States v. Sharpe,* 470 U.S. 675 (1985).

The Court has also ruled on roadblocks used by the police. In several cases, the Court ruled that police may set up roadblocks for informational purposes (a missing person)[13] or for safety purposes (such as DWI checkpoints).[14] Police can also establish roadblocks to check for illegal aliens;[15] but may not set up roadblocks to "detect evidence of ordinary criminal wrongdoing" (drugs).[16] Further, police must have established guidelines in place for the roadblock, such as whether all cars will be stopped or every 10th car, etc. Even here, random stops are not allowed.

Somewhat bridging the gap between a detention and a search, the Court has ruled that police may detain luggage pursuant to an investigation if an officer reasonably believes the luggage may contain contraband.[17] This detention has been more recently extended to allow the "sniff test" of a trained law enforcement dog.[18]

§ 10.4 Searches and Seizures

There is more case law related to searches (particularly vehicle searches) than any other area of law enforcement. This is primarily because there are many intricacies and details involved in searches and because they are generally central to any prosecution. Searches and seizure may occur with a search warrant or without a search warrant. Searches with a warrant are the most straightforward because a neutral magistrate must approve the intentions of the police. There are, of course, procedures and case law that govern searches with a warrant (discussed in Chapter 6); but these are more procedural than instances where a search occurs without a warrant.

Searches and seizures without a warrant can be broken into one of four broad categories: searches of people, searches of things, searches of people in vehicles, and searches of things in vehicles. The separate categories of people and things in vehicles are necessary because of the tremendous number of cases involving vehicle searches.

Searches of people range from temporary searches for the protection of officers—called *Terry* stops or stop-and-frisk—to full searches of a person incident to an arrest. Each of these, as with other searches, must be based on probable cause (or consent); but the level of probable cause varies by the type of search.

A stop-and-frisk is a term that is best understood if thought about as two separate acts. A stop is justified if the police have "reasonable suspicion" (less than probable cause) that "criminal activity is afoot"; that is, an individual has committed, is

---

13 *Illinois v. Lidster*, 540 U.S. 419 (2004).
14 *Michigan Department of State Police v. Sitz*, 496 U.S. 444 (1990).
15 *United States v. Martinez-Fuerte*, 428 U.S. 543 (1976).
16 *City of Indianapolis v. Edmond*, 531 U.S. 32 (2000).
17 *United States v. Place*, 462 U.S. 696 (1983).
18 *Illinois v. Caballes*, 543 U.S. 405 (2005).

committing, or is about to commit a crime. A frisk after a stop is valid for only one reason: officer safety. A frisk is not supposed to be used to look for evidence of a crime. Its sole purpose must be to search for weapons. The Supreme Court specifically ruled that a search that goes beyond looking for a weapon is illegal.[19] In this case, officers had authority to stop and frisk. During the frisk, the officer felt something he believed to be contraband (drugs) but was not a weapon. His seizure of the drugs was ruled a violation of the Fourth Amendment.

There have been many cases related to searches that take place incident to an arrest. The general rule is that police may conduct a full body search of the person who is arrested[20] and the vicinity around the person for evidence of the crime; and any contraband that is found during the search may be used against the person. It is this "area surrounding the person" that is most at issue in these types of cases. The courts have been fairly clear that police may search in the area of the person's spread arms. Some courts have authorized an area within "lunging distance"[21] and other lesser-known measures of area of immediate control. Other factors to be considered in searches incident to an arrest include how immobile the person is (e.g. in handcuffs) and the type of evidence to be searched for (for example, officers should not look "for an elephant in a matchbox").

Warrantless seizures and searches of things is typically based on the assumption that, in the time it would take to obtain a warrant, the evidence would be destroyed or removed.[22] The seizure of things is often related to evidence within a person's body (blood for DWI testing, bullets, etc.). The general rule for searching and seizing things in a person's body is that there must be an exigency that necessitates the seizure without a warrant, and the seizure must not be overly intrusive. For example, courts have ruled that drawing blood from a person is not a violation of constitutional rights as long as it is conducted by a medical person using accepted medical practices.[23] More intrusive seizures, however, such as removing a bullet that requires a general anesthetic, are not allowed.[24] The Supreme Court also ruled that, while taking blood for blood alcohol analysis is acceptable, there is not a blanket rule that it can be conducted without a warrant. If there is time to obtain a warrant in these cases, police are compelled to do so.

Typically, to conduct a search of a person related to a vehicle stop, officers must order the person out of the vehicle. So, the primary concern is the legal authority to

---

[19] See *Minnesota v. Dickerson*, 508 U.S. 366 (1993).

[20] *United States v. Robinson*, 414 U.S. 218 (1973).

[21] See, for example, *State v. Robalewski*, 418 A.2d 817 (1980).

[22] See, for example, *Cup v. Murphy*, 412 U.S. 291 (1973), where officers seized scrapings from under Murphy's fingernails while he was attempting to scrape the blood before police could seize it.

[23] *Schmerber v. California*, 384 U.S. 757 (1966).

[24] *Winston v. Lee*, 470 U.S. 753 (1985).

order people out of the vehicle. At this point, officers can order both the driver[25] and passengers[26] to exit the vehicle. Of course, officers must have probable cause (or consent) for any search that occurs once passengers are out of the vehicle. The ability of police officers to search people related to vehicles also extends to persons on public transportation.[27]

Searches of vehicles and things in vehicles have more case law associated with them than any other part of the criminal justice system. Beginning with *Carroll v. U.S.*[28] in 1925 (not long after cars became readily accessible), police interaction with vehicles has become a large part of the law enforcement function. At this point, a few summary statements can encapsulate the authority of police in conducting searches of vehicles (without consent):

1. Search the passenger compartment of a vehicle based on particularized probable cause;
2. Search a passenger compartment of a vehicle and the contents in the passenger compartment incident to a lawful arrest;
3. Search the entire vehicle (including the trunk) and open any packages or luggage found in the vehicle based on probable cause or as a part of an inventory; and
4. Search a container in the vehicle if there is probable cause to believe it holds contraband, even if there is no probable cause to search the vehicle itself.

Many of these searches are valid even if the vehicle has been moved from its original location to an impound lot or the police station. The cases in Chapter 7 should be read carefully to get a full understanding of this complex line of the law.

§ 10.5 Questioning Suspects

Like search and seizure law, there is a great deal of case law related to questioning suspects since this is also a critical element in many investigations. Often, a case will be "solved" and a conviction obtained because a suspect confesses to the crime. However, these confessions may turn out to be the source of overturning a conviction because they (1) did not happen, (2) did not happen the way presented, or (3) were coerced. It is easy to find examples of cases where a person convicted of murder and serving life in prison or awaiting execution is released because of issues with an interrogation/confession. In one highly publicized case, three boys were convicted of

---

[25] *Delaware v. Prouse*, 440 U.S. 648 (1979).
[26] *Brendlin v. California*, 551 U.S. 1 (2007).
[27] *Florida v. Bostick*, 501 U.S. 429 (1991).
[28] *Carroll v. United States*, 267 U.S. 132 (1925).

brutally killing and mutilating three young boys.[29] The case was largely built on the confession of one of the three suspects. After almost 20 years, the three were released from prison, largely due to questions surrounding the confession. For these reasons, it is important to understand the proper way to interact with suspects and to obtain information from them.

Also similar to case law on searches and seizures, fully covering the case law on questioning suspects is far beyond the page length of this book, and especially a single chapter. Applying this line of law on the streets, however, is more straightforward. For most of the history of the United States, people were free to not talk to the police in criminal investigations—but they had to endure whatever procedures the police used to get them to talk to do so. And if they did talk, even through torture, their confessions were considered legal. It was not until *Brown v. Mississippi* that coerced confessions were declared unconstitutional.[30] The protection of suspects, especially in terms of right to counsel and to remain silent was extended in *Escobedo v. Illinois*, when the Court ruled a suspect had a right to counsel during interrogation once an investigation "begins to focus on an accused."[31] Because courts and the police had differing interpretations of what was meant by "focusing" on an accused, the Court quickly decided one of the most important and far-ranging cases in police law: *Miranda v. Arizona*.[32]

Miranda made law that police must provide proper notice to an accused of his or her rights at any time there is a "custodial interrogation." Custodial interrogation is best understood if discussed as two separate requirements. Custodial means the suspect is under arrest or is deprived of his or her freedom in some significant way. This generally means the person has a reasonable belief that he or she is not "free to leave."[33] Interrogation means that a suspect is asked questions by the police that are likely to elicit an incriminating response. This takes many forms that are important for the police. Even the Supreme Court has not been totally clear about what constitutes an interrogation outside the formal, police station interrogation.[34] There are also a number of exceptions to the *Miranda* requirements that mean police do not have to administer *Miranda* warnings before speaking to a suspect.[35] To ensure the admissibility of any confession, it is best for police, if they wish to question a suspect, to administer the *Miranda* warnings.

---

[29]   For more information, search for "West Memphis Three," or see the movie *Devil's Knot*.

[30]   *Brown v. Mississippi*, 297 U.S. 278 (1936).

[31]   *Escobedo v. Illinois*, 378 U.S. 478 (1964).

[32]   *Miranda v. Arizona*, 384 U.S. 436 (1966).

[33]   See *Kaupp v. Texas*, 538 U.S. 626 (2003).

[34]   See the difference in the opinions of *Brewer v. Williams*, 430 U.S. 387 (1977) and *Rhode Island v. Innis*, 446 U.S. 291 (1980).

[35]   See *New York v. Quarles*, 467 U.S. 649 (1984) and *Michigan v. Bryant*, 562 U.S. ___, No. 09-150 (2011).

There have been many cases decided since *Miranda* that are critical to proper police actions. These cases can be summarized in the following three general statements concerning questioning:

1. Were the *Miranda* warnings given by the police?
2. Was there a waiver by the suspect?
3. If there was a waiver, was it voluntary and intelligent?

If the answer to all three questions is "yes," the admission or confession is likely considered admissible. If the answer to any of the questions is "no," the evidence is possibly not admissible.

§ 10.6 Pretrial Identification

Lineups/showups, photographic identification procedures, fingerprints (and other identifying evidence such as footprints or palmprints), and evidence from the body (dental examinations and DNA) are helpful police practices for suspect identification. The police must be careful, however, that they do not violate the suspect's constitutional rights in the process.

The four constitutional rights usually invoked by suspects in identification proceedings are the Fifth Amendment privilege against self-incrimination, the Sixth Amendment right to counsel, the Fifth and Fourteenth Amendment right to due process, and the Fourth Amendment protection against unreasonable searches and seizures. The courts have determined that suspects do have limited rights in each of these areas. Some of the protections have to do with the place in the process. For example, the Supreme Court has held that an accused who has been formally charged with a crime has the right to have a lawyer present during a lineup.[36] In contrast, there is no right to counsel if the suspect has not been formally charged with a crime.[37] For other types of evidence, the conditions under which the evidence is taken is important. For example, fingerprinting and photographing suspects for identification purposes do not violate self-incrimination provisions, or the Fourth Amendment if there is a legal arrest and no search violations, because they are not testimonial in nature. A court can rule these inadmissible if there was an improper arrest or search in violation of the Fourth Amendment, but not the Fifth Amendment. Finally, the taking of fingerprints, voice exemplars, DNA, and the like have been ruled to be admissible as long as the Fourth or Fifth/Fourteenth Amendment protections have not been violated.

---

[36] *United States v. Wade*, 388 U.S. 218 (1967).
[37] *Kirby v. Illinois*, 406 U.S. 682 (1972).

§ 10.7 When You Are On Your Own

As we have talked about throughout this book, the law governing police actions is one of the most important pieces of knowledge for officers. Whether you are a current police officer, a student who plans to go into law enforcement, or a student whose only contact with the police may be for a traffic violation, it is important to understand the latitude and restrictions of the police in carrying out their duties. It is not necessarily important that you remember all of the case names; but it is important that you fully understand the legal guidelines established by law and the courts.

Appendix

The Bill of Rights (First Ten Amendments to the Constitution) and the Fourteenth Amendment

The first ten Amendments were ratified December 15, 1791, and form what is commonly referred to as the "Bill of Rights." The Fourteenth Amendment was ratified July 9, 1868. Originally intended to address state efforts to limit the rights of freed slaves in the post-Civil War South, the Amendment later was interpreted to apply, in large part, the provisions of the Bill of Rights to the states. These amendments are set forth below:

Amendment I

Congress shall make no law respecting an establishment of religion, or prohibiting the free exercise thereof; or abridging the freedom of speech, or of the press; or the right of the people peaceably to assemble, and to petition the Government for a redress of grievances.

Amendment II

A well-regulated Militia, being necessary to the security of a free State, the right of the people to keep and bear Arms, shall not be infringed.

Amendment III

No Soldier shall, in time of peace be quartered in any house, without the consent of the Owner, nor in time of war, but in a manner to be prescribed by law.

Amendment IV

The right of the people to be secure in their persons, houses, papers, and effects, against unreasonable searches and seizures, shall not be violated, and no Warrants shall issue, but upon probable cause, supported by Oath or affirmation, and particularly describing the place to be searched, and the persons or things to be seized.

Amendment V

No person shall be held to answer for a capital, or otherwise infamous crime, unless on a presentment or indictment of a Grand Jury, except in cases arising in the land or naval forces, or in the Militia, when in actual service in time of War or public danger; nor shall any person be subject for the same offence to be twice put in jeopardy of life or limb; nor shall be compelled in any criminal case to be a witness against himself, nor be deprived of life, liberty, or property, without due process of law; nor shall private property be taken for public use, without just compensation.

Amendment VI

In all criminal prosecutions, the accused shall enjoy the right to a speedy and public trial, by an impartial jury of the State and district wherein the crime shall have been committed, which district shall have been previously ascertained by law, and to be informed of the nature and cause of the accusation; to be confronted with the witnesses against him; to have compulsory process for obtaining Witnesses in his favor, and to have the Assistance of Counsel for his defense.

Amendment VII

In Suits at common law, where the value in controversy shall exceed twenty dollars, the right of trial by jury shall be preserved, and no fact tried by a jury, shall be otherwise reexamined in any Court of the United States, than according to the rules of the common law.

Amendment VIII

Excessive bail shall not be required, nor excessive fines imposed, nor cruel and unusual punishments inflicted.

Amendment IX

The enumeration in the Constitution, of certain rights, shall not be construed to deny or disparage others retained by the people.

Amendment X

The powers not delegated to the United States by the Constitution, nor prohibited by it to the States, are reserved to the States respectively, or to the people.

Amendment XIV
(Ratified July 9, 1868)

SECTION 1. All persons born or naturalized in the United States, and subject to the jurisdiction thereof, are citizens of the United States and of the States wherein they reside. No State shall make or enforce any law which shall abridge the privileges or immunities of citizens of the United States; nor shall any State deprive any person of life, liberty, or property, without due process of law; nor deny to any person within its jurisdiction the equal protection of the laws.

SECTION 2. Representatives shall be appointed among the several States according to their respective numbers, counting the whole number of persons in each State, excluding Indians not taxed. But when the right to vote at any election for the choice of electors for President and Vice President of the United States, Representatives in Congress, the Executive and Judicial officers of a State, or the members of the Legislature thereof, is denied to any of the male inhabitants of such State, being twenty-one years of age, and citizens of the United States, or in any way abridged, except for participation in rebellion, or other crime, the basis of representation therein shall be reduced in the proportion which the number of such male citizens shall bear to the whole number of male citizens twenty-one years of age in such State.

SECTION 3. No person shall be a Senator or Representative in Congress, or elector of President and Vice President, or hold any office, civil or military, under the United States, or under any State, who having previously taken an oath, as a member of Congress, or as an officer of the United States, or as a member of any State legislature, or as an executive or judicial officer of any State, to support the Constitution of the United States, shall have engaged in insurrection or rebellion against the same, or given aid or comfort to the enemies thereof. But Congress may by a vote of two-thirds of each House, remove such disability.

SECTION 4. The validity of the public debt of the United States, authorized by law, including debts incurred for payment of pensions and bounties for services in suppressing insurrection or rebellion, shall not be questioned. But neither the United States nor any State shall assume or pay any debt or obligation incurred in aid of insurrection or rebellion against the United States, or any claim for the loss or emancipation of any slave; but all such debts, obligations and claims shall be held illegal and void.

SECTION 5. The Congress shall have power to enforce, by appropriate legislation, the provisions of this article.

Table of Cases

Index